Creation Unlimited

The remarkable convergence
of Science and the Bible

D1609903

John Allen-Piper

Grosvenor House
Publishing Limited

This book is published by
Grosvenor House Publishing Ltd
Link House
140 The Broadway, Tolworth, Surrey, KT6 7HT.
www.grosvenorhousepublishing.co.uk

A CIP record for this book
is available from the British Library

ISBN 978-1-83975-099-1

Contents

Foreword

The writing of this book was initiated by myself and two other Christians. Philip Foster is an Anglican pastor with a strong interest in environmental sciences, and Michael Young is an evangelist with an engineering training formerly involved with Billy Graham Crusades. We were brought together through a common concern for the damage being done to Christian testimony by denial or falsification of established science. In the event Philip and Michael both had commitments in other areas. Nevertheless, we saw our challenge as a pressing one, and with a long history of university teaching and research in science, complemented by a parallel interest in Biblical interpretation, it seemed appropriate that I should undertake to write and complete the text within a reasonable time frame. Whilst the contributions of Philip and Michael have therefore been limited to advice and editing, the book remains very much a corporate vision. I am very grateful to both of them for initiating a project which I would almost certainly not have undertaken without their encouragement.

Whilst the apparent divorce of modern science from the Biblical narrative has long provided fertile ground for secularists to dismiss and even ridicule adherence to the faith, we believe it is time for re-evaluation of the controversies motivating this division. If the Bible can truly be established to be well beyond the abilities of mortal men to compile and to possess signatures of Divine origin, then we contend that there should be no conflict between Science and the Bible. The two glaring controversies seen by wider society are the origin of life by Creation or Evolution, and the young or old age of the Earth and Universe. It has therefore been our aim to first establish the integrity of the Bible narrative, and then go on to evaluate its impact on these and lesser controversies perceived to be irreconcilable conflicts between the Bible and Science. We also note that the Christian world needs to be reminded that most ministers of the Faith during the great and successful age of Dispensational Evangelism were actually Old Earth Creationists who saw no conflict between the Bible and Science as it was then understood. What has happened in the meantime to produce the conflict we see today reflects both an accelerated attack on Christianity by the media and academia, and a confusing promotion of false science by Christians.

In this book we have aimed to address these divisions and show that there is no fundamental disagreement between the findings of modern science and the Bible, and particularly with the Book of Genesis. We believe this confidently enables us to assign to God the attribute of Universal Creator which motivates the title of this book suggested by Michael Young. To develop our case, we have drawn upon the findings of specialists in a wide range of scientific disciplines, as well as authorities on Biblical history and exegesis. Whilst I have included much information aiming to reinforce the confidence of the Bible-believer, the overriding aim of the text is to challenge the enquiring unbeliever, and especially those willing to consider Intelligent Design, but deterred from examining the claims of the Bible by the influence of Academia and the Mainstream Media. We collectively hope the book will be a foundational text and only the beginning for a ministry seeking to repair the damage caused by the separation of Science and the Bible.

I have included some outline explanations of established scientific methods (with a few simple equations) of items such as methods for determining age in Chapter 6. This is to establish the scientific foundations of the case presented here. It is only by ignoring these foundations that the propagation of false science can continue. However, this material can be readily passed over by those uncomfortable with the scientific groundwork without missing the essential theme of the book. The key aim of the text is to affirm the absolute reliability of the Bible as the Word of God and to show that it is not in conflict with modern science. Whilst this has sometimes forced us to follow a contentious path, our overriding aim is only to glorify the God to whom each one of us is eternally indebted for their Salvation. The author is available to provide talks concerning the issues discussed here. The figures have mostly been drawn specially for the text. Chapter

Six includes four diagrams from the scientific literature whilst chapters 5 and 8 include figures modified from Google images to illustrate appropriate issues described in the text. The Bible quotations are all taken from the Authorised (King James) Version of the Bible.

"Give glory to the Lord your God" (Jeremiah 13:16)

John Allen-Piper, Aughton, Ormskirk, Lancashire. March 2020. Contact: John D.A. Piper, B.Sc., Ph.D., Geomagnetism laboratory, Department of Earth and Ocean Sciences, University of Liverpool, Liverpool, L69 7ZE, U.K. (sg04@liverpool.ac.uk)

Introduction

The Bible reigns supreme amongst books. No other written work of religious or secular origin approaches the majesty and integrity of the 66 books compiled by some 40 authors over a period of ~1500 years. It makes claims for the unique nature of a triune Godhead and embeds an extraordinary amount of evidence to prove the inspired authorship of God Himself. It teaches the promotion of a healthy, ordered and peaceful lifestyle which is the only foundation of a successful society. It documents a history which, although widely derided by a world with a secular mindset, is being substantiated by an expanding body of archaeological and documentary research. It is the only religious text containing multiple prophecies which have so far proved to be one hundred percent accurate. Above all it is the most transforming of books - it provides a sense, a purpose, and a destiny, to those who believe and respond to its message.

Near the end of the 5th Century BC, in a long and unique ministry within two empires (Babylonian and Persian) that included many predictions relevant to all subsequent history, the prophet Daniel was given an extraordinary message: ***"Many shall run to and fro, and knowledge shall be increased....Go thy way, Daniel, for the words are closed up and sealed till the time of the end. Many shall be purified, and made white, and tried; but the wicked shall do wickedly: and none of the wicked shall understand; but the wise shall understand"***. (Daniel 12:4, 9-10). Only in the present age does the full significance of these predictions seem to become relevant. Scientific knowledge is expanding day by day at an exponential rate. At the same time the deeper treasures of the Biblical text supporting a Divine origin, which have hitherto remained the preserve of small numbers of Jewish rabbis, are being widely disseminated throughout the Gentile world, in part by a computer power which has only become available in recent decades. In parallel with this, archaeological research and studies of ancient documents are year by year securing the truth of the Old Testament record.

With the unique veracity of the Bible text now so clearly demonstrated, we should be living in an age where Science and the Bible converge. In reality we see the reverse happening in the developed world where this knowledge is most readily accessible. The Bible is being progressively removed from education, and even banned in sections of society which deem its statements offensive in an environment steeped in political correctness. Many secularists would likely attribute this divergence between Science and the Bible to false science promoted by Christians. Whilst this is doubtless a contributory factor, the underlying causes are much deeper: Jesus (see for example Luke 18:8), the Apostles and Old Testament prophets all warned that there would be a general departure from the faith in the latter days of the present age. We live in a world where there is a dearth of Biblical knowledge, where society is preoccupied with social media and advances in communication, bombarded with consumerism, and where advances in medicine have postponed the likelihood of imminent death. In such an environment many people have little time for issues of their eternal destiny; indeed, many prefer to believe in annihilation, the view that their souls simply disappear when they die. There is also a spiritual dimension to this conflict between the Bible testimony and what we see happening in our modern society: there has been an explosion of interest in fantasy, New Age spirituality, witchcraft and the occult in recent years which has served to generate a world view lacking a code of morality and in total opposition to Biblical Christianity.

As the First World has largely forsaken its Christian foundations we see a society becoming increasingly polarised, more narcissistic, lacking in warmth and sympathy where the womb is the least safe place for a child as abortion surpasses all other causes of death. Social media has the contradictory effect of causing people to feel more isolated and dissatisfied, and suicide rates are increasing everywhere. The frenetic pace of modern life is multiplying problems, especially of a societal and environmental nature, that are seemingly without rational solutions. In the first chapter of the Book of Romans (verses 21-23) the Apostle

Paul laid out seven steps that he recognised under Divine inspiration as applying to the inevitable regression that we see happening around us. He saw society as (i) knowing God but (ii) no longer prepared to glorify Him as the Creator and (iii) neither being thankful for His blessings, so they (iv) became vain in their imaginations, with (v) their hearts becoming darkened, (vi) they professed themselves wise as they became fools, and this resulted in them (vii) changing the glory of an incorruptible God into idolatry - in our age the worship of materialism and selfishness. We can see how these steps have played out in the modern world as we view the contrast between the situation today with ~250 years ago in a Revival which began with preachers such as John Wesley and George Whitfield, continued into the Victorian era, and illustrated the great positive influence of Biblical Christianity. The effects of this Revival extended throughout much of the rest of the world by settlement and colonisation, and produced a wonderful transforming effect on society. It led to the end of slavery in the west, abolition of child labour, universal education, foundation of hospitals, improvement in the status of women and general concern for the well-being of fellow human beings, all of which laid the foundation of a modern prosperous society.

The regression summarised by Paul no doubt has many contributory factors, but it is our concern that the perceived conflict between the Biblical testimony and scientific discovery initiated by the Enlightenment has played no small part. It is the primary motivation of the book to challenge this view. Albert Einstein once said *"Science without religion is lame, religion without science is blind"*. The opening chapters of the book therefore aim to describe the multi-facetted textural evidence that the God who reveals Himself in the Bible is demonstrably real (Chapters 1 and 2). The signatures of a Universal Creator are then demonstrated in both the fine tuning of the Earth and Universe ideal for humankind, and in the perfection of design in nature (Chapters 4 and 5). Blind faith is never good enough for the enquiring mind which instead seeks many lines of testable evidence to support foundational belief. Thus, from these multiple lines of evidence, and in particular the coordinated agreement between the books of the Old and New Testaments written over an interval of ~1500 years, the Bible is considered to be Divinely-inspired. It requires that there should be no conflict between the unchangeable Biblical text and our rapidly-expanding canon of scientific knowledge. In endeavouring to show this, the two fundamental barriers between Science and the Bible perceived by the world at large are addressed in detail, namely the conflict between Creationism and Evolution (Chapter 3) and the Age of the Earth and Universe (Chapter 6).

The majority of the Nineteenth and early Twentieth century evangelists were Old Earth Creationists in so far as they acknowledged the existence of a large, but indeterminate, length of time implied by the second verse of the Book of Genesis where we are told that a perfect created Earth in verse one became desolate and void. This is the GAP concept and seemed able to accommodate the apparent great age of the Earth. Hugh Miller (1802-1856) found no conflict between his epic description of the fossil fauna and flora of Scotland and his profound belief in the Bible. The current era of scepticism and apostasy did not begin with Nicholas Steno (1638-1686) considered the "Father of Stratigraphy", or James Hutton (1726-1797), a geological investigator who saw "no vestige of a beginning and no prospect of an end", and was instrumental in initiating the concept of Unformitarianism, or with William Smith (1769-1839) the canal surveyor who did so much to formulate the science of Stratigraphy and produce the first large scale geological map. Instead, it began with Darwin's 1859 book "The Origin of Species by means of natural selection or the preservation of favoured races in the struggle for life". The issue of contention was not therefore the great age of the Earth *per se*. The Great Controversy derived from Darwin's proposal that selective survival of the fittest members of a species could ultimately transform it into another species if sufficient time had been available. The need for a Creator God would then be marginalised or excluded altogether. Darwin knew nothing of DNA, had only a rudimentary knowledge of the stratigraphic record, and appears to have been ignorant of the Laws of Physics. Nevertheless, so influential has his theory been amongst a modern materialistic fraternity unwilling to acknowledge a Creator, that academic and government institutions enforce it as a fact with, for example, the same status as Newton's Law of Gravity. This in spite of an increasing number of scientists and indeed, the public at large, learning that genetics has confounded Darwin's racist theories, whilst his concept of evolution by natural selection is now widely recognised as totally inadequate to accommodate our modern knowledge of the complexity of living things.

As we explore in Chapter 3 of this book, the Creation versus Evolution controversy which has dominated the debate about mankind's origins since mid-Victorian times, can actually be championed in favour of Creation from straightforward scientific arguments. In contrast, a large body of committed Christians have, mainly since the 1950's, generated another controversy by promoting a Young Earth doctrine. This is primarily a recent development because even the Early Church Fathers such as Irenaeus, Justin Martyr and Clement of Alexandria recognised that a present 24-hour day could never have given Adam time enough to name all the animals, and this only after he had been put into "a deep sleep" and all the preceding acts of Day Six had taken place. The Young Earth doctrine has divorced Christian testimony from mainstream Science. It has resulted in much heart searching in a community of believers which has been prepared to reject Evolution, but now find their confidence undermined by an argument which has been definitively lost. Young Earth Creationism is so intellectually insulated that it can have no impact on secular culture. Because its interpretation of the Bible is associated with Christian belief in the minds of scientifically-engaged non-believers, it presents an insurmountable obstacle to serious engagement with the claims of Christianity (www.godandscience.org/scandal-of-the-evangelical-mind/). Regrettably Young Earth Creationism can leave a trail of devastation in its wake among new Christians when they discover that the scientific claims are untenable; the consequences are transferred to the reminder of Scripture, faith is destroyed and they are absorbed into a secular culture even to the point of arguing for atheism. This is doubly tragic because a major tactic of pagan Marxism is to capture the hearts of the young, the key to the future.

Young Earth Creationism has adopted the false paradigm that time is a constant so that the Days of Genesis Chapter One are present days of 24 hours. We now know from the Laws of Relativity, first proposed by Albert Einstein but since proved by multiple experiments, that time is not a constant but is instead a function of mass, acceleration and gravity. Furthermore, rather than address the events specifically attributed to the Six Days, Noah's Flood, an event lasting for less than a year after the completion of Day Six, has been adopted to explain the whole of the Geological Column. Whilst the primary motivation of Young Earth Creationism has had the laudable aim of precluding time for Darwinian Evolution, the need to abandon a vast canon of modern scientific knowledge has merely served the promotion of Evolution - it avoids the need to mount a scientific defense of Darwinian Evolution. Instead, at a time when we find the scientific foundation of Evolution increasingly questioned by many esteemed academics, the supporter of Darwinianism can dismiss the alternative claims of the Bible because the whole gamut of scientific evidence shows that a Young Earth and Universe are impossible. In Chapter 6 of this book we outline the range of methods, often unrelated, that collectively show that the Earth and Cosmos are very old. We then go on to show how the scientific evidence is entirely in accord with the Genesis record when the Laws of Relativity are acknowledged. In passing, it is also shown that the assertions of Young Earth Creationism do not accord with the original Hebrew narrative: the Bible cannot be defended, nor can the Gospel be effectively proclaimed, if we assert things which the Bible does not say.

C. I. Scofield (1843-1921), who produced the highly-respected Scofield Reference Bible published in 1909 and revised in 1917 noted *"The first creative act refers to the dateless past, and gives scope to all the geologic ages."* He proposed that the Earth had suffered a "catastrophe" associated with Satan's fall and expulsion from Heaven (Genesis 1:2, Isaiah 14:12-14) leading to disastrous results on Earth, but with a subsequent re-creation described in Genesis 1:3 onwards. Other famous preachers from the great age of evangelization and missions such as John Nelson Darby (1800-1882), G. H. Pember (1805-1877), Clarence Larkin (1850-1924), Charles Spurgeon (1834-1892), E. W. Bullinger (1837-1913) and in more recent years Watchman Nee (1903-1972), Billy Graham (1918-2018), as well as many ancient Jewish writers, all embraced this view. These men were not evolutionists. They all acknowledged God as the Creator of all things, and the outstanding results of their ministries is surely testimony that they were not deceived men. In the present age dominated by secularism and a skeptical view of the Biblical record we have fewer ministers with the stature of these men, and, as discussed in Chapter 7, many have unwisely rejected the significance of the GAP between Genesis 1:1 and 1:3. Instead they have developed an alternative narrative that attempts to constrain the whole history of the Universe into a few thousand years with the formation of the modern Earth constrained to Noah's Flood, a claim made nowhere in the Bible. This contrasts with the long-held Old Earth staple of dispensational teaching. Sadly this transition, which can be dated to ~1925, occurred in an environment of panic over Evolution being exclusively taught in schools. This turned Christianity away from examining the Satanic fall beginning in Genesis, and rather rapidly Young Earth theology became a central paradigm of Evangelical Christianity *(see www.ProphecyWatchers/OldEarth/ GaryStearman)*.

The existence of the ancient metamorphic rocks comprising the continental foundations (Chapter 6.13) is alone sufficient to exclude the possibility of a Young Earth. Nevertheless because the Young Earth view has become so widespread amongst a large body of Christians we have been obliged to present the evidence refuting it (Chapter 6), whilst at the same time readily endorsing the evidence that Young Earth Creationists have presented for challenging Evolution and supporting Creation (Chapter 3). It is incongruous that they should have enthusiastically embraced scientific evidence disproving Evolution whilst at the same time ignoring or dismissing so much evidence for the age of rocks, the Earth and the Universe, or reinterpreting it in ways that are readily confounded. This has regrettably repelled many secularists who are now recognising the failure of so much evidence to support Evolution and likely willing to recognise Intelligent Design, from going further and addressing the unique and verifiable claims of the Bible.

The Nobel Physicist Richard Feynman once commented *"In this age of specialisation, men who thoroughly know one field are often incompetent to discuss another"* (*Caltech Forum, 1956*). Whilst we do not deny that Young Earth Creationists include people with an Earth Science education, their interpretive mindset is always constrained to their immovable ~6000-year model, and as we show in Chapter 6, they then fall into the trap embraced by Albert Einstein's sarcastic comment *"When the facts don't fit the theory, change the facts"*. It is surely unworthy of Bible-believing Christians to promote the falsehoods that there was an Ice Age within the last 4000 years or that the Stratigraphic Column is a fiction, for example, and then question why young people are abandoning Christianity.[*] Our Chapter 6 is therefore included to show that Young Earth Creationism has generated a conflict with no substance. Now that we understand the dimension of time in terms of the accelerating expansion of the Universe and in the context of the Laws of Relativity, the Six Days of Creation in Genesis Chapter One are seen to embrace our knowledge of the temporal frame of the Earth and Universe. Furthermore it does not have to appeal to the GAP alone. This is described in Chapters 8 and 9.

The main title of this book "Creation Unlimited" expresses our collective view that this artificial barrier that has grown up between modern Science and Christian testimony in recent decades can now be confidently dismantled. On the one hand the vast knowledge substantiating the great age of the Earth and Universe can be accommodated within our modern understanding that the entire material Universe was created within a fraction of a second of the Big Bang. The ensuing six steps that God took to transform a chaotic medium into order can be explained from our understanding of Relativity when we acknowledge that God is reporting these "Days" from His cosmic timeframe, and outside of our Earth-bound time frame. The latter only begins with the creation of Adam. These six steps can now be shown to correlate with predicted events in cosmic and geologic history. A much younger timeframe for humankind is demonstrated by the science of genetics supporting the view that humankind is a special creation with a recent origin influenced by two "bottleneck" events - just what the Bible claims. Furthermore, the effect of mutations to the human genome not only undermines Evolution, but requires that humankind is both recent and can anticipate just a brief lifespan. These claims are explored in later chapters of the book after we

---

[*] *See: Ham, K., Beemer, B and Hillard, T., 2018. Already Gone, Master Books, Green Forest, Arkansas, 190pp.*

describe the embedded information supporting the Divine authorship of the Bible (2) and the perfection of Creation (4 and 5). In the final chapter (10) we show that Noah's Flood was a very real event with a dramatic implication to the history of humankind supported by a deep divine, archaeological and geophysical signature.

This book could have been one of many written to contend with the multitude of arguments that the secularist-humanist fraternity has used to attack the Bible. Instead it aims to bring together key information gleaned from the many years of research accumulated by outstanding Biblical scholars, notably Ethelbert Bullinger, Grant Jeffrey, James Harrison, Dave Hunt, Kenneth Johnson, Chuck Missler and Victor Pearce to establish the Divinely-inspired truth of the whole Biblical narrative. This is then integrated with the scientific evidence to demonstrate the convergence of recent scientific discoveries with the Bible account. Mentioned in passing are just a few of the impressive recent advances in archaeological research by workers such as Nelson Glueck, Kenneth Kitchen and Douglas Petrovitch, and the translations of ancient documents such as the Armarna and Ebla tablets; year by year these are making great strides to confirm the historical record of the Bible, especially of the Old Testament. Instead the text aims to challenge the reader with a scientific knowledge gleaned from the media and academic training, to see that they can reject the secular view that the Bible is merely a collection of myths in conflict with the findings of modern science. Because the text covers such a vast and diverse range of material, referencing is primarily limited to the major sources, but it is one of the positive facets of the internet that every topic mentioned here can be investigated further by a brief search.

Our explanation for the Six Days of Creation follows the ground-breaking discovery of Gerald Schroeder published in his 1997 book *"The Science of God"* showing that by incorporating relativity into our knowledge of geologic and cosmic histories, we reconcile the time spans implied by Genesis Chapter One with recent scientific knowledge. An understanding of the Biblical Hebrew has been greatly aided by Dr Schroeder's books, and the importance of the original

Hebrew words has been further enlightened by the work of Dr Haim Shore (2005). Dr Schroeder is a follower of Judaism and gained much insight into his analysis from the writings of the ancient Jewish sages. However unlike him, we believe that the Trinity of the Godhead is crucial to understanding the three-fold nature of humankind and Creation. His philosophical approach considers that there are just good things and bad things that happen to people, whereas we prefer to acknowledge the presence of the Satanic realm both in terms of the GAP preceding God's six steps transforming chaos into order, in the numeric properties of the Biblical text, and in the unfolding of each Biblical dispensation. Thus, whilst the subtitles of our respective books highlighting the convergence of science and the Bible are similar, Dr Schroeder deals with the Tanakh, our Old Testament, whereas this book aims to incorporate both Old and New Testaments into the analysis.

Whilst acknowledging the same Divinity, the differing perspectives of Christianity and Judaism have two primary foundations. The first is the interpretation of the Messianic texts, particularly in the Book of Isaiah. The Christian interpretation is that the "suffering servant" of Chapter 53, implied also by other prophecies in the Tanakh, is the Lord Jesus Christ who as the central member of the Trinity became the perfect man to offer Himself as the redeemer for the sin of humankind and restore the relationship with its Creator. In Judaism, and based primarily on the interpretation of the medieval sages, it is the traumas of Israel that represent this suffering servant; the still-anticipated Messiah will be purely human and restore a fallen physical world. The second contrast emerges from the common Hebraic root of the words "sin" and "miss". Whilst this allows sin to be regarded as "missing the mark" and annually dealt with at the appointed time of Yom Kippur in the pattern of repetition of the Old Testament Levitical practises, the Christian interpretation is that sin is an offence and rebellion against a holy God who cannot tolerate sin: beginning in Genesis Chapter Three, continuing through the warnings of the prophets, temporarily covered by the shadow practices instituted by Moses, it is only ultimately dealt with by God becoming man in the form of the Lord Jesus Christ and graciously taking the burden upon Himself for all those who would acknowledge what He has done.

The overwhelming body of the Biblical text is therefore concerned with God's aim of restoring humankind from its fallen condition. It actually has rather little to tell us about His extraordinary supreme act of creating the Earth and Universe. Nevertheless what it does tell us is no longer in conflict with modern Science. It is the primary aim of the book to demonstrate this. The uncertainty of the neutral position between belief and unbelief is not a comfortable one. The person who rejects the need for the Creator God in spite of the evidence He presents in His Creation is an *a^theist*. This is *Greek for* "***without God***". It is condemned in the Scriptures (***"The fool hath said in his heart, there is no God"***, Psalms 14:1 and 53:1) because it produces a mindset leading to the consequences we have noted above in the Book of Romans Chapter One. When obstinate unbelief is adopted in spite of clear evidence to the contrary in the perfection of Creation, God regards this as "wickedness" (Daniel 12:10, Luke 24:25). The neutral position unwilling to reject the claims of either side is described as *a^gnostic* in the *Greek for* ***"without knowledge";*** the unfortunate equivalent in the Latin is ***ignoramus "we do not know".*** On one of his many YouTube postings the late Bible teacher Dr Chuck Missler once said *"I am tired of people telling me that you cannot prove the Bible - quite simply, YOU CAN!"* We hope that the information compiled in this book will help the reader with an enquiring mind to endorse the Book of books and accept the free offering of grace that it promises together with the eternal security that follows.

Chapter 1

The Bible: Integrity and reliability of the Old and New Testament Transcripts

All scripture is given by inspiration of God, and is profitable for doctrine, for reproof, for correction, for instruction in righteousness (2 Timothy 3:16)

Do not My words do good to him that walketh uprightly? (Micah 2:7)

1.1 Introduction: The Book we have Today

The word "Bible" is derived from the Greek word for book, *"biblios"*, which in turn derives from the name of the papyrus reeds (*byblos*) used to make the scrolls on which the texts were originally recorded. The word in the Hebrew Scriptures usually translated as "covenant" in English has several meanings including "testament". God promised the prophet Jeremiah that He would make a new testament (Jeremiah 31:31). The Old (Tanakh) and New testaments are therefore logically included in the same book and we explore allusions to the unity between them in this and subsequent chapters. Each book of the Bible originally ran as a continuous narrative. The chapter divisions that we use today were created by the French friar Hugo Cardinalis (~1200-1263) in about 1240 AD. He wrote a concordance to aid study of the Latin Vulgate Bible which he linked to divisions that have since become chapters. Then between 1437 and 1448 Mordecai Nathan, a Jewish rabbi, subdivided the chapters created by Hugo into the numbered verses that we retain today (Jeffrey 1997). The chapter divisions have not always proved to be ideal because they sometimes interrupt the continuity of a theme. Nevertheless the divisions of the Bible into chapters and verses created in medieval times greatly aids our ability to find our way around the whole book.

In this chapter we outline the histories of the Old and New Testaments of the Bible, emphasizing the integrity and magnitude of the resource base on which they are founded. Throughout this history we see an extraordinary conflict unfolding between the efforts to preserve the precision of the primary revelation, and the efforts to confuse and destroy its message. This would appear to have a spiritual context explored in the concluding comments to Chapter 2 and then later in Chapter 7. That we are able to demonstrate the integrity of the original records after intervals of up to 3500 years is a testimony to the truth that God does indeed oversee the preservation of His Word, just as He declares in the text (Isaiah 55:11, Jeremiah 1:12 and Matthew 24:35), with this theme repeated in the three synoptic gospels of Matthew, Mark and Luke). The Old Testament mentions a number of secular records of ancient Jewish history which have long since vanished from history (Pearce 1993). Instead we have an honest record repeatedly able to record the failures and bad deeds of a people who were nevertheless chosen by God to bring His light to the world. To give His viewpoint he sent inspired prophets who were embraced by good kings but only tolerated, or even executed, by bad kings. Jeremiah tells us there were many false prophets in his time - their views are rarely recorded, and then only to show that they were proved wrong.

The true prophets were men and women of absolute obedience under God's authority. Unlike the priests and scribes who oversaw rituals and copied and interpreted the law, only prophets had the authority to cry "Thus saith the Lord". The Scriptures record that they combined intense prayer with great faith and compassion. They would not be silenced and for this they were often grievously punished. Whilst they seem to have had no major secular responsibilities, they recognized that God's reputation was at the heart of every controversy He had with humankind. They were always confident that their prophecies would be fulfilled either over a near or distant time frame, indeed the Jewish concept of prophecy is pattern, so that a prophecy can be unfolded in future history more than once. The Encyclopedia of Biblical Prophecy records 1,239 prophecies in the Tanakh and 578 in the writings of the Apostles comprising a third of the Bible. Many, including ~300 prophecies concerned with the First Coming of the Lord Jesus Christ, have already been precisely fulfilled (see Johnson 2010 and http://messiahfactor.com); given this evidence, the future fulfillment of the remainder can confidently be anticipated.

1.2 The Biblical Texts

1.2.1 The Old Testament (the Tanakh)

The prophet Jeremiah, the "weeping prophet" who witnessed the final destruction of the nation of Judah by the Babylonians in 586 BC, is regarded by Jewish Talmudic sources as responsible for faithfully compiling and preserving the Tanakh up to his day together with his scribe Baruch. In addition to the Torah, this would have included the history books up to Kings and Chronicles and the record of the prophets that preceded him. Both Jewish and Christian sources then acknowledge that the Hebrew books making up the common Old Testament (Catholic and Orthodox versions include some additional books) were collected by the Prophet Ezra when he returned to Jerusalem in 538 BC with a small rump of Jewish people after their 70 years of exile in Babylon. Ezra divided the writings into three groups comprising the *Torah* (the Law or Pentateuch), the *Nevi'im* (the Prophets) and the *Ketuvim* (the Holy Writings). The younger people returning to Jerusalem were by then only speaking the Aramaic Chaldean language of Babylon; the Scriptures would therefore be read to them in Hebrew and then explained by Chaldean commentaries known as the *Targums.* These Targums have since proved to be a valuable source of ancient commentary on the earlier books of the Bible (Jeffrey 1997). In the overlapping Book of Nehemiah which follows Ezra's own testament, we are told how the unfolding of the Scriptures by Ezra in this way brought new understanding to the people and a temporary spiritual revival (Nehemiah 8:7-12).

This inspired the returnees who found themselves under hostile opposition from unfriendly neighbours. They were encouraged in the work of rebuilding Jerusalem by the additional books of the practical Prophet Haggai and the visionary Prophet Zechariah. The books of these latter authors, together with the last Book of Malachi written during a succeeding time characterised by deterioration into apostasy, completed the canon of Scripture of twenty-two books. This is known by the acronym "Tanakh" derived from Ezra's three divisions **T**orah - **N**evi'im - **K**etuvim. The historian Josephus writing at the time of the Apostles records that just twenty-two books comprised the Tanakh with the number twenty books corresponding to the number of letters in the Hebrew alphabet. The number 22 has extensive numeric significance in the context of Divine revelation and has long been seen as significant of completeness by the Jewish people (http://www.askelm.com/restoring/res003.htmm). However, after the destruction of Jerusalem and the Temple by the Romans in 70 AD and the rebellion of 132-135 AD which excluded Jews from Judea, the centre of Rabbinic authority moved eastward. At some later time for reasons which remain obscure, the rabbis (probably in Babylon) divided the 22 books into the 24 books of the present Hebrew Bible.*

The subdivision of the Old Testament into thirty-nine books in the Christian Bible seems to have originated in Greek translations made in Egypt in the 3rd century. Histories linked by a common timeline for example, were subdivided so that the Book of Judges became Judges and Ruth, whilst the succeeding histories became the books of Samuel 1 and 2, Kings 1 and 2 and Chronicles 1 and 2, and the books of the prophets were individualised. These changes were formalised by Jerome (349-420 AD), a Latin priest who translated most of the Hebrew and Greek originals to produce the Latin Bible, the Vulgate. When added to the 27 New Testament books this transformed the total number of books in the Bible from 49, seen as a perfect number (7 x 7), to 66 which has the stamp of the Biblical number of man (6, see Chapter 5). For this reason, attempts were made from time to time to revise this

---

* *The word "Hebrew" implying "passed over" is probably the equivalent of "Habiru" in archaeological records and first appears in the Bible applied to Abraham (Genesis 14:13) referring to his coming from beyond the Euphrates River which would have crossed to journey to the Land of Canaan.*

numbering by the Catholic Church although the total number of books in the Bible remains sixty six to this day.

Compilation and primary authorship of the first five books comprising the Torah or Pentateuch is usually attributed to Moses which would date it ~1440-1410 BC. The Book of Exodus records that Phineas, a grandson of the High Priest Aaron the brother of Moses, acted as a scribe for him. Deuteronomy, the last book of the five, was subject to some later editing (presumably by Phineas) to conclude the record of Moses' death.* There has also been some editing of place names, probably by Ezra some 800 years later. Thus the "Mount of the Lord" where Abraham went to sacrifice Isaac (Genesis 22:14) was actually Mount Moriah in his day, and only given its new name after the Temple had been built there. The city known as Laish in the time of Moses was renamed Dan after the tribe that later occupied it, and Avaris (Peru-nefu) the city settled by the Hebrews in Egypt, was revised to Pi Ramses, although Pharaoh Ramses II did not reign until ~150 years after the time of the Exodus.

In addition to the giving of the Law and the institution of Levitical worship, the Torah is a book of history. Following a record of ten successive pre-Flood patriarchs from Adam (see Chapter 10.2.3), it notes the descendents of Noah and hints at their subsequent dispersal before focusing on God's call to Abraham (~2150-1990 BC). He was drawn to leave a Sumerian world centered on the idolatrous city of Babylon and move across the Fertile Crescent to a Promised Land where he was to remain a wanderer, but become the progenitor of the Jewish race preserved through tight inter-tribal marriage and the practice of circumcision. His grandson Jacob, later renamed 'Israel' by God (Genesis 32:28) would have 12 sons to father the 12 tribes of

---

* *The timing of the Exodus from Egypt is commonly misplaced and linked to the time of Ramses II (1279-1213 BC) - a line followed by the Hollywood epics. This is due to failure to accommodate the ~340 years occupied by the era of the Judges between the death of Joshua in ~1390 BC and the crowning of Saul, the first king of Israel, in ~1050 BC.*

Israel.* The family of Jacob had expanded to 70 people by ~1875 BC when they moved to Egypt to alleviate the impact of a time of famine. By that time one son, Joseph, had already become a leading authority in Egypt second only to the Pharaoh, and Jacob's families would enjoy a time of blessing, subsequently followed by a period of serfdom as the Egyptians became fearful of the rapid expansion of their population. After a sojourn lasting 430 years they would be led out of Egypt by Moses whose leadership molded them into a nation and returned them to the border of the Promised Land.

The Book of Job is considered to be the oldest book in the Bible because it appears to relate to events that occurred during the interval when the Israelites were in Egypt, or possibly even before. Job may have been a named son of Issachar, who was himself one of the 12 sons of Jacob during the long sojourn in Egypt (Genesis 46:13); this is less likely because the record of Job seems to be unrelated to the family of Israel. The writings of Job were probably collected by Moses, who we are told was trained in all the skills of Egypt which doubtless included literary matters. Modern research indicates that Moses wrote in a form of proto-Hebrew more readily understood by the people than the Egyptian Hieroglyphics or the Sumerian cuneiform. It forms the basis of our modern alphabet, a name derived from the first two letters (*aleph - beth*) preserving its Hebraic origins.**

The etymology of the word "Israel" is composed of two parts. "El" stands for Elohim, the name of God, and the "isra" can either be regarded as derived from the noun "sara", שרה, a noble lady, the verb saral, שרה, meaning "to struggle" or "to contend", or the similar verb, śarar, "to rule" or "to be strong"; collectively the word implies "God Rules", "God Contends", "God Prevails" - all epitomized in the remarkable survival and history of the Jewish people.

**See DVD series by Timothy Mahoney: Patterns of Evidence: Did Moses write the Torah? Also, recent research by Dr Douglas Petrovitch indicates that this script dates from the time when the members of Jacob's family had migrated to Egypt, taken Egyptian hieroglyphics, and transformed them into a writing system of 22 alphabetic letters corresponding to the Hebrew alphabet used today. Translated inscriptions by Dr Petrovitch have found the names of Joseph, his wife Asenath and one of his sons, Manasseh which would date this ancient Hebrew at least as far back as ~1800 BC. Dr Petrovitch concludes that the Israelites in Egypt sought to communicate in writing with other Israelites in Egypt by simplifying Egypt's complex hieroglyphic writing system. (www.bit.ly/oldestalphabet).*

Whilst leading the Israelites through the wilderness, Moses had to communicate to a population likely exceeding two million people and the Tribe of Levi was set aside to copy the law and transmit it to the people (Deuteronomy 31:24-26). The Torah as completed by Moses' scribe Phineas, was placed in the Ark of the Covenant. The Book of Joshua follows the books of the Torah and describes the movement into, and the occupation, albeit incomplete, of the Promised Land at ~1410 BC. Characters in the story of Joshua were evidently still alive when his book was being compiled (Joshua 6:25) and the phrase "unto this day" appears several times to endorse a contemporary account. Joshua housed the Ark at Shiloh and is recorded as reading it to the people when they entered the Promised Land (Joshua 8:31-35). The archaeological record has identified the signature of this invasion, whilst the Tel el Armana tablets record pleading by the indigenous Canaanite people to the Pharaoh for aid in dealing with the Israelite invasion; he did not respond, likely due to his memory of the damage already inflicted on Egypt by the Israelite Exodus (Pearce 1998).

Once the tribes had moved to occupy their allocated portions of the Promised Land serious observance of the Torah largely lapsed as they fought to fend off the hostile inhabitants already present, and often became absorbed into their pagan cultures. The history recorded in the Book of Judges covers approximately 340 years of rule by 7 major and 6 minor judges falling into seven cycles of apostasy and defeat followed by repentance and revival, then rapidly sinking back into apostasy. It embraces the history of Israel from the death of Joshua in ~1390 BC to the penultimate judge, Samson, who ruled during an era of Philistine domination, and then the crowning of Saul, the first king of Israel, by the last Judge Samuel in ~1050 BC. Samuel likely compiled the books of the Tanakh up to his time; an indication of this is the absence of any serious mention of Jerusalem, then a little-known place of small significance, which would go on to become at the heart of the Jewish people. To ensure a faithful continuing record, Samuel established a school of scribes and prophets (1 Samuel 19:20-21) which was still active more than 300 years later in the era of the prophets Elijah, Elisha (2 Kings 6:1) and probably Jonah. A unity of purpose of the tribes (now expanded from 12 to 13 to include descendants of the two sons of

Joseph) was only finally achieved under the strong leadership of Samuel. It was to turn them into the nation of ancient Israel but with a unified history lasting only until the death of King Solomon in ~931 BC. King David was zealous in worship, adding much poetry and music now included in the Book of Psalms, and bringing order to the Levitical priesthood. His son Solomon known as a brilliant and wise king, built the first temple and added much wisdom to the accumulating scriptures. Sadly the influence of his wives, many from surrounding pagan nations, later soured his commitment to the Torah and his arrogant son Rehoboam tore the kingdom apart.

The subsequent formation of the separate nations of Israel in the north and Judah in the south divided approximately on tribal lines; ten of the tribes inherited from Jacob's 12 sons occupied Israel and two (Judah and Benjamin) occupied Judah. The successive kings of Israel are all recorded as bad kings. They established an alternative worship system which quickly lapsed into the Baal worship that the Prophet Elijah had to contend with. Whilst the kings of Israel endeavored to prevent their people from visiting Jerusalem to worship according to the ordinances of the Torah, intermingling evidently took place. The more zealous members of all tribes believed that their worship would only be acceptable if it took place in the Temple established by the kings David and Solomon in Jerusalem which now lay in the nation of Judah (2 Chronicles 15:9). The histories of these two nations from the time of Samuel until their destructions by the Babylonian and Persian empires are documented in detail by the books of Samuel, Kings and Chronicles. The nation of ancient Israel disappears from history completely in 722 BC with the defeated people scattered throughout the Assyrian Empire. In keeping with the Assyrian policy of destroying enemy power structures, they conducted ethnic cleansing by dispersing the Jews throughout their empire and replacing them with the Samaritans. The Samaritans were nevertheless influenced by a relict Jewish heritage and acquired a Biblical record up to the time of the Judaic king Hezekiah (reigned 715-686 BC); this scroll comprises the Samaritan Old Testament and provides a further record of the books preserved by the Jews up to that time.

The judgment of the nation of Judah was delayed by a number of righteous kings, notably Jehoshaphat, Hezekiah and Josiah, that aimed to achieve revival by restoring the teaching of the Torah. When King Josiah reopened the closed Temple after a long period of neglect, the Torah was rediscovered (2 Kings 22:8) and this may well have been the original transcript from the time of the Exodus. However, within 40 years of the end of a 55-year reign by the particularly wicked king Manasseh, final judgment and destruction by Babylon became inevitable; the nation had by then become so decayed by strife, famine and disease that Nebuchadnezzar found only ~4,600 Jews worth taking into exile. Whilst Jeremiah was left behind to observe the devastation of his nation, Daniel of the Royal line and the priest Ezekiel were amongst the exiles. Daniel is recorded as having access to the Torah and the books written by Jeremiah, and likely to the remainder of the scriptures secured by Jeremiah (Johnson 2010a). After an interrupted story comprising 70 years of exile, a rump of ancient Judah was allowed to return from Babylon, albeit under oppression; this is traditionally interpreted by Bible scholars as a concession by God due to His promise to David that a descendent of His would sit on the throne of a future united Israel (2 Samuel 7:16).

Whilst all ancient manuscripts compiled first by Jeremiah and then by Ezra were destroyed with the destruction of the First and Second Temples, or lost with the passage of time, we can be confident that they record events close to the times at which they occurred. The Abrahamic record for example, incorporates the Hittite legal code still used when Moses compiled the Torah in ~1400 BC, although abandoned in later times (Pearce 1998). Moses is recorded as keeping a record of the forty years of wandering through the wilderness (Numbers 33:2) even to the point of recording one item on the same day (Deuteronomy 31:22). The details of Levitical worship practice and the trials during this long sojourn indicate a record close to the time of the events they describe, both because the ordained festivals have been kept by Jewish people ever since, and because they accord with archaeological evidence discovered in the Arabian desert at the site of the ancient land of Midian where much of the wilderness experience was played out. The history books of Joshua and Judges following the Torah include frequent references to items that were with them "to this day" implying that long-vanished features were there when the texts were compiled.

Frustratingly, Moses does not name the Pharaoh of the Exodus, but this was characteristic of the writing style in his times when the word "Pharaoh" referred to a status and not to a man; ~700 years later during the age of the Israelite Kings, when Pharaohs were no longer supreme figures, the Pharaoh Nechoh is specifically named (2 Kings 23:33). Moses does not even name his adoptive and protective mother, although this was probably Hatshetsup because she was the only surviving child in the Royal line of Thutmose 1, the Pharaoh at the time of his birth in ~1526 BC. Hatshetsup would go on to become the most important queen in the history of ancient Egypt and was perhaps favored by God because of her special relationship to Moses.*

Hatshetsup either died or fell from grace in ~1488 BC and probably within two years Moses would flee into the wilderness of Midian in north west Arabia. It seems that once he had begun God's commission of leading the Israelites out of Egypt and turning them into a nation, his past life as a Prince of Egypt, covered by just fourteen verses in Exodus Chapter 2, was to be discarded. We rely on the historian Josephus writing at the time of the Apostles to provide more details of this era. From the Bible record alone it is evident that Moses had the most extraordinary life occupying three 40 year periods beginning with an exalted position in Egypt, followed by a long, essentially personal, wilderness experience accompanied by Divine encounters. He would then return to Egypt to lead the now greatly-expanded family of Hebrews out of bondage, turn them into a nation, and after a tumultuous 40-year history of wilderness wanderings, take them to the borders of

---

*The precise chronologies of the Pharaohs of this 18th Dynasty are disputed. Here we follow recent revisions proposed by Dr Douglas Petrovitch. The historian Josephus records the part played by Moses in the conquest of the southern kingdom of Cush leading to annexation of Nubia in ~1504 BC, whilst a tablet from the Temple of Serabit records thanks given to Queen Hatshetsup by Moses for allowing the Hebrews ('Habiru') to build a worship site remote from the Egyptians (Pearce 1998). The Egyptians revered animals and the Hebrew sacrificial practices originating as far back as Cain and Abel in Genesis Chapter Four would have been anathema to them.

the Promised Land. His final words to the nation are recorded in the last chapters of the Book of Deuteronomy and include great wisdom and prophecy. Of particular interest to the theme of this book is Deuteronomy 32:7 where he divides time into "the days of old" and "the years of many generations". As we explore in Chapters 8 and 9, this apparent division of time before and after Adam becomes instrumental in understanding Genesis Chapter One.

Beginning with Ezra's return to Jerusalem there is a short final record of the ancient history of the Jewish people covering the closing of the fifth century BC (~538-510 BC). The Book of Nehemiah is a pivotal narrative concluding this history and the Book of Maccabees notes that he established a library to secure the Biblical record up to his time. Nehemiah's book is the only one recorded throughout in the first person singular and his mission becomes a type of the forthcoming Messiah. It had two purposes. Firstly, he rebuilds the Walls of Jerusalem and secures the future of the Jewish remnant, initiating this task in 444 BC.[*] Secondly, he anticipates the Messianic era to follow by including the last Biblical record of the Jewish people, and then coinciding his ministry with the beginning of the countdown of the remainder of history; this is covered by the outstanding "Seventy Weeks of Years" prophecy given to the Prophet Daniel in 536 BC and recorded in Chapter 9:24-27 of Daniel's book (see Johnson 2010a). It may be for this reason that God provides no more history of Israel, although we know much more from the Books of Maccabees covering the interval 175-134 BC, and the writings of the historian Josephus. Also, the final Chapters Eleven and Twelve of the Book of Daniel describe a further prophetic revelation given to the prophet in 533 BC predicting with remarkable precision the events that would take the Jewish people into the Messianic era. Daniel recorded part of his book (Chapters 2:4 - 7:28) in Aramaic (Syriac), a language already in use when the Assyrians invaded Israel; he likely did this because the prophetic subjects concern the gentile world. In contrast now an old man, from Chapter eight onwards he returns to the Hebrew with prophecies of primary concern

---

[*] *This is recorded in Persian records as a decree of the Persian Emperor Artaxerxes Longimanus on March 14th 444 BC.*

to the Jewish people. In Chapter nine, after an intense period of repentance for the sins of his people he is given the Seventy Weeks of Years prophecy predicting the death and resurrection of the Lord Jesus Christ. Three years later after an intense spiritual struggle spanning three weeks covering the 6th and 7th Levitical festivals of Atonement and Tabernacles, he is given the future of his people recorded in Chapter 10 onwards; this time no mention is included of the death and resurrection of the Messiah, presumably because the Jews as a nation would reject Him at His first coming.

The books of the earlier prophets (Isaiah, Jeremiah, Ezekiel, Hosea, Joel, Amos, Micah Nahum, Habakkuk and Zephaniah) comprise messages given to a succession of men (for which most of them were persecuted and sometimes killed) during the waning years of the nations of ancient Israel and Judah as these nations sank more and more into apostasy. However, their collective messages include not only warnings of the dangers of this apostasy, but also many predictions concerning the First and Second comings of the Lord Jesus Christ, as well as the distant future of the Jewish people. As carefully documented by Johnson (2010b), many of these prophecies have already been precisely fulfilled and provide a key facet for confirming the Divine inspiration of the Scriptures (see also Table 5.1 footnotes in Chapter 5).

Ezra's group of "wisdom books" comprise Job, Psalms, Proverbs, Ecclesiastes and the Song of Solomon. Collectively they seek to praise and thank God, understand His character, and follow His advice for leading a righteous and fruitful life. They give us an understanding of the character and prefect righteousness of the Creator and enable us to develop the personal relationship that He desires. The Psalms also include important prophetic messages of which the most remarkable is Psalm 22 which describes in detail the agony of crucifixion that Jesus would go through during His time on the cross. The ultimate Jewish punishment at that time and continuing into the apostolic era (Book of Acts, Chapter Seven) was death by stoning. Death by crucifixion was only devised by the Persians some 550 years after this Psalm was given prophetically to King David, and was then adopted by the Romans.

The Book of Esther records the threat of persecution overshadowing the Jewish Diaspora in the Persian Empire during the reign of Ahasuerus (Xeres 1, 486-465 BC) and their remarkable deliverance. Ahasuerus would take the Jewess Esther as a wife and there is a time gap between his third (Esther 1:3) and seventh years (Esther 2:16-17) accounted for by his disastrous invasion of Greece where he was heavily defeated (480-479 BC). This book is the only one in the canon of the Scriptures that does not mention God and for this reason its inclusion was disputed by reformers such as Luther; however, it has since been shown to embed textural features of Remez (see Chapter 2.3) which confirm a Divine inspiration. This deliverance of the Jews in the Persian Empire is commemorated as the appointed time of Purim, the ninth and last festival of the religious year.

The books written before the time of Ezra weathered several crises. Their scrolls were suppressed for many years under a succession of apostate kings notably Manasseh (~687-642 BC), who executed his maternal grandfather the Prophet Isaiah. It was only his grandson, the godly king Josiah (~640-610 BC), who restored the reading of the Torah. We read in Chapter 36 of Jeremiah that King Jehoiakim (609-598 BC) tried to cut up and burn a Biblical scroll; it required the swift intervention of the prophet to ensure that a copy was made. During the fierce rule of the oppressive Greco-Syrian King Antiochus Epiphanes IV reading of the Scriptures was banned in 168 BC as he aimed to aggressively Hellenize the Israelite culture. He ordered the burning of the scrolls in the Temple which he transformed into a temple for Zeus and sacrificed a pig on the altar, an ultimate abomination to the religious Jews. Jews who failed to reject their Hebraic origins and transform to a Grecian life style were treated mercilessly. His plans were only thwarted by the rebellion and victories of the Maccabees in 165 BC. This enabled the Levitical practices to be restored according to the procedures instituted in the Torah. As the temple was cleansed and rededicated, the priesthood relit the Menorah lamp with just one day's supply of the required oil; this was to last for eight days whilst new oil was prepared and gave rise to the miracle celebrated as Hanukah, now to become the eighth appointed time of the religious year.

The Old Testament repeatedly asserts its divine inspiration with statements such as *"thus saith the Lord"* and *"the Word of the Lord came..."*. David declares this in the Psalms whilst Moses records that God actually wrote the Commandments Himself on the two tablets of stone (Exodus 31:18). Paul the Apostle reaffirms the Old Testament as the "oracles of God" (Romans 3:1-2) and inspired by God Himself (2 Timothy 3:16). The historian Josephus was emphatic in his assertion that all the original 22 books of the Old Testament were written under Divine inspiration.

However, it is the conduct of the ancient Hebrew scribes that provides the highest level of confidence in the accuracy of the copies of the Old Testament books passed down from generation to generation that we inherit today (Jeffery 1997). Initially there were no gaps between the words on the scrolls. The copyist would be expected to count the number of times each of the 22 letters of the Hebrew manuscript that occurred on each page; he would note these figures in the margin to ensure that no letters had been added or taken away. A priest-inspector would oversee the copyist and check each character, carefully counting every letter to ensure that there were no errors. A single error would be allowed but must be corrected. Two or more errors would require the master scribe to destroy the entire scroll and the copyist would face the onerous task of starting again from the beginning of Genesis. This proven reliability of the Old Testament texts far surpasses that of any other ancient documents. Jesus confirmed the significance of "every yod and tittle" in the Old Testament Scriptures (Matthew 5:18) where the *yod* is the smallest letter of the Hebrew alphabet written like an apostrophe, and the *tittle* is the curved taper that embellishes the terminations of the letters. It is the supreme quality of work of the ancient scribes that has enabled the recovery of the Divine signatures in the text (Chapter 2.3), particularly the multiple example of equi-distant letter spacing.

The Essene scholars of Qumran were particularly assiduous in preserving the sanctity of books they held in Divine respect. It is thanks to them that we have the Dead Sea Scrolls. With discoveries beginning in 1947, there is now a wealth of Biblical documentation dating mostly from the last two centuries before Jesus Christ. The manuscripts, including the treasured Isaiah Scroll, have been able to confirm the precision and reliability of Hebrew Bible texts that could previously only be dated back to about 900 AD. The Book of Isaiah contains the greatest Messianic prophecies and more copies of this book than any other Old Testament prophet have been recovered from Qumran; he was evidently their most revered source and goes on to be the most quoted Old Testament book in the New Testament. The precise transcription of the Tanakh continues up to the present day where all scrolls in synagogues are hand-copied by master scribes. An extraordinary number of rules have to be observed to undertake the copying task. If the name of the "Lord" appears in the text for example, the scribe should take a bath to ensure that he is ritualistically clean. If a mistake is discovered that cannot be corrected the scroll must be burnt or buried.

By the third century BC as a result of the conquests of Alexander and the widespread dispersal of Greek settlements throughout the Mediterranean region, Greek had been adopted as the vernacular language. Following the destruction of the nation of Israel in 720 AD and of Judah in 606 and 587-586 BC, the Jewish populations were now widely dispersed with the use of Hebrew becoming restricted to religious practice. Emperor Ptolemy II Philadelphus (285–247 BC) of Egypt was a scholarly ruler concerned with gathering literary sources for the Great Library at Alexandria and he brought together Hebrew scholars to produce a Greek translation of the Old Testament. This version, known as the "Septuagint" after the 70 members of the Sanhedrin of Alexandria, the highest Jewish law court in Egypt that confirmed it, dates from about 285 BC. All events described, including prophecies concerning the First Coming of the Lord Jesus Christ, have to predate this time. Jesus, His disciples and the Early Church Fathers confirmed their respect for the Septuagint version of the Old Testament by most commonly quoting from it. The Septuagint contained some books now called the Apocrypha ("Apocrypha" meaning "those hidden away") which became a source of dispute over their Divine inspiration. Believers centered on the Holy Land tended to exclude them from the canon of Scripture and Martin Luther holding to ancient Jewish precedent spoke out strongly against them. Those affiliated to Rome have tended to include them and in reaction Rome declared the Apocrypha to be canonical at the Council of Trent (1546). Catholics still uphold the Apocrypha whilst the Reformed churches do not regard them as Divinely-inspired.

Meanwhile the residue of Israel became a vassal state, first of Greece and then of Rome, with the exception of a short period of independence following the Maccabean Revolt. The pressures of subjection caused the system of the Levitical priesthood to fade away as the Temple practise became dominated by men with monetary influence. The priestly system now split into three divisions. The Sadducees became the liberal scholars who rejected miracles and resurrection, but usually managed to dominate the Second Temple priesthood and give a token acknowledgement to the Levitical practises. The Pharisees accepted the Scriptures literally but became legalistic and adopted 613 Oral Laws which rapidly became the main focus of their religious practise. This observance, and their demands for esteemed status in society, came under severe criticism from Jesus. Nevertheless, He would usually agree with their interpretation of the written word of the Tanakh. A third group, the Essenes, would have nothing to do with what they considered to be the apostasy of both Sadducees and Pharisees. They moved into the country, particularly to the Qumran area in the Dead Sea region, to zealously practise their faith. They kept strictly to the written word of the Hebrew Scriptures, whilst at the same time preserving many other ancient writings which are continuing to provide a valuable source of ongoing scholarship. It is likely that John the Baptist was associated with the Essenes. They understood the Triune nature of the Godhead and from their study of the prophecies in the Tanakh they were anticipating the soon coming of the Messiah in the guise of the Suffering Servant (Johnson 2017). The Essenes disappear from history in the first century AD and it is probable that they were amongst the First Century Messianic believers.

Following the destruction of the Temple in 70 AD the Levitical blood sacrifices could no longer be performed and within a few decades Judaism had been revised into its modern form. This has involved a bloodless ritual observance accompanied by study of the Tanakh, sometimes to intense detail. Nevertheless, Judaism continues to deny much of the interpretation emerging from the depth of the Biblical text as described in the next chapter. This requires a triune Godhead with a Suffering Servant Messiah that has already appeared to fulfil the Levitical blood sacrifice once and for all. The Apostle Paul, himself once a dedicated Pharisee with great intellectual abilities, attributes this to *"a blindness in part has happened to Israel, until the fullness of the Gentiles be come in"* (Romans 11:25). The continuing survival and preservation of the Jewish people over 2000 years during which much larger nations and numbers of peoples have come and then vanished from history, is however, a testimony of God's special concern for their past witness and their future purpose (Jeremiah 31:35-36 and 31:10, Ezekiel 36:24, Hosea Chapter 3). The unique scale and intensity of Anti-Semitism amongst global persecutions is the outworking of attempts by the satanic realm to frustrate these purposes.

The ongoing trials of the Jewish people, especially throughout the Church Age, have been accompanied by repeated judgements that carry a Divine signature. These have always occurred on the identical day of the year, the 9th day of the 5th month, Av, of the Jewish religious calendar, and they span both the Old and New Testament dispensations. When the Prophet Zechariah referred to this date in the statement: *"Speak unto all the people of the land, and to the priests, saying, when ye fasted and mourned in the fifth* (Av) *and seventh* (Tishrei, including Yom Kippur) *month, even those seventy years, did ye at all fast unto Me, even to Me?"* (Zechariah 7:5) only two tragic events had been recorded on this date, namely the return of the spies from the Promised Land with a negative report which consigned the Israelites to 40 years of wandering in the wilderness (Book of Numbers Chapter 14), and the destruction of Solomon's Temple in 586 BC. In the Messianic era cataclysmic events have continued to take place on this same day of the Jewish year beginning with the destruction of Jerusalem and the Second Temple in 70 AD (Predicted by Jesus in Luke 19:41-44, 1,100,000 Jews killed and 97,000 taken into slavery) and the plowing under of Jerusalem with salt exactly a year later on this date in 71 AD (predicted in Micah 3:12). Subsequent destructive events with the same annual date include the destruction of the army of the false messiah Bar Kochba in 135 AD (500,000 Jews killed during this rebellion with thousands sold into slavery), the destruction of the Jewish community in Mainz by the Crusaders in 1096, expulsion of the last Jews from Austria in 1282, expulsion of Jews from England in 1290, expulsion of the Jews in France in 1306, massacres of the Jews in Catalonia, Spain, in 1358, the expulsion of Jews from Spain in 1492, the initiation of pogroms against the Jews in the Pale of Settlement in western Russia in 1914, initiation of the Göring-Himmler–Heydrich plan for the "Final Solution" in 1942, the final crushing of the Warsaw Rising on this day in 1943 and the evacuation of Gaza, which would subsequently become a terrorist base for attacking Israel, in 2005 (the latter date was deliberately postponed by a day so that it would not coincide with the 9th of Av). The odds of all these disastrous events for the Jewish people occurring by chance on the ninth day of Av, rather than by God's design, are impossibly large. This prolonged wilderness experience of punishment for the Jewish people is expressed by prophecies given to the Prophet Ezekiel in Chapter 4 of his testimony. It is interpreted as leading to a seven-fold multiplication of a period of time of punishment for the grievous sins of ancient Israel and Judah when most of the people failed to repent after the 70 year exile in Babylon. This exilic period was then extended to 2520 prophetic 360-day years comprising the 'servitude of the nation' and the 'desolation of Jerusalem,' periods of judgment that only finally expired in 1948 and 1967 respectively (see footnote to Table 5.1 in Chapter 5).

1.2.2 The New Testament

It is fairly certain that all four gospels in the New Testament were compiled before the cataclysmic destruction of the Second Temple accompanying the slaughter and dispersal of the Jews in 70 AD because, apart from the prediction of this event by Jesus and the prophets, there is no indication that the writers knew that it had happened. Matthew and Luke required the Temple records in order to compile their genealogies of the Lord Jesus Christ and this would not have been possible after 70 AD. Matthew was a scribe and likely recorded the events of Jesus' ministry whilst it was in progress.

Furthermore, the historian Luke tells us that the other gospels (implying Matthew and Mark) were written before his gospel, and that the Acts of the Apostles is his second book (after his gospel). His extensive documentation of Paul's missionary journeys ends abruptly before the execution of Paul in Rome; he would almost certainly have recorded Paul's death if he had been writing at a later date. Christian influence in the capital of the empire was evidently profound by 64 AD when much of Rome was destroyed by fire and Emperor Nero blamed the Christians. Following mass arrests, he had his victims covered in the skins of wild animals and torn to death by dogs, set on fire or crucified, and Church tradition records the martyrdom, first of Peter probably in 65 AD and then of Paul in 66 or 67 AD at the hands of Nero. At the time of the Crucifixion the Apostles were a fearful and reclusive group of men; the transforming record that all but one of them would subsequently be willing to undergo the cruelest of martyrdoms for the cause of the Gospel of Jesus Christ is the most remarkable witness to the truth of their testimonies (Morison 1967).

Obviously, the Epistles were written before their authors, the Apostles, were martyred and the Book of Hebrews would have made no sense if it had been written after the destruction of the Temple in 70 AD. The exception is the Book of Revelation since John, the only Apostle not to be martyred, lived until the end of the First Century. The evidence for the time of writing of this book fits most closely to a time around 90 AD when John was on the Island of Patmos during the exiles imposed by the Emperor Domitian. This accords with the testimony of the Early Church Father Irenaeus (120-202 AD) writing in about 180 AD; Irenaeus was trained by Polycarp who in turn, worked with the Apostle John for 20 years. Eusebius a later church historian, confirms the record of Irenaeus *(The Ecclesiastical History of Eusebius Pamphilus, translated by Isaac Boyle)*.

The secular world makes extraordinary historical and archaeological demands for evidence confirming the Ministry of the Lord Jesus Christ, but totally fails to apply these standards to other historical records represented by a mere handful of sources, usually compiled long after the events they purport to record. There are for example, over 20,000 manuscripts of all dates and ages confirming a record of the New Testament preserved over 2000 years. A comparison with some key ancient writings which form the bedrock of classical education is striking:

Author	Date written	Earliest copy	Approximate time span between original and copy	Number of copies	Accuracy of copies
Pliny	61-113 AD	850 AD	750 yrs	7	----
Plato	427-347 BC	900 AD	1200 yrs	7	----
Herodotus	480-425 BC	900 AD	1300 yrs	8	----
Suetonius	75-160 AD	950 AD	800 yrs	8	----
Caesar	100-44 BC	900 AD	1000	10	----
Tacitus	circa 100 AD	1100 AD	1000 yrs	20	----
Aristotle	384-322 BC	1100 AD	1400	49	----
Homer (Iliad)	900 BC	400 BC	500 yrs	643	95%
New Testament	~50-96 AD	~130 AD and following	less than 30 years except for the Book of Revelation	5600	99.5%

This table includes the New Testament documents of the Byzantine world in Greek and their internal consistency is over 99.0%. The Early Church Fathers showed remarkable discernment in separating the canon of inspired new scripture from invented works by writers with supposed secret knowledge (the Gnostics), and by the early third century only a handful of books that comprise our New Testament were in question. In western regions of the Roman Empire, the book of Hebrews faced opposition, and in the east Revelation was unpopular. The church historian Eusebius (263-339 AD) records that James, 2 Peter, 2-3 John and Jude were the only books questioned by part of the body of Christian believers. By 367 AD differences had largely been resolved and Athanasius, the bishop of Alexandria, wrote an Easter letter that contained mention of all the twenty-seven books of the present New Testament canon. In 393 AD at the Synod of Hippo a group of devout men studied the many manuscripts then circulating among the churches. With much research and prayer, they separated writings they could certify as genuinely written by the original apostles of Jesus from a host of unverifiable manuscripts. They ended their work by including just the 27 books of the present New Testament, and in 397 AD the Council of Carthage published this same list.

In most respects this team was affirming work already done nearly a century before when a Greek New Testament had been compiled by Lucian of Antioch, and before the Edict of Constantine brought an end to the tyranny against the Church culminating in the Diocletian Persecution (303-305 AD). Lucien's compilation was widely circulated when the Emperor Constantine came to power. He ordered 50 copies to be distributed to the growing churches in his capital of Constantinople. With the 27 New Testament books established, the Bible in Latin and Greek spread rapidly and motivated extensive missionary activity throughout the Roman Empire before it fell apart in 476 AD; after this everything changed as an authoritarian Church government took over in the West. In the East missionaries moved out from a training school in Antioch and the 27 books of the New Testament quickly became established as the standard Byzantine text. For nearly a thousand years the great majority of the New Testament manuscripts were produced in Greek in the Byzantium world. They were used by Erasmus to compile the Greek text produced on the early printing press in 1525. This became known as the *Textus Receptus* or "Received Text". In addition to the Byzantine texts, over 19,000 copies of the New Testament in the Syriac, Latin, Coptic and Aramaic languages have survived. The total number of ancient manuscripts supporting the New Testament record exceeds 24,000. A minority group of texts originating from the Alexandrian School, are regarded as somewhat older but were exposed to textural alterations by Gnostics, particularly those influenced by Arianism. Origen and other scholars of this school denied the deity of the Lord Jesus Christ and their manuscripts differ from the traditional *Textus Receptus* in 8,413 places (Missler 1999).

1.3 The Bible in the Church Age

The history of the Bible during the 2000 years since the Apostolic Age has been a complex and turbulent one. The Bible has been seen not only as the most important of books, but also as the most dangerous one. It has survived efforts to eradicate its influence by conquest and genocide, attempts to keep it hidden in a language the common people could not understand, Church edicts to destroy it and burn at the stake those who tried to read it in their own language, and now in our own times, rewriting to mute or compromise its message. This history has followed many different paths and is documented by a vast amount of scholarship elsewhere. Here discussion is limited to an outline of key events, focussing primarily on the influence of the Bible on Western Civilisation.

The compilation of the Bible texts in Greek, Aramaic, Syriac and Armenian languages saw a remarkable explosion of belief throughout the Roman Empire. It carried the nascent Church through persecutions imposed by ten Roman emperors for the refusal of Christians to worship Caesar and sacrifice to the pagan gods. More than two centuries of oppression culminated in the persecution (303-305 AD) by Diocletian (reigned 284-305 AD) which involved mainly exiling, but served to further distribute the message. The pivotal change occurred with the accession of Constantine (reigned 306-337 AD) who issued an edict of toleration in favor of Christians in 313 AD. Now that Christianity was an accepted religion of the Empire it was no longer under pressure to preserve the purity of its doctrine and it became increasingly influenced by the surrounding environment of pagan worship. Pagan festivals were adopted to include Christmas and Easter, and the remaining Jewish heritage was abandoned. The Second Commandment was rewritten to permit iconography and other imagery which has dominated much religious practice ever since.

Constantine was concerned primarily with preserving an orthodox unity amongst Christians and called a number of Church Councils with the aim of achieving a consensus. The First Council of Nicaea in 325 drew up the first Nicene Creed and declared Arianism (the belief that Jesus was begotten at some later date by God the Father and therefore subordinate to Him) a heresy. Arianism was widespread through the Empire at this time and had been embraced as the leading doctrine by Germanic tribes, notable the Goths. Although Arianism largely disappeared within these communities several centuries later, it never

CREATION UNLIMITED

totally went away and the core doctrine was to emerge in more recent times in forms such as Unitarianism, Mormonism, Christadelphianism and the Jehovah's Witnesses; although differing in beliefs, these more recent developments share a common rejection of the Trinity, a central pillar of Christian belief (see Chapter 5.12).

The third Council of Ephesus in 431 was called by the Emperor Theodosius II to address a conflict between two church patriarchs, Cyril of Alexandria (~376-444 AD) and Nestorius (~386-450 AD). Cyril was influenced by pagan mother-goddess worship and campaigned for Mary to be called "Mother of God". To Nestorius this was heresy; he regarded Mary as a privileged virgin chosen to give birth to the Messiah, but otherwise a sinner like everyone else. Nevertheless, Cyril successfully carried his opinion forward and this has remained Catholic doctrine ever since. Nestorius moved into exile but his orthodox Biblical Trinitarian values seeded numerous churches. The teachings of Nestorius and his pupils were taught from the School of Edessa based in the Persian city of Nisibis (modern-day Nusaybin in Turkey) from 489 AD. Their church planting flourished eastwards across Asia reaching China in 635 AD. Subsequent centuries saw periods of revival when even Mongol leaders and one Chinese emperor became Christians, alternating with periods of repression as Chinese emperors sought to enforce indigenous religions. Christian influence became very widespread across Asia surviving here for nearly a thousand years until mostly swept away by the Mongol and Islamic invasions. By the end of the fourteenth century it had been largely destroyed, although minority communities such as the the Assyrian Church of the East are relict survivors of this remarkable missionary activity. Sadly, even many of these precious remnants are currently falling victim to the depredations of ISIS and the resurgence of militant Islam.

Although the Church in Rome had developed a hierarchy of bishops, these enjoyed no temporal power until the time of Constantine. When he moved the capital from Rome to Byzantium (later Constantinople) a power vacuum allowed a line of popes to take over leadership, assert an influence over secular powers and engage in worldly matters. With the fall of the Roman Empire in 476 AD, this Papacy had become embroiled with rulers surrounding the Italian Peninsula and then made territorial claims of its own. Its expanding influence was able to subsume most of the more Biblically-based Celtic churches long established around the fringes of Europe. Succeeding centuries saw important Roman families seizing control, claiming authority over Kings and Princes, and disputing for the position of Papal leadership. Increasing conflict with the Byzantine Empire and the Church in Constantinople over issues including the claimed dominance of the Pope, resulted in the Great Schism of 1054 which seeded the Eastern Orthodox Churches.

By this time essential Catholic doctrine had been articulated, notably by Augustine of Hippo (354 - 430 AD) the most influential of the Later Church Fathers. Augustine became a powerful orator and advocate of critical thinking. He taught that the Church comprised a threefold entity comprising the Institutional Hierarchy, the Catholic Sacraments, and the Laity. He developed an amillennialist viewpoint of history in which Christ presently rules the Earth spiritually through a triumphant church, a view later adopted by reformed theologians such as John Calvin. His attitude to the Jewish people were ambivalent: in some writings he called for them all to be slain whilst in others he considered that God had chosen them as a special people and believed that they would be converted to Christianity at "the end of time". He correctly contended with Pelagianism, a doctrine originating from an obscure monk of possible British origin who taught that people could choose right or wrong without God's help, and that His grace was unnecessary. Pelagianism was duly condemned by the Councils of Carthage (418 AD) and Ephesus (430 AD). However, much of Augustine's theology was diametrically unbiblical. He supported the view that purgatorial fire was necessary to purify those that died in communion with the Church, and his view of Mary as the sinless "the Mother of God" predates Cyril of Alexandria and the Council of Ephesus; Augustine also held the view that Christ could become a real presence in the Eucharist and be sacrificed for sin again and again by performing the mass. He also insisted that baptism and these sacraments could only be performed within the Catholic Church.

The alienation between Christianity and its Jewish heritage commenced in the late Apostolic Age as Christians, still primarily Jewish, began to be excluded from the synagogues; it culminated following the Jewish revolts of 70 and 132 AD. Now becoming predominantly a gentile faith, this alienation rapidly morphed into a rampant anti-Semitism fuelled by the writings of Church Fathers such as Justin Martyr (100-165 AD), Origen (184-253 AD), John Chrysostom (349-407 AD) and Augustine. Much later a virulent anti-Semitism was adopted by Luther when the Jews failed to respond to the Reformation. A grievous legacy of hostility of much of the Church to the Jewish people continues to our own time and is articulated in "Replacement Theology". This regards a triumphant Church as totally replacing the Jewish people in God's purposes. The future implications of the prophecies of Jesus and the Book of Revelation are dismissed, and there will be no Millennial Reign - this is "amillenialism".

A more rigorous interpretation of the Scriptures limiting the need for allegory sees a dual but separate, interpretation of the purposes of God for the Church and the Jews. This discerning analysis of the Scriptures sympathetic to the Jewish people, was adopted and articulated by all the great dispensational preachers of the 19th and early 20th century noted in the Introduction. Long before the establishment of modern Israel in 1948, the 17th century puritan John Owen understood that multiple prophecies implied that the Jewish people would ultimately be returning to their ancient homeland, albeit in unbelief. Ministers who were able to probe a deeper understanding of the Scriptures accordingly abandoned the amillenialist view of history carried over by all the main Christian denominations from the Reformation. Although rejected by the Later Church Fathers such as Augustine, modern scholarship has found that this "dispensational" view of history was merely recovering what the Early Church Fathers had been taught by the Apostles. Papias (70-155 AD), Tertullian (190-210 AD) and Irenaeus (~178 AD) all taught that there would be a literal millennial reign as foretold in the Book of Revelation, whilst Barnabus (~100 AD), Irenaeus (~180 AD) and Hippolytus (~205 AD) taught that this would happen after six thousand years of history from Adam; some of these and others from their era, taught that the millennial period would happen after restoration of the Jews to their homeland and the reign of a man of apostasy, the antichrist (see Johnson 2010a, b). These are key facets of modern prophecy teaching, although they do not tend to figure prominently in the teaching of the established Christian denominations which mostly remain amillennialist in outlook.

St. Jerome completed the Vulgate Latin translation of the Bible in 405 AD in his monastery in Bethlehem. Regrettably Jerome was also vociferously anti-Semitic and, together with later insertions of Catholic doctrine, his Bible remains the official version used in Catholic churches to this day. As additions caused the original Vulgate to become more and more corrupted, the Emperor Charlemagne drew together a group of scholars in the 9th century with the aim of recovering the original, although with no lasting impact. In reality when the Roman Empire collapsed many regional languages developed and Latin became a dead language; most people were then denied access to Scriptures in a language that they could understand. The imposition of an exclusive Latin liturgy transmitted by a sacerdotal priesthood (i.e. essential mediators between God and humankind) throughout the domains under Papal control - essentially the former Roman Empire - ensured that the next thousand years were to become the true "Dark Ages" in the context of a real absence of Biblical understanding by the common people. Nevertheless, throughout this long period of ignorance God graciously preserved nuclei of believers scattered throughout Europe and Asia. This "Pilgrim Church" would assiduously preserve the Biblical texts and adhere to their teaching (Broadbent 1999).

In contrast, the dominant power granted to the established Church hierarchy caused it to become increasingly worldly, oppressive and corrupt. To translate the Bible into a local language became a crime that could cost the scholar his life; church agents would aggressively track down any translations and burn them. A typical law was the Decree of the Council of Toulouse (1229 AD): *"We prohibit also that the laity should be permitted to have the books of the Old or New Testament; but we most strictly forbid their having any translation of these books".* This corruption continued with ever increasing severity for a thousand years during which the Church created its own literature, traditions and practices and placed them on the same level of authority as the Bible. In effect this followed the pattern of the latter part of the Old Testament era when the rabbis developed a complex oral law and gave it a status equal or superior to the Scriptures. The commissioners sent by Henry VIII to oversee the dissolution of the monasteries in England reported widespread immorality; they found that the priests were avaricious in their exploitation of the laity, whilst unable to repeat the Ten Commandments or even know in which part of the Scripture they were to be found; similarly, with the Lord's prayer, many did not know where it was written or even who the author was. The tragedy for the common person was that he or she were banned from owning a Bible, let alone one in their own language. They were then told that they could only reach God through confession to a priesthood which would then be able to hold them to ransom.*

Peter Waldo (1140-1218) commissioned a translation in the vernacular language in France and his followers, the Waldensians, branched out all over Europe waging a campaign to get the Bible to the people. They were to become the subject of a relentless Church inquisition and had been largely annihilated by the 17th century. Nearer the peripheries of the Papal domain preachers had sometimes been able to minister more freely in the common language. In England John Wycliffe (1330-1385) was a seminary professor of Oxford grieved with the corruption in the established church. Concerned that the populace should be able to read the Scriptures in a language they could understand, he personally translated portions of the Vulgate Latin Bible into English. He saw literacy as the key to the emancipation of the poor and sent preachers called "Lollards" (a derogatory nickname given to preachers without an academic background) far and wide throughout the land to preach and teach. Like Luther who was protected from Catholic wrath by German princes, Wycliffe was able to operate due to patronage of John of Gaunt the Duke of Lancaster; he was called upon to advise Parliament in its negotiations with the Pope, a position which only increased his contempt for the Papacy. However, with the succession of new

---

* *What do we owe to the Reformation? by J.C. Ryle, Protestant Truth Society, Gospel Press, South Molton, Devon (undated).*

monarchs more assiduous at enforcing Church discipline, this freedom had ended by 1404.

Jan Hus (1372-1415) a Czech theologian from the University of Prague, became an influential preacher committed to the authority of the Bible and exposing Church corruption. Although tried and burned at the stake, his example seeded a strong Bible-based movement, the Moravian Brethren, which ultimately achieved a world-wide influence and became instrumental in the conversion of the Wesley brothers. William Tyndale (1494-1536), who must surely rank as one of the greatest Englishmen of all time, devoted his life under great oppression to translating the Bible into English from the Hebrew and Greek originals. He employed the printing press introduced into England by William Caxton in 1476 to print and distribute the Bible in English. A conflict with Henry VIII enforced an exile where he was hounded and ultimately murdered by the agents of Sir Thomas Moore. Nevertheless, in an environment of expanding education and enlightenment, demand for a Bible to be understood by the common person could not be held back. The invention of the Gutenberg printing press in 1450 was crucial to this transformation because Bibles were soon being printed much faster than the Church could find and burn them. A year after Tyndale's death the Matthew Bible, most of which conformed to Tyndale's translation, was chained to the lectern of every church in England. This was followed by the Great Bible (1539), the Geneva Bible (1560), the Bishop's Bible (1568) and ultimately the King James Bible (1611).

Thus, although the beginning of the Reformation is traditionally attributed to the posting by Martin Luther (1483-1546) of his 95 theses on the doors of the Castle Church of Wittenberg, in Saxony in 1517, widespread dissention with the established church was already pervasive. The supreme success of the early reformers such as Hus, Luther and Zwingli was the recovery of Biblical truth and Apostolic teaching that salvation could not be earned - it is a supreme free gift of God achieved by grace through faith alone. This doctrine was quickly condemned by the Catholic Church with an anathema at the Council of Trent (1545-1563). Nevertheless, the early reformers mostly carried over unbiblical practises such as child baptism and largely left the subject of eschatology (God's prophetic intentions for winding up His plan for the history of the Church Age) untouched. Not until the nineteenth century would this become a serious issue for Bible study. However, access to the Scriptures in the vernacular language did enable people such as Oliver Cromwell and John Owen to realise God's continuing purposes for the Jewish people who gradually gained a more favoured status in Protestant societies.

The first two centuries following the Reformation were characterised by much internecine strife between the various Protestant sects mostly over degrees to which they held on to Catholic doctrines. John Calvin (1509-1564) established a legalistic church in Geneva that advocated exclusive salvation of an elect and persecuted the Anabaptists who insisted that only adult baptism was meaningful. In England disputes raged between the Anglicans of the established church, who retained much of the Catholic ritual, and the Puritans who maintained that the Church of England needed to be purified of Catholic practices. In Scotland John Knox (1513-1572) formed a successful partnership with the Scottish Protestant nobility and established the Presbyterian Church. Although much conflict was to occur in subsequent years, the Reformation had been firmly established in both countries with the accession of Elizabeth the First in 1558 who succeeded her half-sister Mary I ("Bloody Mary"), a Catholic who had executed nearly 250 Protestants during her short reign. Elizabeth affirmed the legitimacy of her father Henry VIII's Anglican Church, but maintained a settlement by which Protestants and Puritans were allowed to practice their own varieties of the religion.

Nearer to the Papal heartland the Reformation followed a less successful path. The Jesuits (Society of Jesus) founded by Ignatius of Loyola in 1534 and approved by Pope Paul III, became the key arm of the Counter Reformation. By clandestine invasion of Protestant societies they sought to keep alive Catholic influence and even undermine governments, whilst engaging in aggressive evangelism in pagan and newly-colonised countries to extend the influence of the Pope. In France Catherine de Medici was able to secure a Catholic monarchy, initiate the St Bartholomew's Day Massacre, and enforce the exile of the remaining Huguenots, many of whom moved away with a range of skills that enhanced the growing prosperity of Protestant societies. France remained in the grip of an enforced church system that was ultimately to suffer terrible retribution in the French Revolution and lead to a society that readily embraced atheism. The Thirty Years War (1618-1649) started as a Catholic-Protestant conflict but morphed into a dynastic struggle that developed into one of the most destructive wars in the history of Europe. It ultimately did little to advance the Reformation. The exception was the Dutch Republic which was at last able to break free from the stranglehold of Catholic Spain and go on to enjoy a period of great prosperity and development. In Britain the Reformation followed a turbulent path with conflicts, including a Civil War, between the different Protestant divisions and a Catholic-sympathising Stuart monarchy. Not until The Glorious Revolution of 1688, which enforced a permanent Protestant monarchy with limited power, was a greater measure of stability achieved.

Access to the Bible however, proved to be no guarantor of a stable moral society. History has shown that this can only be achieved by Bible study and the free practise of Godly preaching, what Jesus referred to as "building disciples". By the early 1700's many writers including Daniel Defoe, Samuel Johnson and Alexander Pope confirm that Britain and the American Colonies were on the point of moral collapse. The official Church of England had used the Act of Conformity and then in 1714 the notorious Schism Act to restrict, and ultimately expel, all non-conformist preachers. These were always much more assiduous in keeping to the Biblical testimony than establish clergy; these enjoyed secure parish stipends and were often indifferent to preaching from the Bible. With a depravity vividly portrayed by the engraving of William Hogarth, so many gin houses populated the towns that public drunkenness was endemic and many adults and even children died of alcoholism. Abuse of women and children was rampant and they were forced to work long hours in dangerous conditions in mines and factories for pitiful wages. The moral debasement of society was reflected in multiple severe laws for those who violated them; both adults and children were subjected to 160 laws that could lead to hanging.

God graciously transformed this moral and spiritual wasteland with great revivals initiated by the evangelists John and Charles Wesley. In 1769 John Wesley (1703-1791), who also opposed slavery in a time when its horrors were not strongly challenged by society, founded a Sunday School Movement that was to flourish throughout the land and teach the Bible to children. Forced out of the traditional churches, the open air preaching of John Wesley declared the Bible unto audiences of hundreds and sometimes thousands. Other influential Christians such as John Bunyan, John Milton, Jonathan Edwards and George Whitfield emerged at this time of great spiritual energy to both preach and write in ways that had a remarkably positive effect on society. The laws restricting mission outside of the established church were repealed and the transformation of lives by preaching led on to a desire to fight the injustices that lay at the root of the moral decay. The imprisonment of debtors and children was made illegal, schools were founded in every parish for the education of children, and harsh laws and child labour in mines and factories were abolished. Universal free education, charities and free hospitals were all established by lives transformed by the Biblical message. The Primitive Methodist movement was particularly successful in evangelising the emerging industrial regions of the nation and the renowned preacher Charles Spurgeon was converted at one of their meetings. Missionary societies were founded to carry the Biblical message to the colonies and elsewhere with William Carey initiating Christian mission in India and Hudson Taylor in China. The British and Foreign Bible Society was established in 1804 by the Clapham Sect, a group of Church of England social reformers which included the famous anti-slavery campaigner William Wilberforce. They gave their society the mission statement of providing Bibles in every language to every individual in every nation throughout the world, and they received support from the entire class spectrum of society from the aristocratic down to the poorest. The wider influence of this great revival on Britain was to lay the foundations of a stable society rooted in Biblical morality; this turned the nation into the world's leading power that defeated the autocratic Napoleon and went on to champion technological innovation and forge an empire.

It was the version of the Bible authorised by King James I that embraced this revival and dominated Christianity in the English-speaking world for more than 300 years. The Geneva Bible, formerly the most popular translation, had supplanted the co-called Bishops' Bible, but appeared to challenge the primacy of secular rulers and bishops' authority; a typical scathing annotation compared the locusts of the Apocalypse to swarming hordes of "Prelates" dominating the Church. Translation of the new version was initiated in 1604 to address problems of the earlier translations perceived by both Puritans and the established church; whilst King James was concerned to achieve unity, he also aimed to see that it conformed to the Episcopal structure of the Church and his belief in an ordained clergy. The task of translation was undertaken by 47 Churchmen who, although ranging in outlook from High Church to Puritan in theology, were united in their reverence for the Scriptures as the Word of God. Mindful of the edict not to add or take away from the original (Deuteronomy 4:2, Revelation 22:18-19). Hence theirs was a word for word translation from the Majority Texts of the New Testament (the Byzantine *Textus Receptus)* with insertions to refine the sense of statements distinguished in italics. These were scholars of a kind that simply do not exist today. Lancelot Andrewes, the chairman, spent 5 hours a day in prayer and mastered 20 different languages, whilst John Boys is reported to have been able to read Biblical Hebrew as a child and was a proficient Greek scholar at the age of 14; he would spend up to 16 hours a day studying manuscripts in the library at Cambridge. When the texts of the Torah covering Genesis to Deuteronomy were discovered in the Dead Sea Scrolls only 169 Hebrew letters were found to differ from the texts used by the King James Bible translators, and none of these changed the meaning of a single word. Problems with the King James Version (KJV), later to become the Authorised Version by Act of Parliament, mainly relate to King James who, believing himself to be a sovereign ordained by God and sensitive to his headship of the Church of England, insisted on phrases noting established church structure and hierarchy. Nevertheless some 80% of the King James Bible emerged to publication in 1611 essentially the same as Tyndale's 1526 Bible.

The KJV was the defining translation of the Bible in English covering the great age of revival and missions. According to Jesus' guideline *"by their fruits you shall know them"* (Matthew 7:20) it has been an unqualified success and as long as Shakespeare was an essential part of the education curriculum, the 17th century language was not a notable problem; the language remains poetic and readily memorised. Some key words have changed their meaning in the intervening ~400 years. For example, in the famous verse John 3:16 the word "belief" now has a general detached meaning whereas in Tyndale's day it had a stronger implication, closer to "total commitment" today; this helps us to understand why the early Protestant martyrs were prepared to be burnt at the stake to confirm their commitment to the reformed faith. As with all translations, the KJV is imperfect but today there are multiple resources available such as *BlueletterBible.org* where the in-depth meaning of the Biblical words can be explored.

Subsequent efforts to translate the Bible, mostly with alternative manuscript sources, began when Brooke Wescott and John Hort published "The New Testament in the Original Greek" in 1881. They employed manuscripts of the Alexandrian School presumed to be older than the Majority Texts used for the KJV. This translation has been more critically received, in part due to the secular beliefs of the authors who were evidently unbelievers, and evidence that their sources, including the Codex Vaticanus, have been influenced by Gnostics with an Arian leaning seeking to undermine the deity of Christ. However, most translations published since then have shared the preference of Westcott and Hort for the manuscripts sourced in the Alexandrian School rather than the *Textus Receptus*. This is primarily based on the assumption that the more recently-discovered (1844) *Codex Sinaiticus* is the oldest complete preserved Bible (~350 AD); unfortunately this copy has been subject to multiple editing.

The plethora of Bible translations that have emerged in the past 140 years vary from the scholarly and laudable with the aim of refining the true meanings of the words, to versions that have aimed for commercial success or followed the agenda of pressure groups. The mindset of the translators has ranged from committed believers to agnostic but the pressures of the modern world have produced none measuring up to the standards of the KJV translators. Reflecting the Gnostic influences on its sources, the New International Version (NIV) has become notorious for muting or omitting passages concerned with the Redemptive mission of the Lord Jesus Christ and His equality in the Godhead (Salliby 1994). The addition of footnotes, whilst pretending to show scholarly endeavor, has merely added to confusion concerning exactly what the original texts actually said. There can be little doubt that the multiplicity of the modern translations and doubts surrounding their sources have contributed to the apostasy and moral confusion of the present day. It prompted even the secular commentator Melvyn Bragg to note that the Church of England lost the plot when it abandoned the KJV *(Bragg, M., 2011, The Book of Books: The Radical Impact of the King James Bible 1611-2011, ISBN: 9781408480700).*

References and Further Reading:

Broadbent, E.H., 1999. *The Pilgrim Church*, Gospel Folio Press, Grand Rapids, Michigan, U.S.A., 448pp.

Jeffery, Grant R., 1997. *The Signature of God: Astonishing Biblical Discoveries*, Frontier Research Publications, Toronto, Canada, 278pp.

Johnson, Kenneth, 2010a. *The Ancient Book of Daniel*, Charleston, South Carolina, ISBN 1456306561,172 pp.

Johnson, Kenneth, 2010b. *Ancient Prophecies Revealed: 500 prophecies listed in Order of when they were Fulfilled*, Charleston, South Carolina, ISBN 143825346X,174 pp.

Johnson, Kenneth, 2017. *Ancient Testaments of the Patriarchs: Autobiographies from the Dead Sea Scrolls,* Charleston, South Carolina, ISBN-10: 978-1975887742,167 pp.

Miller, Hugh, 1857. *The Testimony of the Rocks: Geology in its bearings on the two theologies natural and revealed*, reprinted in 2001 by St Matthew Publishing, Cambridge, ISBN 1901546 1 1 X, 402pp.

Missler, Chuck, 2004. *Cosmic Codes: Hidden Messages from the Edge of Eternity*, Koinonia House Publications, Coeur d'Alene, Idaho, U.S.A., 535pp.

Morison, F., 1967. *Who moved the stone?* Faber and Faber, London, 192pp.

Pearce, E.K.V., 1998. *Evidence for Truth: Archaeology*, Eagle Publications, Guildford, Surrey, U.K., 272 pp.

Salliby, Chick, 1994. *If the Foundations be destroyed: what does the New International Version of the Bible have against Jesus?* Word and Prayer Ministries, Fiskdale Maryland, U.S.A., 101 pp.

Chapter 2

The Bible: a unique narrative with multi-level interpretation

2.1 Introduction: A Divinely-Inspired Narrative

In former times the Bible could be preached as a straightforward and simply-understood message from God promoting the heartfelt trans-formation of the individual and promotion of a moral and ordered society. In contrast, the times since the Enlightenment, often considered to have begun in a major way with the publication of Isaac Newton's *Principia Mathematica* in 1687, have witnessed an explosion of scientific know-ledge. This has been accompanied by a more skeptical and enquiring mindset that in educated circles seeks to challenge, and frequently condemn, the Biblical narrative. To counter this, God has provided signatures in the text to confirm that only an Infinite and Divine mind could have embedded them. During past centuries much of this evidence was the exclusive preserve of small numbers of Jewish rabbis and was simply unnecessary for mission and testimony. However, as if to counter the attacks of a cynical and skeptical modern world, the careful study and publications of a range of authors in recent years, both Jewish and Gentile, has disseminated much information requiring a Divine authorship. As outlined in this chapter, the evidence is unraveled within four levels of interpretation of the primary Biblical text. In order of increasing depth and breadth of interpretation these levels are referred to respectively by their Hebrew names **P'shat, Remez, Midrash (derash)** and **Sod**.

2.2 The P'shat Level

The plain meaning of the text at this level includes all that the individual needs to know for the personal relationship that God desires. It covers the key message of redemption and all that is necessary for eternal salvation. This personal relationship is the unique claim of Christianity - the gods of all other religions are remote, potentially duplicitous, and can only be followed with blind faith. However, to substantiate this extraordinary claim the P'shat level is underscored by the three deeper levels. These require interpretation and are emplaced to confirm for us that God, and He alone, is the author.

2.3 The Remez Level

This is a "hint" interpreted from within the specific passage of text. It can include the systematic use of numbers, gematria and equidistant letter spacing. An example of a "hint" or Remez purely involving words alone, occurs in the Gospel of John 19:21 where we are told that the priests were furious when Pilate refused to change his assignment on the cross of "Jesus of Nazareth King of the Jews". They were able to see in the Hebrew statement **Y**eshua **H**anatsri **V**melech **H**yuhudim (Jesus the Nazarene and King of the Jews) the letters **YHVH**, the proper name of God known personally to a holy people; this is why they were so angry.*

The Remez seen in the use of numbers is entirely consistent throughout the text. We find that each number up to 12, and then certain numbers

---

* *There are two Hebrew names used for God in the Old Testament. The plural word for God, "Elohim", is most commonly translated as "Lord" in English. This is the generic name for God as Creator of the material Universe and the source of life where He stands outside of His Creation. The Hebrew has no vowels and the alternative four letter name YHVH, יהוה , (the tetragrammaton) is a proper noun abbreviated from "Yahweh", and would not normally be uttered by observant Jews; today they usually refer to Him as "Hashem". Yahweh is the proper name of God both as known in a personal way to a holy people, and expressing His personal involvement with His Creation. It is closest to the common modern use of the name "Jehovah". Yahweh is first used together with Elohim in Genesis 4:2 where we are told "The Lord God made the Earth and the Heavens". They are used together again when God makes a covenant with Adam and Eve in Genesis 3:1 and then again in Genesis 3:8 onwards when they break this covenant. During the Genesis era God would normally introduce Himself to the individual Patriarchs as "El Shaddai", "the Almighty One". See also note on the Trinity in Chapter 5.12, Chapter 8.9 and Chapter 9.1.*

above that, have consistent usage throughout the Bible with a significance summarised in the Table 5.1 of Chapter 5. The consistent use of numbers in both the Old and New Testaments has been extensively documented by Ethelbert Bullinger (1837-1913) in his monumental work "Number in Scripture". Born in Canterbury, Bullinger was a direct descendent of the Protestant reformer Johann Bullinger who succeeded Zwingli, founder of the reformed church in Zurich in 1531; he was educated at King's College, London and went on to become a distinguished scholar of Biblical languages.

Particularly important is the recurrence of multiples of 7 which creates the heptadic structure of the Scriptures found some 600 times pervading both Old and New Testaments. Seven is the 5th prime number where 5 is the Biblical number of grace and 7 is used to express perfection and completeness. The seven Days of Creation is just the obvious first example; a few additional examples include 21 (3 x 7) Old Testament authors, 7 (Moses, David, Isaiah, Jeremiah, Daniel, Hosea and Joel) are named in the New Testament; the numeric value of these 7 names derived from the gematria described below is 1,554 (= 222 x 7), the Name of David occurs 1,134 times (162 x 7) in the Old Testament, the name of Jeremiah occurs in 7 times in 7 different forms in Hebrew a total of 147 times (21 x7) and the name of Moses occurs 847 times throughout the Bible (121 x 7). Seven becomes a significant number in the natural world. Seven colors make up the rainbow. Most mammals and birds have gestation periods which are multiples of seven. The human pulse beats faster in the morning than in the evening while on the seventh day, the scriptural day of rest, it beats slower. Although attempts have been made to change it, there continue to be seven days in the week. The succeeding number 8 has the implication of "starting again" after 7. Eight people were saved by the Ark of Noah. Eight occurs repeatedly in the Scriptures in the context of resurrection and the ministry of the Lord Jesus Christ. He rose from the dead on the 8th day after appearing in the Temple on 10th of Nisan to be presented as the perfect "Lamb of God" to fulfil the ultimate Passover. It is the first cubic number (2 x 2 x 2) and is extensively associated with dimensions and furniture of the former Temples in Jerusalem, and with the dimensions of the New Jerusalem in the Book of Revelation.

The number nine occurs in the context of the end of man's works and is recognised as the number of finality, whilst ten is the number of Divine order. We find it in the context of the ten tribes of the divided nation of Israel, the ten plagues, the Ten Commandments, and the significance of the person of the tenth generation attained in the cases of Noah and Abraham amongst the line of Old Testament Patriarchs. Eleven becomes the number of disorder, notably in Old Testament events and generations; it adds to Divine Order (10 + 1) but takes away from Divine Government (12 - 1). Twelve becomes representative of Divine Government and is associated with the tribes of Israel, the number of the Apostles, the number of servants of the Lord and dimensions of the New Jerusalem in the Book of Revelation (144,000 = 12 x 12 x1000), the months of the year, the twelve signs of the zodiac and the circle of the heavens (360 = 12 x 30). Many other occurrences of this number are found in the Scriptures, often in the context of governing or judging peoples. The number 13 is specifically associated with the Satanic kingdom; it is the 6th prime number and adds to the number of God's Divine government. Higher but more widely spaced numbers that have a critical Biblical significance are summarised in Table 5.1 of Chapter 5.

Gematria is the study of the assignment of numbers to letters. The Hebrew of the Old Testament and the Greek of the New Testament are the two languages where each letter is equivalent to a number. This was essential for day to day commerce before the adoption of our modern numerals together with the use of zero that we employ today (Chapter 5.1). When these numbers are assigned to words and phrases in the Hebrew and Greek texts profound patterns emerge. The gematria of the name of Jesus in the Greek is **888** for example, and is elevated above the gematria of "cross" 777, and "Antichrist", 666.

Although long known by many Jewish rabbis, it was the remarkable work of the outstanding mathematic and Hebraic scholar Ivan Panin (1856-1942) that first brought the extraordinary numeric properties of the Scriptural to the attention of a wider gentile audience. Panin was a Russian Jew, an atheist and revolutionary; forced to flee to America, he pursued an academic career. His discoveries of the gematria properties of the Hebrew Old Testament and Greek New Testament led him to faith and he spent nearly 60 years of study describing his results in 40,000

Figure 2.1: The 7-branched Menorah

Figure 2.2: Ivan Panin

pages of material incorporating well over a million calculations. To demonstrate the exceptional nature of the Scriptural gematria, Panin and two other Hebrew scholars tried to compose a passage with just 7 meaningful features but had to admit defeat when it lapsed into nonsense well before this could be achieved - they collectively acknowledged that only God could achieve such perfection of design. Panin also challenged the most influential secular scholars of his day, including the greatest mathematical brains, to refute his findings; no one took up the challenge.

The letters in the Hebrew and Greek languages routinely used to double up for numbers in order to express quantities are listed in Figures 2.3 and 2.4 below:

The Hebrew Alphabet		
Units	Tens	Hundreds
Aleph א = 1	Yod י = 10	Koph ק = 100
Beth ב = 2	Kaph כ = 20	Resh ר = 200
Gimel ג = 3	Lamed ל = 30	Shin ש = 300
Daleth ד = 4	Mem מ = 40	Tau ת = 400
He ה = 5	Num נ = 50	Koph ך [1]- 500
Vau ו = 6	Samech ס =60	Mem ם [2]= 600
Zavin ז = 7	Avin ע = 70	Num ן [3]= 300
Cheth ח = 8	Pe פ = 80	Pe ף [4]= 800
Teth ט = 9	Tsaddi צ = 90	Tsaddi ץ [5]= 300

Figure 2.3: Letters of the Hebrew Alphabet with their numeric equivalents. The last five letters indicated by the superscripts are variants of five preceding letters and used only when they occur at the end of a word. (Adapted from Harrison, 1994).

The Greek Alphabet		
Units	Tens	Hundreds
Alpha	Iota	Rho
A α = 1	I ι = 10	P ρ = 100
Beta	Kappa	Sigma
B β = 2	K κ = 20	Σ σ ς[4]= 200
Gamma	Lambda	Tau
Γ γ = 3	Λ λ = 30	T τ = 300
Delta	Mu	Upsilon
Δ δ = 4	M μ = 40	Y υ = 400
Epsilon	Nu	Phi
E ε = 5	N ν = 50	Φ ω = 500
Stigma	Xi	Chi
ς[1] = 6	Ξ ξ[2]= 60	X γ = 600
Zeta	Omicron	Psi
Z ζ = 7	O o = 70	Ψ ψ = 700
Eta	Pi	Omega
H η = 8	Π π = 80	Ω ω = 800
Theta	Koppa	Sampsi
Θ θ = 9	o[3] = 90	ϡ [5] = 900

Figure 2.4: Letters of the Greek Alphabet with their numeric equivalents. [1]Stigma is not in the Greek alphabet and the origin of its use for 6 is uncertain. [2]This has the shape of a serpent and is rarely used. [3]This is an obsolete letter with the lower case form is the same as omicron. [4]The two lower case forms have the same value with the latter only used where it occurs at the end of a word. [5]Also an obsolete letter and used only as a number. Otherwise omega is the final letter in the written Greek alphabet. (Adapted from Harrison 1994).

Equidistant Letter Sequencing (ELS) is a further key example of Remez. The original Old Testament documents were recorded by scribes as continuous successions of Hebrew letters (Chapter 1.2.1) and ELS expresses the ability to recover key words or phrases by selecting letters at regular intervals moving forwards or backwards through the text. This property has long been known by Jewish rabbis but they could only recover examples by laboriously counting out the intervals and recording the letters; even then the result would only likely have been meaningful if the correct starting letter had been selected. Since the starting letter is generally not known, much trial and error would have been required to recover something significant. Rabbinic research on this topic has been focused primarily on the five books of the Torah with results collectively grouped as the "Torah Codes". Two popular examples can illustrate the significance of ELS in the Torah. The word **Torh** (in Hebrew the 4-letter word for Torah) occurs as every 50th letter going forward through the books of Genesis and Exodus beginning from the first letter *tau*, ת, in each case. The same word is encoded in reverse (**hroT**) going backwards through the Book of Numbers every 50th letter and then through Deuteronomy every 49th letter. This word in not encoded in the central book of Leviticus but instead we find that the word **YHWH**, the personal name of God encoded every 7th letter from the first *yod*, י, (Missler 1999). Leviticus is the pivotal book in this 5-fold set of books where God describes the way that He required the ancient Israelites to worship Him. The word "Israel" appears encoded in the first Chapter of Genesis at intervals of 7 and 50 letters; these are two key numbers of special Biblical significance - Forty nine is the number of days counted to lead up to the 50th Day of Jubilee, the day of restoration when debts and bondage are cancelled and land is restored. Chapter 23 of Leviticus defines the 7 **moedem** (a word meaning "fixed appointment" and incorrectly translated into the English as "feasts"); these seven dates span the agricultural year with the first four embracing the grain harvests and the last three the fruit harvests, and the Jewish people were required to observe them in perpetuity. The four (grain) appointments: Passover, Unleavened Bread, First Fruits and Pentecost, were precisely fulfilled during the first coming of the Lord Jesus Christ in 32 AD as recorded in the four gospels.

A second example is found in Chapter 38 of Genesis reporting the sordid story of the adultery between Judah and his daughter in law. Judah was to be the progenitor of the line of kingship leading ultimately to the Messiah, but due to this sin God cursed the line for 10 generations as unfit to succeed to this elevated position. However, anticipating restoration, at 49 letter intervals in the Hebrew text of this chapter the names of Boaz, Ruth, Obed, Jesse and David are given in correct chronological order leading up to David who would become king when the 10 generational curse had finally expired. This record was recorded by Moses in the Torah some 400 years before these people were born to become key personalities in the Book of Ruth dating from the end of the time of the Judges (~1100-1050 BC, see Chapter 1.2.1).

Nowadays we have the ability to use computers to rapidly recover examples of ELS by successively testing multiple examples of starting letters and counting intervals to the next significant letter. If the theme of the investigation is specified the computer program will know when to focus the investigation. Unfortunately, ELS has also been misused in recent decades to try and predict the future. This should not be anticipated because the evidence is typically embedded in a way that events can only be recognised after they have occurred. A suitable target word is always required to initiate the search and the event must first happen before it can be identified. Using this approach, Rabbinic study has since recognised numerous ELS records in the Torah of political personalities and terrorist attacks such as the 2001 New York 9-11 event; these can be explored by internet search. We are not to expect that any information would be secreted away in these deeper levels of the Scriptures that would not ultimately be exposed over the course of time. Jesus made clear that *"nothing is secret, that shall not be made manifest; neither anything hid, that shall not be known"* (Luke 8:17). Instead the ELS examples of Remez are properties of the Bible embedded to confirm God's authorship of His Word.

Critics of ELS have implied that it is possible to find examples in almost any book in English if the text is long enough. However, English with 26 letters has many more possible permutations of letters than Hebrew with just 22 letters. Furthermore, the significance of the discoveries from ELS in the Old Testament is confirmed by three observations. *Firstly*, there is the sheer density of Biblical examples in *close proximity* within the text. *Secondly*, there is their association with the *theme of the text*. We note examples of this below where the Suffering Servant Chapter of Isaiah 53 has multiple features of the Ministry of the Lord Jesus Christ during His First Coming embedded within it. Another example would be the names of 26 seed-bearing fruits and trees found in Genesis 2:9 where the text tells of God giving seeds, herbs and trees for the benefit of mankind. *Thirdly*, as noted above, the numbered *spacing of the letters often has obvious significance*.

Numerous examples of ELS are noted by Jeffrey (1997, 1999) and Missler (2004). They fall into two categories. The first includes multiple examples of historical events and people, usually of a secular nature although mostly related in some way to the Jewish people. Examples of this category include the first investigations passing review to publication in the secular journal *Statistical Science* in 1988 and 1994. The latter study found the names and birth dates of 34 (subsequently extended to 66) prominent 9th to 18th century rabbis in close proximity embedded within the Torah. Subsequent study found 15 allusions to the names linked to the Holocaust, the greatest tragedy to impact the Jewish people in the modern era, in the Book of Deuteronomy. Words such as "Hitler", "Auschwitz", "Genocide" and "The Fuehrer" were found to be embedded at regular intervals either forwards or backwards. Other examples explored by Jeffery (1999) include multiple names, and sometimes dates, associated with the false 1993 Peace Process between Israel and the PLO, the assassination of Prime Minister Rabin in 1995 and the Gulf War of 1991. The locations of these ELS codes is also sometimes noteworthy. Thus the Israel-PLO treaty is found embedded in Deuteronomy 9 where the Jewish people provoke God to anger because they did not have faith that He would enable them to possess the whole of the Promised Land.

The probability of all of these patterns occurring by chance is vanishingly small. Of special interest is the recording of the word for equidistant (*shalav*) and the phrase "the latticework of the equidistant letter sequence" in every one of the five books of the Torah. These discoveries confirm the care taken to record the original manuscripts described in Chapter 1:2:1: if even one Hebrew character had been missed or incorrectly inserted, the search for ELS would have completely failed. The search for ELS has been tested in other Hebrew texts but predictably, no such multiple patterns have been discovered in any other literature.

The second group of ELS discoveries relate directly to the confirmation of the Biblical narrative where discoveries of ELS in the Old Testament specifically refer to subjects in the New Testament. It is these discoveries which have so far emerged mainly from the research of the late Biblical researcher Grant Jeffrey (1999) and his colleague Yacov Ramsel that are especially noteworthy. Although the frequent occurrence of the Hebrew name of Jesus, *Yeshua*, in the Old Testament could be viewed sceptically because it is a short and common name, it occurs adjacent to the phrase "lamp of the Lord" in the famous Suffering Servant Chapter 53 of the Book of Isaiah. Furthermore the identifying statement "Yeshua (Jesus) is my name" is also encoded as a phrase counting every 20th letter left to right. This Chapter written down by Isaiah in about 740 BC contains a remarkable number of ELS codes relating to the First Coming of Jesus as the Suffering Servant Messiah and to His death and resurrection. He is encoded as a "Nazarene", a person chosen for a sacred purpose and dedicated to the service of God. Galilee, the place where He lived most of His life and performed much of His ministry, is encoded every 32nd letter starting in Isaiah 53:7. The words "Yeshua" and "Messiah" (*Mashiach*) are both encoded together in Isaiah 53:8, the former with the 3rd letter in the second word and the latter in the 3rd letter of the 10th word, both at 65 letter ELS intervals.

There is a special treasure associated with the name of "Yeshua" linking both gematria and ELS. The gematria value of His name is 386 and it is spelt out 12 times (the number of governmental perfection) at 386 letter intervals in the Torah. The occurrence in Leviticus 22 has two adjacent words also spelt out at 386 letter intervals; these words are "Truth" and "Wisdom".

Three woman called "Mary" were present with the disciple John at the Cross and the names of these three Marys and John are encoded at 20 letter intervals reading left to right beginning in Isaiah 53:10. The phrase "tremble Mary" is recorded by ELS in Isaiah 53:9, whilst the preceding Chapter 52 has the expression "the Marys weep bitterly". In John 19:26-27 we learn that Jesus committed His mother to the care of John, presumably because the remainder of His earthly family did not then believe in Him. The names of all the disciples are further encoded at different intervals and starting verses in this pivotal chapter of Scripture with the exception of Judas Iscariot. Two apostles called James, James son of Zabbadai and James son of Alphaeus, are recorded but a third James, his half brother, who would later go on to become a leading figure of the Church in Jerusalem, is evidently not recorded because he was not a believer at the time of the Crucifixion. The time of the Crucifixion is recorded in Chapter 52:1 of Isaiah as "Aviv of Mount Moriah" counting every 27th letter from right to left; Aviv is the alternative name assigned to the month of Nisan. It is used in the Bible when the Jewish people are in the land of Israel and present to judge the time of the barley harvest, the grain essential for the institution of the third appointed time of First Fruits. Adjacent letters in this chapter spell out *"rosh"* meaning head of the year (the first month of the religious year).

Jeffery (1999) records that the religious and secular authorities responsible for the Crucifixion are all encoded by ELS in Isaiah 53. They include the high priests Ananias and Caiaphas, the words "Pharisee" and "Levi" and the phrases "the man Herod", "the evil Roman city", "wicked Caesar to perish", "pierce" (in Isaiah 52) and "let Him be crucified", with the latter encoded by ELS every 50th letter starting with the 2nd letter in the 6th word of Isaiah 53:8. The ability of the Jews to execute the death penalty had been taken away by the Romans in 7 AD making that the act of Crucifixion a corporate Jewish and Gentile responsibility (see Chapter 8.9.1).

Investigations up to the present time have barely touched on the likely wealth of Biblical confirmation embedded by ELS. The Messianic Psalms will no doubt provide a fruitful field of research and Jeffery

(1999) notes the results of his own study focussing on verse 16 of Exodus 30 which deals with God's commands to Moses concerning the atonement price for the sins of the people. In this Chapter he finds 17 names of the people directly associated with the ministry of Jesus and five examples covering place names and events. Unfortunately, it seems unlikely that many significant examples of ELS will emerge from study of the Greek New Testament because the documents were never copied (mostly by Gentiles) with the extreme diligence shown by the Jewish scribes.

2.4 The Midrash Level

The Midrash Level of the Scriptures is understood by wider knowledge spanning the different books of the Bible, both Old and New Testaments. The word is derived from "derash" meaning "investigation" and seeks a consistent pattern spanning the whole of Biblical history. There are numerous examples. In Chapter 22 of Genesis after three days Abraham went to Mount Moriah on God's instructions to sacrifice his son Isaac when God instead provided a ram for the sacrifice once Abraham's faith had been proved; the ultimate sacrifice (described in Psalm 22) would be fulfilled 2000 years later by God sacrificing His Son at the same location. Later in Genesis Joseph became a type of the Suffering Servant Messiah. The favoured son of his father, he was rejected by his brethren and separated from them. An innocent man suffering for the sins of others, he was later raised to an exalted position, marries a gentile bride and goes on to save the whole known world from death; lastly his brothers recognise him and he forgives them. Missler (1999) identifies 101 events in the story of Joseph repeated in the ministry of the Lord Jesus Christ. Four hundred years later Moses is promised that God will send a prophet like him (Deuteronomy 18:15) and again we find many events played out in the life of Moses that are repeated by Jesus. The Book of Ruth is a love story where Ruth a gentile from the reprobate nation of Moab, is taken to be the bride of a Jewish Kinsman Redeemer - Ruth discovers her redeemer through Naomi a Jewess whilst Noami recovers her land through Ruth the gentile. The mental anguish of the Old Testament prophet Jonah followed by three days in the belly of a whale becomes symbolic of the anguish in the Garden of

Gethsemane and subsequent death and resurrection of Jesus and is another example of Midrash.

2.5 The Sod Level

This level implies a secret level of information embedded in the Scriptures. It has been central to Cabalism and widely misused by Gnostics and secret societies to lead to all sort of dubious conjectures. Nevertheless, if approached with correct Biblical authority embracing both Old and New testaments it can yield remarkable confirmation of Divine Authorship. As noted in the discussion of the Remez level of interpretation, we see *Yeshua*, the Hebrew name of Jesus, embedded extensively by ELS throughout the Old Testament. Although dismissed by Rabbinic authors as fortuitous on the grounds that it was a common name in Old Testament times merely comprising four letters, the strength of the case that it does indeed represent Jesus as the Creator and Author of redemption, comes from the observation that it occurs at very short ELS intervals of just 3, 4 of 20 letters, and more frequently than any other common name. Likewise as alluded to above, the times when it occurs in expanded and meaningful phrases at key point in the Scriptures endorses the view that it is of fundamental Messianic significance.

The most important example of the sod level of scripture surrounds the *aleph* and the *tau*, את, the first and last letters of the Hebrew alphabet equivalent to the *alpha* and the *omega* in the Greek. These two letters occur as the central (fourth) letter in the seven-word menorah verse of Genesis 1:1 (Figure 2.1). This word is untranslatable but nevertheless occurs extensively throughout the Old Testament including seven times in Genesis Chapter 1 describing God's work of Creation. It is often referred to as the "Word of Creation" in rabbinic literature. John's Gospel identifies Jesus as the Word of Creation: *"In the beginning was the Word, and the Word was with God, and the Word was God. The same was in the beginning with God. All things were made by him; and without him was not anything made that was made"*. (John 1:1-3). Here John becomes the second witness of David's declaration in Psalm 33:6: *"By the Word of the Lord were the heavens made; and all the host of them by the breath of his mouth"*. The extraordinary properties of the first verse of Genesis are central to God's claim to be the Creator. The scientific grounds for this claim are explored in Chapter 4.

The Hebrew word for "truth", *emet*, begins with **aleph** and ends with **tau**. If we remove the aleph, the first letter of the alphabet with the value of unity and always symbolic of God (Table 5.1 and Chapter 8.1), we have *met* the word for "death". *Emet* has a gematria of 9, the Biblical number of finality. The opposite word for "lie" is *skelet* and has a value of 6, or 9 turned upside down; the gematria of the component letters to this latter word has no order.

Further in the Book of Revelation Jesus describes Himself as the alpha and omega (Revelation 1:8, 21:6, 22:13), symbolically endorsing God's claim in the Book of Isaiah that *"I am the first and I am the last"* (Isaiah 44:6 and repeated in Isaiah 48:12). The confirmation of the את as representing Jesus, the Second member of the Trinity, as the Messiah who was dead and is now resurrected occurs twice in the Book of Revelation: *"And when I saw him, I fell at his feet as dead. And he laid his right hand upon me, saying unto me, Fear not; I am the first and the last .(את) I am he that liveth, and was dead; and, behold, I am alive for evermore, Amen; and have the keys of hell and of death"* (Revelation 1:17-18); *" These things saith the first and the last, which was dead, and is alive"* (Revelation 2:8).

Of the many places where the את is inserted into the Hebrew Old Testament one of the most intriguing noted by Missler (1999) is in the Book of Zechariah. It is inserted in the English translation as follows *"... they shall look upon me (את, the aleph and the tau) whom they have pierced, and they shall mourn for him, as one mourneth for his only son, and shall be in bitterness for him, as one that is in bitterness for his firstborn"* (Zechariah 12:10). The repeated insertion of את in the context of mankind's redemption is particularly noteworthy. A further example occurs in the Book of Habakkuk: *"Thou wentest forth for the salvation (את) of thy people"* (Habakkuk 3:13). It is a feature of the crucial verses recording the virgin birth in the Book of Isaiah

7:12-14 and is in the great vision of Isaiah Chapter 6 (verse 1): *"In the year that king Uzziah died I saw also the Lord (את) sitting upon a throne, high and lifted up, and his train filled the temple"*.

Although the understanding of the Old Testament scriptures by Orthodox followers of Judaism is often based on a lifetime of study typically unsurpassed in depth, these become examples of "secrets" which are spiritually-discerned. They become examples of the Sod level of Scriptural knowledge only apparent to the Messianic believer.

2.6 The Unity of the Old and New Testaments

2.6.1 Genesis and Revelation: gematria of the Beginning and the End

Genesis, the book of beginnings, and the Book of Revelation enclose both testaments and collectively define the Biblical beginning and end of God's control of humankind's story. When considered together these two books provide remarkable examples of the sod level of scripture and serve to enclose and endorse a holistic message. The first verse of Genesis is *"In the beginning God created the heaven and the earth"*. The *Hebrew* gematria of this verse is **2701**. This is the 73rd triangle number (Table 5.1) and 2701 is equal to 37 x 73. Three and seven are the Biblical numbers of the Trinity and perfection/completion respectively. In these first 7 words there are 7 gematria relationships involving the number 37. In addition, the (Hebrew) number **2701** = 888 + 888 + 888 + 37 where **888** is the gematria of "Jesus" and 37 is the gematria of "The Word" in the Greek.

The Book of Revelation is the 66th book of the Bible and the last verse is numbered 21 (both of these are triangle or trinity numbers as explained in Chapter 5.12). The last verse of the book is: *"The grace of our Lord Jesus Christ be with you all. Amen"*. (Revelation 22:21). The *Greek* gematria of this verse is **8991** where **8991** has the Stamp of Finality because **8991** = 999 + 999 +.....+ 999 (**9** times) and the last digit 9 is the Biblical number of finality. The gematria of this verse is also a multiple of 37 and the Trinity number 3. The gematria link between the first verse of Genesis and the last verse of Revelation is remarkable (Harrison 1995). They are linked together because both are made up of the gematria of the Lord Jesus Christ (888), the sacred combination (37), and the Trinity number (3):

Genesis 1:1: **_2701_** = 888 + 888 + 888 + 37
Revelation 22:21: **_8991_** = [37] + [37] + [37] + 888 x 10
(Jesus x Ordinal perfection)
Revelation 22:21: **_8991_** = **2701** + **2701** + **2701** + 888
(Genesis 1:1 x 3 + Jesus)
Also in Revelation 22:21: **_8991_** = [37] + [37] + [37]+…….+ [37] = 3
+ 3 + 3…….+3 (The Trinity multiplied)

The authorship Book of Revelation is confirmed in Chapter 1 by verses 11 and 18: *"I am Alpha and Omega (את), the first and the last: and, what thou seest, write in a book". "I am He that liveth, and was dead; and, behold, I am alive for evermore, Amen; and have the keys of hell and of death".*

2.6.2 *Genesis and Revelation - Unity of Purpose*

The histories described in the books of Genesis and Revelation begin and complete the story of humankind's Redemption in a way that collectively confirms the holistic Biblical message of both testaments:

In Genesis Earth is created (1:1), *in Revelation Earth passes away (21:1); in* Genesis the Sun governs the day (1:4), *in Revelation there is no more need for the Sun (21:23)*; in Genesis there is day and night (1:5), *in Revelation there is no more night (22:25);* in Genesis the sea is created (1:10), *in Revelation there is no more sea (21:1);* in Genesis sin enters in and humankind falls (4:7), *in Revelation these is no more sin (1:5, 21:8);* in Genesis humankind is driven out to Eden (3:23), *in Revelation humankind is restored to Eden (20:4);* in Genesis the curse enters (3:17, 4:11), *in Revelation the curse is ended (22.2);* in Genesis sorrow enters (3:16), *in Revelation there is no more sorrow (21:4);* in Genesis Babylon is founded (10:10), *in Revelation Babylon (religious and economic world order) is destroyed (18:21)*; in Genesis Satan's dominion over Earth is established (3:14) and *in Revelation it is taken away (20:2).*

* * * * * * *

2.7 Conclusion

From the times of the Apostles up to and including the great era of Victorian and Early 20th Century revivals, the Bible was generally accepted in the Western World as the inspired and authoritative Word of God. Rare exceptions were vocal opponents such as Thomas Paine and Voltaire, although even these men were prepared to support the freedom to debate opposing values. It was the rise of "Higher Criticism" beginning in Germany in the middle of the nineteenth century that began the relentless attack on the authority of the Bible by academia, liberal theologians and the media that has accelerated in intensity up to the present day. Although masquerading as liberal, this attack is intolerant of the Biblical viewpoint. We have now reached a point where anti-Christian bigotry is the only acceptable prejudice remaining in a politically-correct society of the so-called "First World". Elsewhere, as much as one-third of the world's population is now suffering persecution for its religious beliefs and more than 80 percent of these victims are Christians; indeed, the persecution of Christians is now reported to be reaching genocidal proportions (https://pjmedia.com/faith/shocking-report-persecution-of-christians-worldwide-close-to-genocide/).

However, whilst Christianity may be dying in the First World, it is flourishing elsewhere, often under conditions of severe oppression. During 2019 on average eight Christians were murdered every day for their faith, nearly 4000 more were arrested daily and imprisoned and more than 9000 Church buildings desecrated; seven of the ten worst countries for persecuting Christians are Islamic societies ruled by Sharia Law (https://www.gatestoneinstitute.org/15507/christians-persecution-global-catastrophe). The First Book of Corinthians (3:7) makes clear that *"neither is he that plants anything, neither he that waters, but it is God that gives the increase".* Hudson Taylor saw a mere handful of converts from his missionary efforts; now there are untold millions of Christians in China, possibly the largest national body of believers in the world; this is perceived to be such a threat to the Communist Party that they are now rewriting the Bible to give it "socialist values". It is believed that Iran, where the people live under an oppressive Mullocracy, has the fastest growing number of Christian believers today.

These societal conflicts can only logically be understood in the context of a spiritual battlefield. Just as this condemnation of Christianity and the Bible has reached such an intensity in the present generation, the Dead Sea Scrolls have been discovered, Israel has been re-founded in fulfillment of multiple Biblical prophecies, and high-speed computers have revealed that the text incorporates an extraordinary amount of order and predictive information that could only have been emplaced there by a divine power. Outstanding Biblical gentile scholars have emerged to investigate the depth and beauty of the text. Digital software called "ParaText" now speeds up translation to enable the spreading the Gospel to indigenous peoples the world over at a rate never achievable before and permitting completion of the Great Commission of Jesus (Mark 16:15). The concomitant improvement in communication, particularly over the airwaves, can now make available to the whole world mysteries of the text that were formerly the privilege of small numbers of, mostly Jewish, scholars. The fourfold depth of interpretation of the Bible explored in this chapter defines for us a book that we should hold in unparalleled reverence. It provides an unchanging framework in which scientific discovery, which is always expanding and changing, can be evaluated. It is the purpose of the remainder of this book to make this comparison.

"And the Lord said... O that there were such an heart in them, that they would fear Me, and keep all My commandments always, that it might be well with them, and with their children forever!" (Deuteronomy 5:28-29).

References:

Bullinger, E W., 2009. *Number in Scripture: Its Supernatural Design and Spiritual Significance*, Kregel Publications, Grand Rapids, Michigan, U.S.A., 303pp.

Cahn, Jonathan, 2016. *The Book of Mysteries*, FrontLine/Charisma House Book Group, Florida, 365pp.

Harrison, James, 1995. *The Pattern and the Prophecy*, Isaiah Publications, Peterborough, Ontario, Canada, 399pp.

Jeffery, Grant R., 1997. *The Signature of God: Astonishing Biblical Discoveries*, Frontier Research Publications, Toronto, Canada, 278pp.

Jeffery, Grant R., 1999. *The Handwriting of God; Sacred Mysteries of the Bible*, Frontier Research Publications, Toronto, Canada, 280pp.

Johnson, Kenneth, 2010. *Ancient Prophecies Revealed: 500 prophecies listed in Order of when they were Fulfilled*, ISBN 143825346X, 174 pp.

Kitchen, K. A., 2003. *On the Reliability of the Old Testament*, Eerdmans Press, Grand Rapids.

Missler, Chuck, 2004. *Cosmic Codes: Hidden Messages from the Edge of Eternity,* Koinonia House Publications, Coeur d'Alene, Idaho, U.S.A., 535pp.

Missler, Chuck, 2016. *Beyond Newton*, Koinonia House Publications, Coeur d'Alene, Idaho, U.S.A., 111pp.

Pearce, E.K.V., 2000. *Evidence for Truth: Archaeology*, Eagle Publications, Guildford, Surrey, U.K., 272 pp.

Schroeder, Gerald, 1990. *Genesis and the Big Bang*, Bantam Books, New York, 212pp.

Schroeder, Gerald, 1997. *The Science of God: The Convergence of Scientific and Biblical Wisdom*, Broadway Books, New York, 226 pp.

Shore, Haim, 2007. *Coincidences in the Bible and in Biblical Hebrew*, iUniverse Publishers, New York, 319pp.

Chapter 3

The Case for Creationism

3.1 Introduction: Evolution - an irrational belief

In the Apostle Paul's last and most profound letter, in this case addressed to his faithful protégé Timothy, he prophecies that *"In the last days perlous (in the Greek this word has several meanings including "insane") times will come"* (2 Timothy 3:1). Insanity is the absence of reason and appropriately describes the modern embrace of Evolution. The academic world now requires that all education is predicated on the belief that we evolved by random mutations out of a primeval slime. We are expected to ignore the fact that there is no case of DNA transmutation across the species barrier. We are expected to ignore the fact that mutations and permutations necessary for evolution have mostly negative consequences and ultimately lead to the extinction of the species. We are expected to ignore the fact that there is a total absence of transitional forms in the fossil record. We are then expected to admire in secular amazement that every living thing starts at conception from a single cell of almost infinite order and complexity programmed to produce a whole living creature from toe nail to pancreas. *Surely this is insanity.*

Every molecule in our bodies contains the equivalent of three feet of DNA cells with each one containing the information necessary to create the complete individual. The cells contain their own language to interpret the instructions encoded in each DNA cell. A language can only be produced by intelligence and it requires a creator to produce it. Beginning with the union of egg and sperm, a human cell rapidly reproduces into millions and then billions of cells. Within two weeks through instructions contained within the DNA cells, they differentiate to become everything from the retina to an earlobe. Considering just one aspect of the remarkable progress of human development: the body ends up with just 2-4 lbs pounds of calcium with nearly 99 percent stored in the bones and teeth. But the rest is required for blood clotting, nerve transmission, muscle contraction and heart function, and when the body needs calcium for these applications it draws from the large area of tiny mineral crystals within the bone. Meanwhile marrow in those bones, of which the body has about 200 to accompany 600 muscles, creates a trillion blood cells daily that travel through 60,000 miles of blood vessels. As for the brain, it holds 10^{14} bits of information with a storage capacity 1,000 times that of a supercomputer and equivalent to 25 million books, enough to fill a bookshelf 500 miles long (https://onenewsnow.com/perspectives/robert-knight/2019/07/23/). We are expected to believe that all this can, purely by chance, achieve a human being that also possesses feelings and emotions? *Surely this is insanity.*

Living in an age when ethnic cleansing has gone on in a genocidal scale, we are also expected to ignore that this belief was the basis of Hitler's holocaust and continues to be the justification for abortion and euthanasia. After seizing control of Russia, Marx's disciples enforced the denial of the Triune God by way of terror, murder, psychoactive drugs and enforced teaching of Darwinism; his disciples still use the same methods today. The concept of Evolution as formulated by Darwin was not only racist, but has philosophically pagan materialist implications. The idea that humans evolved by chance working on primordial water and lifeless chemicals is in direct conflict with the very foundation of the Genesis account of creation *ex nihilo*. It has provided the scientific framework to support the economic infrastructure on which Marx could build his godless communist utopia: "...*the biggest thing going for Darwinism was that it finally broke the tyranny in which Christianity had held the minds of men for so many centuries.*" (F. Hoyle and C. Wickramasinghe, *"Evolution from Space,"* 1983, pp. xiii-xxii, 81 and 145). The arguments summarized here aim to refute this view.

3.2 Biology refutes Evolution

Multiple biological arguments refuting Evolution are extensively covered by ministries such as *Creation Moments* and *Answers in Genesis*. We endorse these factual presentations and do not need to cover them here. Instead we note key observations that challenge any residual belief in a false concept by reiterating that the mathematical odds against life forming by random chance verge on the impossible. Dr Harold Urey awarded a Nobel Prize for his research in chemistry wrote about this: *"All of us who study the origin of life find that the more we look into it (life), the more we feel that it is too complex to have evolved anywhere"*, but then in an extraordinary comment which sadly encapsulates the mindset of much of the scientific community, he adds *"We believe as an article of faith that life evolved from dead matter on this planet. It is just that its complexity is so great, it is hard for us to imagine that it did"*. This is a tacit admission that the doctrine of Evolution survives despite lack of evidence because people want to believe it - the alternative solution, a divine Creator, is unacceptable. Sir Fred Hoyle admitted that the spontaneous emergence of a single-cell organism from random coupling of chemicals with his famous comment that it was about as likely as *"the assemblage of a Jumbo 747 by a tornado whirling through a junkyard"*. With scientists such as Dr Frances Crick, Hoyle subsequently proposed that life originated in some far part of the universe only to be imported to Earth by some extra intelligence; in a verbal interview Richard Dawkins, the most aggressive campaigner against belief in God, retreated into the same explanation. This novel "panspermia" solution borders on fantasy: it is merely pushing the solution to the problem out to some unknown time and place.

Darwin admitted that vast numbers of transitional life forms, "missing links", would have to be discovered in the geological record to validate his theory. Instead more than a century and a half of intensive investigation of rock successions all over the world have failed to locate a single convincing example. As summarized by Pearce (1993): *"The absence of linking fossils is not a lack of knowledge. It is a record of the absence of links. The fossils are there but there are no evolutionary links......There are no gaps in the records, the records merely show that missing links do not exist"*. Life appeared with the first oceans and stable continental crust, and for more than three billion years single celled organisms called "prokaryotes" and "eukaryotes" (the former without a nucleus, the latter with one, see Chapter 9.4) comprise the biological record. Throughout this time these organisms, predominantly bacteria, showed no tendency to evolve greater complexity. It has now been established that eukaryotic cells with a nucleus could not have evolved from the more primitive prokaryotes because *"the total energy required to process eukaryotic DNA is far more than any bacterial system could produce"* (Nature, Oct 2010. 467 (7318): 929-934).

An explosion of varied multi-cellular soft bodied organisms appeared abruptly in geological terms in the Ediacaran Period beginning 635 Ma (Million years) ago. These are preserved as impressions resembling segmented worms, disks and immobile bags in fine grained sediments (see the history documented in Chapter 9.6 and Figure 9.2) and have no apparent analogues in later animals. They were soon to disappear to be replaced at the beginning of the Cambrian Period 543 Ma ago *by examples of all the phyla (basic anatomies) that are still present with us today*: although different classes of animals developed within each phyla, they always retained the basic body plan unique to their phyla. Some species such as the brachiopod *Lingula* have remained practically unchanged since the beginning of Cambrian times. More commonly, species have a much shorter life span before abruptly becoming extinct; they likely show morphological changes as they adapted to changing environments but remained the same species. According to the stratigraphic record the species barrier is apparently unbreachable.

The popular argument for Special Creation is that the disparate organs of living things are useless unless fully formed. Fully-functioning complex eyes for example, appeared abruptly at the beginning of the Cambrian (Chapter 9.6, Figure 9.3) - there was simply no times to repeatedly test, an albeit useless, partial eye until perfection was achieved. Indeed, some trilobites which spent their lives grubbing about in soft sediment lost the use of eyes - *but they remained trilobites*. The simultaneous creation of unrelated organisms is often required because they depend on one another. Thus pollen-seeking insects appear at the same time as pollen-bearing flowers (angiosperms) in Early Cretaceous times because one could not exist without the other.

Proteins are amino acids that carry out the work of cells to build every part of a living organism. Each DNA cell contains 4 nucleotides which combine in instructed ways to produce the twenty-two different amino acids required to produce the proteins in the smallest living cell and all experiments seeking to create these in the laboratory have failed. Proteins that make up living cells are composed of long thin lines of amino acids just one-millionth the size of a human hair and the smallest living thing contains more than 500 amino acids. More than 100,000 proteins are made up of amino acids attached to side groups of atoms. In non-living amino acids some 50% of the side groups of atoms are attached to the left side and the other 50% to the right side. However, proteins within living cells are entirely "left-handed" - all living cells have amino acids with their side group of atoms on the left side only. Amino acids produced in the laboratory are entirely unlike those found in non-living matter, about 50% being left-handed and 50% right-handed. Yet living cells can only exist when the atoms are solely "left-handed". The odds against a chain of only left-handed atoms forming a single protein have been calculated as one chance in 10^{123}; this is less than the possibility of locating one atom in all the atoms of the universe. The chance of forming the staggering number of complex proteins that make up the multitude of living things becomes quite simply impossible (Jeffrey 1993).

Proteins in living creatures are composed of long chains of different amino acids that can only support life if they are linked together in a precise sequence. The odds against hundreds of amino acids lining up in the correct order to produce one single living cell is just one chance in 10^{200}. Jeffrey (1993) continues: "The odds against a single living protein being formed by chance alone is equal to the chance that a blind-folded man could locate a single grain of sand painted gold within a universe composed of fifty billion galaxies of two hundred stars apiece composed of nothing but sand"

In fact, life requires much more than structures composed of simple amino acids and proteins. DeoxyriboNucleic Acid (DNA) creates the genetic code that commands the various elements in a cell to create the building blocks of life. The odds against a single DNA gene forming by chance has been calculated as equal to one chance in 10 followed by one hundred and fifty-five zeros. The highly intricate DNA language controls every element and cell in the body of all living creatures and contains incredible amounts of information, far more complex than computer software currently controlling vast and intricate operations. Fred Hoyle found that *"If one counts the number of trial assemblies of amino acids that are needed to give rise to the enzymes, the probability of their discovery by random shuffling turns out to be less than one in 10^{400000}"*. The study of human DNA provides much evidence to support Creation in relatively recent times. The International HapMap project which has examined DNA similarities between humans finds that the difference in DNA between any two humans is amazingly, only ~0.1%: the genetic evidence shows that humans vary only slightly in DNA levels. Only a small proportion of this variation separates continental populations and refutes Darwin's unsavory racial theories. This genetic evidence becomes highly relevant to the Genesis record of humankind's origins and is explored in more detail in Chapter 8.13 and 8.14.

As an extensive literature and the few selected examples noted above illustrate, the biological arguments refuting Evolution and requiring Special Creation are extensive and profound. Many people skeptical of Evolution will note that it is "just a theory". However, a theory needs observation to give it this status: scientific endeavor involves observation, measurement, experiment, and the formulation and testing of a concluding hypothesis. Since this is not possible for Evolution it has become a philosophy, a way of thinking about the origin of life. Although posing as a science, it is actually *scientism*, a speculative ideology (for which we can read "religion"). However, in spite of the many arguments refuting Evolution, the atheist will always likely point out that the biological examples depend on chance possibilities and could claim that given the enormous periods of geological and astronomical time, it is still possible that a fluke event could cause one species to evolve into another. To demonstrate that Evolution is quite simply a lie rather than a theory we need to refer to the Laws of Physics.

3.3 Evolution excluded by the Universal Laws of Physics

The word "creation" has only entered the domain of the physical sciences during the last few decades. Until the early 1960's most scientists believed in some variation of the "steady state theory". This regarded the universe as always existing as we observe it today, a view recorded at least since the time of Aristotle 2300 years ago. A humanistic concept, it was clearly in contradiction to Genesis 1:1 attributing Creation to God. However, new discoveries in astronomy and astrophysics forced a radical change in views and today virtually all scientists accept some variation of the "Big Bang Theory" proposing that the whole universe came into existence at a singular point in time. This has forced the word "creation" into the literature of the physical sciences (see for example: *"Creation of the Universe from Nothing" by A. Vilenkin, Physics Letters, 1982*). Nevertheless, the philosophical implications of Creation are considered outside of the realms of scientific discussion by Editors of leading science journals, and by academics such as Stephen Hawking. Physics considers the creation of the mass of material in the Universe, as shown by Edwin Hubble and others to comprise more than fifty billion galaxies, outside of our present rational understanding; instead it is assigned to the realm of quantum mechanics. In contrast the Bible affirms that God created everything with absolute purpose and intelligence. Issues concerned with Creation at a specific point in time are taken further in Chapter 8.5 to 8.7 where we aim to show that the physical sciences can correctly accommodate the origin of the Earth and Universe in the context of the Six Days described in Genesis Chapter One.

The great names of the modern physical sciences from Newton and Boyle, Pascal to Kepler to Pasteur to Kelvin, Rutherford and Faraday were uniformly believers in an intelligent creator and most were professing evangelical Christians. *"Men became scientific because they expected Law in Nature, and they expected Law in Nature because they believed in a Law Giver"* (C.S. Lewis, *Miracles*). Even Einstein, the greatest scientist of the last century, acknowledged that *"God does not play dice"*. Their confidence in their belief in a divine Creator came from observation of the perfection of natural design and from the two immutable Laws of Thermodynamics. The first law as explained by the science writer Isaac Asimov states that *"Energy can be transferred from one place to another, or transformed from one form to another, but it can neither be created nor destroyed"*. The entire amount of energy in the universe remains constant and can never change. A nuclear explosion for example, is simply converting molecular energy into an equivalent amount of heat and light. *The very existence of energy requires a Creator in the first place*.

The other universal law of the physical sciences, the Second Law of Thermodynamics, is even more devastating for Evolution. It states that every item of matter in the universe tends to disintegrate to a lower order of energy organization. *The natural creation always goes progressively from order to chaos - it is only possible to go from chaos to order if there is a Creator to do this.* The implication of the Biblical account is that God moved into His creation six times as described in Genesis Chapter One to convert chaos into order. The Book of Genesis declares that we are now in Biblical Day 7 when God's creative work is complete, order is pro-gressively dispersing as the universe moves towards a state of infinite entropy known as "universal heat death": energy will then be uniformly distributed throughout space and all motion between, and within, atoms will cease. By denying that a creator is required to bring order to creation Stephen Hawking had a problem with God that defied logic; we can only assume that he indulged in obfuscation by refusing to acknowledge implications of his own Laws of Physics.[*]

The so-called "Darwin Day" (12th February) now passes virtually unnoticed with polls showing that between 30 and 50% of the population no longer believe that his "theory" explains Evolution. By 2019 more than 1050 doctoral scientists had signed a statement publicly expressing their skepticism about the contemporary theory of Darwinian Evolution (*www.dissentfromdarwin.org*). *"Darwin's theory of evolution is the great white elephant of contemporary thought,"* said Dr. David Berlinski, one of the original signers, a mathematician and philosopher of science with Discovery Institute's Center for Science and Culture (CSC). *"It is large, almost completely useless, and the object of superstitious awe."* Since

---

[*] See: *God and Stephen Hawking - whose design is it anyway?* by John C. Lennox, Lion Hudson publications, 2011.

most of these scientists work within an apparently rational framework which precludes the possibility of miracles, the only alternative, namely that life is a Divine Creation, is unacceptable. The evidence covered in the next section implies otherwise.

The irony of the continuing frenetic promotion of Darwinism by the media is the substantial documentary evidence showing that Darwin, who came from a family tradition dominated by atheism and married to a wife committed to Unitarianism, rejected his own theory and underwent a conversion to Christianity late in life. Whilst the secular-humanist fraternity has done much to obscure or condemn this evidence, it appears to be well established by Croft in his book *"The life and Death of Charles Darwin"*; the evidence is documented in detail by Pearce (1993). The primary testimony comes from his association with the Temperance campaigner Lady Elizabeth Hope. Darwin had an abhorrence of alcohol because of the damage that it had done to his own family. Lady Hope was an acquaintance of the great reformer Lord Shaftesbury and records her conversations with Darwin declaring his conversion, his love of the Book of Hebrews, and his support of local revival meetings, with the latter confirmed by evangelists James Fegan and Ishmael Jones. At this late stage in life Darwin also became a supporter of Christian missions and expressed his delight at the transforming effect that these missions were achieving in primitive societies that he had seen with degrading practices including human sacrifice. He refused to grant Karl Marx permission to dedicate *Das Kapital* to him and in a letter to a Dr Scherzer he is recorded as stating his concern about the ideas developing in Germany linking Socialism and Evolution. He apparently became grieved with Haeckel's false racial ideas and fabricated drawings of a developing baby in the womb used to promote evolution. Sadly the damage that his 1859 book had started could not be undone and these developing ideas were to have devastating consequences, particularly in Germany in the 20th century.

3.4 God declares that He is the Creator

God actually has very little to say about His act of creation. What He does say is confined to the first chapter of Genesis, plus a few verses mostly in the books of Job, Isaiah, Jeremiah, John and Colossians. The real "Answers in Genesis" are concerned with His plans for the redemption of the human race from its fallen condition. That the Creator of a Universe comprising millions of galaxies should be primarily concerned with rescuing us, His ultimate act of creation, should be both awesome and humbling. Nevertheless He makes it clear that He is the Creator in the first verse of His Word:

Figure 3.1: The First verse of Genesis in the Hebrew and English

This single verse (Hebrew reading from right to left) declaring God to be the Creator has remarkable properties of numerology and gematria (Chapter 2.3) proving that only God himself could have dictated it to his servant Moses, to whom authorship of the Torah is generally attributed. The symmetric word pattern reflects the 7-fold Menorah with seven being the Biblical number of perfection and completion. The central word of this first verse of Genesis is composed of *aleph-tav*, the first and last letters of the Hebrew alphabet, equivalent to *alpha-omega* in the Greek - the untranslatable "Word of Creation" with special attributes explored in Chapter 2.4. In the Menorah the central lamp is called the *"Servant Candle"*. In Isaiah 53 Jesus is the "Suffering Servant" in His first coming as the Redeemer of humankind.

Referring to the gematria (Chapter 2.3) of Genesis 1:1 each letter has the following numeric value:

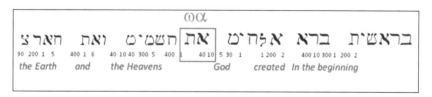

Figure 3.2: The first verse of Genesis Chapter One with the gematria

Properties of this single verse reflecting the sacred scriptural number **7** include the following:

- The number of Hebrew words = 7
- The number of letters = 7 x 4
- The numeric value of the three nouns (God, heaven and earth) = 7 x 111 = 777
- The number of letters in these three words = 7 x 2
- The number of letters in the four remaining words = 7 x 2
- The first three Hebrew words contain 7 x 2 letters
- The last four Hebrew words contain 7 x 2 letters
- The numeric value of the first, middle and last letters = 7 x 19
- The numeric value of the first and last letters of all seven words = 7 x 199
- The middle word and words to the left and right each comprise 7 letters

There is just one chance in 282,475,249 that all these properties could be present in this one verse by chance. However at least 21 other combinations of the number 7 have been discovered in this one verse alone. Evidently God has embedded these properties in His first words to humankind to make it clear that He is the Creator.

References:

Pearce, E.K.V.,1993. *Evidence for Truth: Volume 1, Science*, Evidence Programs, Eastbourne Sussex.

(For references to the extensive arguments by Grant Jeffrey (1993, 1998) see the Bibliography in Chapter 2. Much further information refuting evolution can be found in *Answers in Genesis* and various Creation Ministries on the Internet).

Chapter 4

The Perfection of Creation

In the beginning was the Word, and the Word was with God, and the Word was God. The same was in the beginning with God. All things were made by Him; and without Him was not anything made that was made. (Gospel of John 1:1-3).

For by Him were all things created, that are in heaven, and that are in Earth, visible and invisible, whether they be thrones, or dominions, or principalities, or powers: all things were created by Him, and for Him: And He is before all things, and by Him all things consist. (Book of Colossians 1:16-17).

"All matter originates and exists only by virtue of a force which brings the particle of an atom to vibration and holds this most minute solar system of the atom together. We must assume behind this force the existence of a conscience and intelligent mind. This mind is the matrix of all matter" (Max Planck, the "Father" of Quantum Physics).

4.1 Introduction

The observation that the properties of the Earth and Universe are constrained by a wide range of properties that are collectively so finely-tuned that life would be impossible without them has been a subject of intense enquiry for over a century. To the Bible believer this is a natural consequence of God designing the perfect world for humankind. To the secular humanist a fine-tuned Universe is a proposition that has to be explained within an extraordinary confluence of chance events, normally within a mindset that a group of values of fundamental physical constants will by chance be suitable for allowing life to form by *abiogenesis* - the view that living things can somehow arise from non-living matter such as simple organic compounds. This is usually articulated within the so-called "Anthropic Principle". Several some-what confusing variants of this principle have been proposed, but all have been accused of discouraging the search for a deeper physical understanding of the universe; it lacks the ability to prove its falseness and is in essence a non-scientific concept.

In this chapter a list of parameters and observations is compiled of items so precisely constrained that life, and specifically humankind, would not be able to exist if these values were significantly different. The sources have mainly used Wikipedia and YouTube entries with references quoted therein where the content of this chapter can be further investigated by a brief search. In some cases, investigation will find that contrary arguments have been raised to refute the need for the very special nature of some of the parameters required to constrain the Universe, Earth and life. It is not the intention to contend with these here. It is acknowledged that finer and more specialized brains are better able to address these issues. Instead it is the extraordinary number of so many finely-tuned parameters that support the existence of the Creator. This chapter accordingly occurs between chapters 3 and 5 reinforcing Biblical truth, not because fine-tuning is necessary to prove the existence of God, but rather because it shows that His perfect Creation is a clear demonstration of His creative handiwork.

4.2 THE UNIVERSE

The Universe is not only material. Its formation and preservation are controlled by operation of the Laws of Physics - immaterial realities that specify the properties and behavior of the material world. These are in turn expressed by a number of universal parameters. Most important are the four primary forces, namely *gravity, electromagnetic, strong nuclear* and *weak nuclear*. The force of **Gravity** is required on a cosmic scale to pull matter together to form planets; on smaller scales it is required to retain our atmosphere and enable us to move comfortably and function on a rotating planet of modest size. The gravitational force, F, between two bodies of mass m1 and m2 is expressed by Newton's Law of Gravitation: $F = G(m1 \times m2)/r^2$ where G is the

Gravitational Constant and r is the distance between the masses m1 and m2. The precision with which G is constrained for the survival of life, indeed the very existence of a Universe, is at least 1 part in 10^{40}. This has been likened to a ruler spanning the visible width (10^{28} inches) of the Universe: if the value were increased by just a few millimeters the Universe would collapse, stars would become too hot and burn up and life would be crushed; if the value were decreased by just a few millimeters the Universe would blow apart, no nuclear fusion to produce elements beyond hydrogen would then be possible and no stars or planets could form (e.g. https://www.youtube.com/watch?v=4NMz WvlMYys).

The ratio of the electron to the proton mass (1:1836) is tightly constrained; molecules would be unable to form if this ratio were perceptibly larger or smaller. The **strong nuclear force** is required to pull protons and neutrons together in the nucleus of the atom - without it there would be no atoms and no chemistry. It is 10^{39} times stronger than gravity but has a very short range (~ 1 to 3 x 10^{-15} meters). If this force were to be just 2% stronger (with the other constants unchanged), protons would stick together so that helium and the other high elements could not form. If the strong nuclear force were decreased by just one part in 10^{30} only hydrogen could exist and this would likely have been consumed within the first few minutes after the Big Bang. The **Weak Nuclear Force** controls the interactions between subatomic particles and is responsible for the radioactive decay of nuclei. It plays an essential role in nuclear fusion: if the weak nuclear force were slightly weaker no nuclear fusion could occur and hydrogen would be the only element in existence; helium would not be present as the first step for generating the heavier elements in the stars and there would be no nuclear fuel to power the stars. If it were slightly stronger the stars would burn out too quickly and supernova explosions could not scatter heavy elements across the universe to form the building blocks of rocky planets like Earth.

The possibilities for combining elements into compounds, and thus producing the chemical complexity of Earth and Life is also dependent on the masses of the basic components of matter, electrons and quarks

(Chapter 5.12). If the mass of a down quark had been greater by a factor of 3, the Universe would have contained only hydrogen. If the mass of an electron had been greater by a factor of 2.5, the Universe would have contained only neutrons - no atoms at all, and certainly no chemical reactions.

The **Electromagnetic Force** binds electrons to protons in the atoms. It is approximately 10^{20} times stronger than the gravitational force, but has a very short range; it dominates only over the atomic width where it supplants the strong nuclear force within the nucleus. If it were slightly smaller fewer electrons would be held, whereas if it were larger the electrons would be held too tightly to bond with other atoms - no molecules for producing the numerous compounds essential to life could then form. A fifth parameter, the ***Strength of Electromagnetism, N***, is a dimensionless physical constant defined as the ratio of the strength of the electromagnetic interaction between elementary charged particles, to the strength of gravity between a pair of protons. It has a very large value of approximately 10^{37} and if it were significantly smaller it is reckoned that only a small and short-lived universe could exist.

The origins of these forces holding the Universe together are of course, ultimately a mystery. The rational mind of humankind cannot go beyond noting that they are an observational reality. Here we meet one of the most extraordinary boundaries between the limits of scientific experiment and the beginning of a spiritual reality. The Bible has a Divinely-inspired explanation: the Book of Colossians 1:17 tells us that everything consists in the Lord Jesus Christ and is held together by His power (literally "strong force"). This is the implication of the first verse of John's Gospel quoted at the start of this Chapter. If He lets go of the atom, the present universe will cease to exist. This is also implied in the Epistle of Peter (2 Peter 3:10-12) where Peter uses the Greek word for "loosing" for the force that, if released, would dissolve the atom and lead to the destruction of the Universe.

Three other parameters used to define the physical properties of the Universe also prove to be exceptionally finely-tuned:

The parameter **Epsilon** (ε) is a measure of the efficiency of the process of nuclear fusion from hydrogen to helium. When four nuclei fuse into helium, 0.007 (0.7%) of their mass is converted to energy and it is this fusion energy that powers the stars like our Sun. The value of ε is determined in part by the strength of the strong nuclear force. If ε were reduced to 0.006, only hydrogen could exist and complex chemistry including the chemistry of life would be impossible. If ε were 0.008 or higher all the hydrogen would have fused and used up shortly after the Big Bang.

Omega (Ω), is a density parameter and describes the importance of the force of gravity relative to the expansion energy in the universe. It is defined as the ratio of the measured density divided by a critical theoretical density derived from the expansion of a homogenous and isotropic space. It is used to define the fine balance between an expanding and a contracting Universe. With the discovery that the Universe is expanding and that this expansion is accelerating, it has been necessary to invoke the existence of dark matter (Chapters 5.9 and 8.5) with repulsive gravitational energy ('antigravity') to explain observed properties of galaxies and the formation of the Universe. The assigned name "dark" implies ignorance of a medium which is unknowable although its creation appears to be recorded in the Scriptures (Chapter 8.5). Its properties have to be finely balanced: if gravity had been too strong compared with the influence of the dark matter the Universe would have collapsed in on itself early in its history; if gravity had been too weak no stars and our Solar System could have formed. A related cosmological constant, **Q,** is used to define the ratio of the gravitational energy required to pull a large galaxy apart to the energy equivalence of its mass. It has a very small value of around 10^{-5} and is also considered to be finely-balanced: if it were much smaller no stars could form but if it were much larger the cosmos would be too violent for any stars to survive.

Lambda (λ) is assigned to the *Cosmological constant*, is the energy density (the vacuum energy) of space. Lambda was originally introduced by Einstein as a factor in his General Theory of Relativity (Chapter 8.7) to allow a static Universe. When the expansion of the Universe was understood it was reckoned to become unnecessary and from 1930 to 1998 was assigned the value of zero. However, when the acceleration of the Universe was discovered it was reintroduced as the ratio of the density of dark energy to the vacuum energy density of space. Since dark energy is not directly observable, it is poorly understood but is considered to operate like a force of anti-gravity which dilutes much more slowly and clusters more weakly than the observable matter as the universe expands. Advancing cosmological data now assign it a miniscule value of about 10^{-122}. It has to be extremely small otherwise it would prevent the formation of cosmic structures expanding to their present sizes of more than a billion light-years across and stars and galaxies would not then be able to form.

The collective fine tuning of six of the most important parameters that have permitted our Universe to form and exist, and then allow higher forms of life to flourish, are considered to be collectively fine-tuned to an unimaginably high degree. An estimate of these precisions include: Gravitational Constant: 1 part in 10^{40}, Strength of Electromagnetism (N): 1 part in 10^{37}, Cosmological Constant (λ): 1 part in 10^{120}, Mass Density of universe, (Ω): 1 part in 10^{59}, Expansion Rate of Universe: 1 part in 10^{55}, and Initial Entropy: 1 part in 10^{123} (*https://evolutionnews.org/2017/ 11/ids-top-six-the-fine-tuning-of-the-universe/*).

4.3 EARTH

4.3.1 The best position in the Galaxy

Our Solar System is sited at a favorable position in the Milky Way. If we were too close to the center of the galaxy (and closer to the black hole at the centre), harmful radiation would make life impossible. Conversely, if our planet had been sited too far out in the periphery there would not be enough heavier elements available to form a habitable planet, and specifically find the necessary carbon and oxygen necessary for life. The controlling star also acts as the energy source for life and most stars are too large, too bright or too unstable. The size and age of our Sun preferentially makes our planet inhabitable and enhances its hospitality. The brightness of a larger sun would change too quickly and there would be too much high energy radiation, whilst a much smaller sun would restrict the range of planetary distance able to support life; a distance amenable to life would be so close to the star that tidal forces would disrupt the planet's rotational period, and the ultraviolet radiation would be inadequate to allow photosynthesis to occur. Our Sun is also the right colour to permit photosynthesis: if it was redder or bluer, any photosynthetic response would be weaker and unable to produce the atmospheric changes that have characterised the history of our planet since its formation. This history is described in Chapter 9.

As more and more exoplanets are being discovered it is becoming apparent that the properties of our Solar System are rare, and perhaps uniquely favourable to life. Compared with other systems, ours seems to be exceptionally large. Most others are characterised by huge gas giants very close to their suns. Unlike our Solar System, all examples discovered to date seem to have gas giants closer to the sun (or suns) than terrestrial planets. The seven worlds around the system TRAPPIST-1 for example, are tightly packed within a radius of just six million miles, or one-sixth the distance between the Sun and Mercury. In our Solar System the planets, and notably Earth, travel in near-circular orbits whereas about half of the exoplanets have distinctly oval-shaped orbits; some are wildly eccentric. Our Sun is a middle-aged, relatively hot star but less than 10 percent of stars in the Milky Way fit this description; instead, most are red dwarfs—older, colder, and smaller. Furthermore our Sun formed alone, whereas other stars are typically paired; most stars in the galaxy seem to have been born in pairs with some having many companions. *(Forbes Magazine, Innovation contribution by Bill Rutherford, January 2018).*

4.3.2 The right size

A large planet has high gravity and is able to gather hydrogen and helium, as well as unfriendly gases like methane and ammonia, and then become a gas giant like Jupiter and Saturn. If it is too small it has insufficient gravity to hold onto its atmosphere including the water vapor; this is the situation with Mars. Earth has just the right size and mass to hold on to its atmosphere. The atmosphere of Earth has also achieved a finely-calibrated ratio of oxygen to nitrogen, as well as just enough carbon dioxide and adequate water vapor levels to promote advanced life and allow photosynthesis. Currently our atmosphere does not possess an excessive greenhouse effect but it retains sufficient water vapor and circulation to allow for widespread rainfall. The atmospheric pressure is also important because too much pressure causes water to turn into a solid whilst too little pressure will cause it to turn into a gas.

4.3.3 A Magnetic Field

Unlike Mars, Earth is large enough and still hot enough to retain a liquid iron-nickel Outer Core which by circulation and convection is able to generate a significant magnetic field. The influence of this field extends well above the Earth as the *magnetosphere;* this field deflects charged and harmful cosmic radiation from the Sun and elsewhere in space that would otherwise be very damaging to life. Although the magnetic field collapses to only 10-20% of its average value during reversals (Chapter 6.11), it has not reversed during the past 720,000 years, an interval which embraces the history of humankind.

4.3.4 Perfectly placed within the Solar System

Life relies on liquid water but water has only a relatively narrow temperature range of 100°C at surface pressures between freezing into a solid and evaporating into a gas. The habitable zone of the Solar System has to be where liquid water can exist in abundance. Earth lies inside this habitable zone beginning at ~0.9 AU from the Sun (one Astronomical Unit, AU, is the distance between the Earth and the Sun, or approximately 150,000,000 km) and extending out to about 1.3-1.5 AU away from the Sun. Fortunately too, the Earth has a nearly circular orbit so the difference between the closest and most distance proximities to the Sun vary by only about 3%; this compares with most planets which have much more elliptical orbits (see Figure 5.7 in Chapter 5). It means that Earth is rare in not experiencing extremes of temperature. The rate of planetary rotation also matters: although habitable limits are not easily constrained, a slower rotation would make days too hot and nights too cool to support life whilst a faster rotation would also cause wind speeds to increase, ultimately to very damaging levels (Chapter 5.9).

4.3.5 Earth has reached the right age for life to prosper

The age of the universe is relevant to the existence of life on Earth. It must be neither too young nor too old. If it were one tenth of its present age there would not have been sufficient time to build up significant amounts of the elements beyond hydrogen and helium. This applies especially to the carbon and oxygen crucial to life, and small rocky planets would not yet exist. On the other hand if the universe were 10 times older than it is now (and the "universal heat death" of infinite entropy had not yet been attained) most stars would be too old to remain on the main sequence of planetary evolution (see Chapter 6.5); they would have burnt up and turned into white dwarfs. With the exception of the dimmest red dwarfs, all stable planetary systems would have ceased to exist. The formation of Earth also occurred at the right time to escape the effects of the intense solar blasting during the *T Tauri* phase of the star formation. If this had occurred earlier in the history of our Sun all material would have been blasted away into space and no Planet Earth would likely have formed; if it had occurred too late the first seas and cloud cover would have been swept away to leave a lifeless Mercury-like rocky ball.

4.3.6 Earth has attained an ideal Crust and Ocean

Because the Earth has reached an appropriate planetary maturity we have a continental crust of the right age covering about a third of the planet and allowing an optimum area for oceans. During its early history the crust of the Earth would not only have been thin and hot, but also intensely radioactive. Now that the radioactivity has greatly declined and the thickness of the crust has increased to ~30 km conditions are appropriate for supporting life. The earlier thinner crust would also have experienced intense volcanic activity and highly unstable tectonic behavior as well as intense radiation. The crust has now thickened to a point at which ocean crust can be subducted back into the Mantle, and Plate Tectonics within wide oceans can control planetary behavior (Chapter 6.12). This allows for the continuing recycling of elements and compounds accumulated in the seas, the ocean crust and the sediments depositing around the continents, back into the cycle of life. By ongoing volcanic activity, the crucial elements required for life are recycled back into the atmosphere, oceans and hydrosphere. At the present time Plate Tectonics allows limited seismic activity, provides nutrient recycling and carbon dioxide release without destroying all life on the planet; it keeps gas and mineral concentrations within life-permitting ranges. A much thicker crust would inhibit subduction and negatively-impact the quantity of oxygen in the atmosphere.

4.3.7 Protected from frequent impacting by dangerous space debris

Space is a hazardous environment. The multitude of material from the Asteroid Belt impacting a planet the size of Earth would make the planet uninhabitable. Fortunately, we have a massive planet, Jupiter, within a proximal distance able to capture the vast majority of this debris. Although small sized particles are entering Earth's atmosphere all the time where their small size ensures that they are largely or wholly burnt up, the presence of Jupiter ensures that it attracts the bulk of the larger material and means that catastrophic impacts on Earth have only been occasional events. The position of Mars behind Earth has also served to shield us from much bombardment from the Asteroid Belt.

4.3.8 Earth has the optimum tilt

The tilt of the Earth's spin axis of 23.4° with respect to the plane of the orbit about the Sun is essential for producing the four seasons required for the annual renewal of plant, and much animal, life and for restoring the soil and waters on which life depends. Whilst interplanetary forces could have caused the axial angle to change over time, it appears that the stabilizing effect of the single large and nearby Moon has kept the spin axis of the Earth in a stable configuration able to provide a long-term uniform climatic cycle in which life can flourish. Without a large moon, the axis of our planet would likely have wobbled dramatically, perhaps by as much as 90 degrees. The angle of tilt also appears to be close to the optimum value for ensuring that most of the globe is habitable; this allows for seasons that are well balanced and prevent temperature extremes.

If the Earth had not been tilted early in its history the ice caps would be more extensive and permanent; places much further north or south of 50 degrees could not be cultivated, and monsoons would disappear leaving areas near the tropics uninhabitable. If the acquired tilt had been significantly larger the "Torrid Zone" would cover the largest area of the globe and the most productive temperate zones would be much smaller. A higher tilt would also mean more extreme seasons, warmer summers and colder winters, and this would increase the intensity of the storms that counteract the north-south temperature differences.

4.4 The importance and unique properties of Water

Water is essential for life - it is required to dissolve and transport nutrients. It has several properties that make it unique amongst compounds and thus possible for all known forms of life to function. It is the only natural substance found in all three physical states within the narrow range of temperatures that occur naturally on Earth. It is also unique amongst compounds because the solid state (ice) is less dense than liquid water. Because ice floats on water, seas and lakes freeze from the top downwards; this is crucial for animals that live partly on ice because their habitats would either be greatly reduced or vanish altogether if ice sank. Fish and other pond-life could not flourish if lakes and ponds froze from the bottom upwards; instead the layer of frozen water at the top provides insulation and produces a barrier between the cold air and the water below. This means that large bodies of water can retain equitable temperatures at depth where life can survive for winters or even millennia. However, if temperatures were significantly colder than the range currently experienced on Earth the seas would all be ice, there would be no rain and nothing for plants to collect and animals to drink. Seas, lakes and rivers maintain a much more constant temperature than air; this means that animals can live in water throughout the year without having to adapt to large temperature changes.

The rare properties of water valuable for life arise from the special bonding between the two hydrogen atoms to the one oxygen atom in the water molecule. This is a high energy bond and is only broken with great difficulty; it is responsible for the high melting and boiling points of water compared with compounds such as methane. A great deal of energy is required to break this bond down, and it is so arranged that the oxygen sector of the molecule is slightly negatively charged and the hydrogen atoms are slightly positively charged. This give the water molecules electrical polarity and causes water molecules to 'stick'; it is responsible for the high surface tension and the ability of water to move laterally and upwards by capillary action. Small insects are able to land on water and provide food for higher organisms, and plants are able to tap water drawn up through the ground. The polarity properties of water are also responsible for its special solvent properties which enable it to be a source of nutrients for life. A substance will dissolve in water if it has electrical polarity. Salt, NaCl, for example, dissolves because it too, is ionic (has polarity) but oil which is not polar, will not dissolve; it would otherwise make water inimical to life.

4.5 The importance of Carbon and Oxygen

Life on Earth is based on the element carbon because its unusual chemistry allows it to bond to itself, as well as to other elements and create highly complex molecules. These are stable over prevailing terrestrial temperatures and pressures, and are able to convey genetic information through the code comprising the DNA. Carbon is the 6th element in the fusion sequence above hydrogen and 6 is the Biblical number of man (Table 5.1). The special property of carbon is expressed by the *Hoyle State* and refers to the spin resonance value of carbon-12. This is an energy level recorded as 7.7 MeV (million electron volts) and is the unique value required for carbon to form from nucleosynthesis during star formation. If it were lower than 7.3 or greater than 7.9 MeV insufficient carbon would exist to support life. To explain the abundance of carbon in the Universe the Hoyle state must be further finely-tuned to a value between 7.596 and 7.716 MeV.

A similar calculation, focusing on the other fundamental constants concludes that the strong force must be tuned to a precision of at least 0.5% and the electromagnetic force to a precision of at least 4%, to prevent either carbon or oxygen production from dropping significantly below the amounts required to support life. The oxygen essential for all higher forms of life is produced by photosynthesis: carbon dioxide and water are synthesized by sunlight to produce food (glucose) for the plants which generate oxygen as a byproduct. Oxygen is readily consumed by chemical oxidation and the processes of production and consumption must be finely balanced by nature to sustain the ~21% in the atmosphere necessary for higher forms of life to thrive: when the oxygen level falls to ~15% suffocation ensues; when it increases to ~25% oxygen becomes poisonous and spontaneous combustion occurs.

4.6 Overview: The place of Humankind in the Cosmos

In the earlier decades of the last century there was little speculation about the possibility of alien life. H.G. Well with novels such as "War of the Worlds", was an early motivator of thoughts of alien life and when Hollywood began to seriously produce films on extra-terrestrial themes in the 1950's the ideas were mainly centered on meetings with human-like aliens. The 1960's began to see much interest in the search for extraterrestrial intelligence (SETI) by American and Soviet scientists. Carl Sagan was a particularly strong advocate of the likelihood of finding alien life. Given just the right kind of planet at a suitable distance from a sun, he speculated that there would be a high probability of finding extraterrestrial life; this was before any planets outside of our own Solar System were known to exist. Since then large numbers of radio telescopes have had the primary or secondary purpose of seeking signals from alien life, the number of identified exoplanets is increasing all the time with programs such as Project Kepler, and probes have been sent to nearby planets and moons with the aim of detecting life-supporting elements and compounds. As the decades with a total absence of evidence for alien signals have accumulated and the highly specialized conditions required for life to survive have become evident, it is becoming clear that the early hopes for discovering alien life were drastically over-optimistic. The chance that the unique range of factors, including those documented in this chapter, which have allowed higher forms of life to survive and prosper on Earth being repeated anywhere else in the Universe is remote in the extreme.

This has not checked the overwhelming necessity for evolution embedded in the mindset of the Mainstream Media which requires that every newly-reported space investigation has to have the motivation, or at least the expectation, of finding signs of alien life. In reality the special combination of the enormous number of factors required to allow any form of life on Earth is so unique that the hope of finding life elsewhere has to be living an illusion. Just as the probability of Evolution been found to be so improbable that the humanist is required to force its origin out into space as "panspermia", the only hope of finding another universe fine-tuned for life has to be accommodated by postulating multiple universes, where at least one might have the perfect combination of properties to allow for life like our own. Not only is there not the slightest evidence for multiple universes, but this is merely pushing the question of the original Designer further away into a more comfortable distance of time and space.

Within the limits of our prospective technology it would take more than 80,000 years or ~2,700 human generations to traverse the 4.24 light years to our nearest star neighbor, Proxima Centauri. In view of the insuperable distances involved, UFO phenomena are regarded by those prepared to acknowledge a spiritual realm as demonic apparitions from another dimension. As discussed in Chapter 8.3, multiple dimensions beyond the four we are constrained to, are recognized by both Biblical and secular sources. We need to face the reality that we really are alone in the Universe. A study by scientists at Oxford University has determined that aliens do not exist and concludes that humankind is alone in space. Researchers at the Future of Humanity Institute came to this conclusion whilst examining the so-called "Fermi Paradox" which ponders why scientists believe in extraterrestrials despite having zero proof (Sandberg et al. 2018). Their conclusion is that "We find a substantial probability of there being no other intelligent life in our observable universe, and thus that there should be little surprise when we fail to detect any signs of it". There is likely no intelligent life outside of Earth and there is no need to waste time theorizing about humanity's relationship with aliens, notes the paper, dubbed "Dissolving the Fermi Paradox". The paradox, named after physicist Enrico Fermi, questions how there could be "a high probability" of extraterrestrial life when there's no evidence. "Where is everyone?" Fermi asked in the

1950s while pondering the possibility of interstellar travel. "There should be little surprise when we fail to detect any signs of aliens", the Oxford report notes: "there is simply no one else out there". It is our assertion here that humankind on Earth is a unique creation of God.

It is appropriate to conclude this summary with quotations from some of the experts:

Sir Fred Hoyle who coined "the Big Bang": *"My atheism was greatly shaken by these developments".*

Paul Davies, theoretical physicist: *"The appearance of design is overwhelming".*

Christopher Hitchens, ardent atheist: *"Without question the fine-tuning argument is the most powerful argument of the other side".*

John Lennox, Christian mathematician: *"The more we get to know about our Universe, the more the hypothesis that there is a Creator gains credibility as the best explanation of why we are here"*

Even that ardent denier of the need for God, *Stephen Hawking*, had to observe: *"The laws of science, as we know them at present, contain many fundamental numbers, like the size of the electric charge of the electron and the ratio of the masses of the proton and the electron....... The remarkable fact is that the values of these numbers seem to have been very finely adjusted to make possible the development of life."*

Reference:

Sandberg, A., Drexler, E. and Ord, T., 2018. Dissolving the Fermi Paradox, Arxiv.org, physics, arXiv:1806.02404, also Published June 26, 2018, by New York Post.

Chapter 5

The Perfection of Design - Fibonacci Numbers and the Trinity

5.1 Introduction

If the fine tuning of the Earth for human habitation is an expression of the Creator, we should anticipate that the numerical order He also designed should express this perfection and ordering. We indeed find that the numbers used every day and taken for granted, each have special properties and are expressed in the natural world. The usage of numbers in the Bible carries a consistent meaning throughout the text and they appear in Creation in a way that proves to be so perfect that we can readily acknowledge that the Creator is responsible for them. Numbers of course, are also the expression of time and we recognize an intimate relationship between the numbers of time and their signature in Creation. This relationship is a key facet for understanding Creation and the nature of the Six Days of Genesis Chapter One. In this chapter we examine the Biblical properties of numbers, explore their links to the natural world, and define a key relationship for determining the durations of the Six Days.

5.2 Numbers, Fibonacci Series and the Golden Proportion

The decimal, or base-10 system on which our modern numbering system is founded has its origin in Indian (Hindu) usage dating back to at least the 8th century AD. Following adoption by Arabic scholars, it seems to have reached the west via contacts with Byzantium and Middle Eastern pilgrimage. The adoption of zero and Arabic (Gobar) numerals then spread rapidly throughout Europe, notably by the promotion of Gerbert of Aurillac (~946-1003) who later became Pope Sylvester II. Our modern numbering system employing ten digits with its decimal point and a symbol for zero, was first popularized in the western world by Leonardo da Pisa (Fibonacci, 1170-1250) in a pioneering book entitled *Liber abbaci* ("Book of Calculating" or "How to do Arithmetic in the Decimal System"). It was soon seen to have many benefits over the cumbersome Latin numeral system, and also over the Greek and Hebrew number-letter equivalence system described in Chapter 2.3.

Fibonacci's book also introduced the properties of a sequence of numbers where each succeeding number is the sum of the preceding two numbers. Although it did not originate with Fibonacci, the sequence of numbers that has carried his name since 1877 obeys the simple equation $X_{n+2} = X_{n+1} + X_n$ where n is the number in the sequence. It proceeds to define a succession of numbers:

1, 1, 2, 3, 5, 8, 13, 21, 34, 55, 89, 144, 233, 377, 610, 987...

This sequence contains a special property: the ratios between each successive pair of numbers rapidly approaches a constant known as the "golden proportion" designated **Phi**, ϕ and approximating to 1.618; although often referred to as the "golden ratio", it is an irrational number and therefore not a true ratio. An irrational number is any number that cannot be written as a simple fraction, only expressed as an infinite number of decimal numbers that never repeat themselves. A unique property of Phi is that its reciprocal is 1 less than itself, or 0.618, whilst its square is 2.618 one more than itself. The numbers 1.618 (**Phi**) and 0.618 (**phi**) can be used interchangeably by doing multiplication or division. The golden proportion defines a rectangle known as the "golden rectangle": if the short side is **x** the longer side (**L**) will be **1.618x** and L and x satisfy the equation **L/x=(x+L)/L**. The exact value is $(1 + \sqrt{5})/2$. This rectangle permits a progressive multiplication, always preserving the golden proportion (Figure 5.1) and every time we take away a square from a golden rectangle we end up with another golden rectangle:

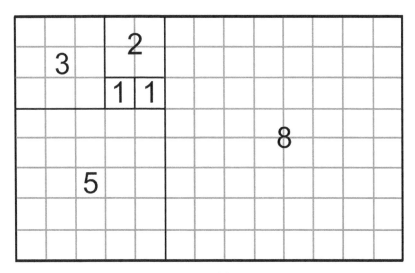

Figure 5.1: The Golden Rectangle

The golden proportion is an intrinsic property of the Scriptures. As if to confirm this, the words "Fibonacci Series" and "Genesis" have the same gematria number of 913. The research of Rabbi M. Glazerson, which can be explored in his books and website, identify the remarkable way in which the Fibonacci Series is reflected in the Hebrew names of the numbers. Beginning with the first letter of the Hebrew alphabet *aleph*, which contains the abbreviated name of God *"El"* and is spelt with the three letter *aleph*, *lamed* and *pei*, the names of these three letters comprise 8 Hebrew letters altogether. Doubling and writing out the new number in its constituent letters in the manner of the Golden Rectangle generates successively 21, 55, 144, 377 etc. letters all following the Fibonacci Series (*https://www.youtube.com/watch?v= OEitTICcVko*). Furthermore the first three numbers of the series are 1,1, and 2 where 112 is the combined gematria of the names of the personal name of God, *YHVH* (26), and Lord, *Elohim* (86). The next three numbers are 3, 5, and 8 where 358 is the gematria of "Messiah" as well as "God is King". Many further properties linking the Fibonacci Series with gematria and the Hebrew alphabet can be explored on rabbinic websites covering these topics.

5.3 Perfection in God's Creation of Man

The golden proportion is often called "Divine" because of its ubiquity in nature. It is present at several levels in the dimensions of man. The famous image of Leonardo da Vinci is embraced by a pentagram within a circle linking the two key irrational numbers showing order in Creation: Phi (ϕ), and Pi (π) (Figure 5.2). The pentagram contains four different lengths denoted AB, AC, AD and BC in the figure and the ratio of each length to the next larger length equals 1.618: AD/AC = AC/AB = AB/BC = 1.618. The inverse property is AC/AD = AB/AC = BC/AB = phi (0.618). A regular pentagram also has five golden triangles at each corner and the ratio of the longest to the shortest sides is equal to Phi. No other comparable figure incorporating any number of points displays this ratio. The three major triangles are frequently used in Palladian architecture and commonly seen above entranceways always supported below by two or more pillars. Although the pentagram, especially in its inverted form, has been widely misused for occult purposes, it has a genuine Biblical significance. Five is the Biblical number of grace (Table 5.1). Here it encompasses man - he is only required to acknowledge God's provision of that free gift of grace and its repentant implications.

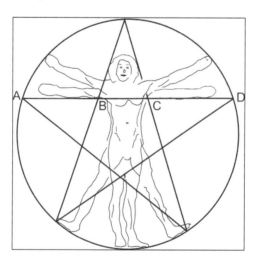

Figure 5.2: The image of Man after Leonardo da Vinci's Man as the "Measure of All Things" in the Pentagram after Agrippa's "De Occulta Philosophia". Note the relationship between the two irrational numbers of the creation, Phi and Pi.

It will be observed that the center of the circle is located at man's navel and the navel divides the human body from the base of the feet to the top of the head in the ratio 1.618. The study of human biometrics (life measurements) shows that the navel changes position during growth continuously from slightly above to slightly below this position, as it approximates closer and closer to this central point by an age in the mid-twenties. Whilst there are several views on the Biblical significance of the navel, symbolically it is the signature of every fallen descendent of Adam. We argue in Chapter 8.1 that Adam was a unique creation of God; presumably he did not have a navel.

Other features approximating to the Golden proportion are found in details of the human makeup. The mouth and nose are each positioned at golden sections of the distance between the eyes and the bottom of the chin. Other proposed relationship are seen in the features of the human makeup as diverse as the length of the forearm to the length of the hand, the ratio of the lengths of the digits in the fingers and foot, the dimensions of the foot and the ear, the ear and in fingerprints. When women are at their most fertile between the ages of 16 and 20, the ratio of length to width of a healthy uterus during the culmination of pregnancy is 1.6, a good approximation to the golden proportion. The Fibonacci signature continues down to the microscopic level: the DNA molecule measures 34 angstroms long by 21 angstroms wide for each full cycle of its double helix spiral (1 Angstrom = 10^{-10} metres); these numbers, 34 and 21, are numbers in the Fibonacci series, and their ratio 1.6190476 closely approximates to Phi. The Golden Proportion has even been recognized in the field of quantum mechanics where quanta are observed to resonate according to this value (*Science, January 2010*).

However, it must be stressed that since natural growth occurs under imperfect conditions, when these propositions are investigated experimentally in humans they typically yield approximations to Phi, and always with associated errors. As with the migration of the human navel noted above, the occurrence of the Fibonacci Series in nature always has the implication of striving towards the ultimate irrational number. This is evident in the addition of the squares in Figure 5.1: for every square we create we use the sum of the length of the sides of the two squares that went before. When the ratio between each number of the series to the previous number they converge more closely towards the ultimate Golden Ratio:

$1/1 = 1$ (61%), $2/1 = 0.5$ (76.4%), $3/2 = 1.5$ (92.7%), $5/3 = 1.666$ (96.99%).....$610/377 = 1.618037$ (99.9998%)

5.4 God's Perfection copied in the Works of Man

It is hardly surprising that perfection of the natural world created by God should be copied by humankind. Artists who incorporated the Golden Rectangle into their art include Leonardo da Vinci (seen for example in his Mona Lisa), Van Gogh, Rembrandt, Vermeer, Monet and Renoir. The properties of Phi were known to the ancients. In the Great Pyramid of Giza, the ratio of the slant height to the vertical height is exactly Phi to √Phi giving it the special property that the area of a triangular face is equal to the square of the height; other dimensions relating the external and internal features of this pyramid incorporate Phi, and the other universal irrational number, Pi (π). The golden proportion of the rectangle has long been regarded as the most pleasing shape to the eye and has correspondingly been incorporated into the works of numerous artists, as well as forming the proportions of many works of architecture. The ancient Greeks sought it as a factual perfection of beauty called the "essence". The Greek sculptor and architect **Phi**dias, who gave his name to the golden proportion, incorporated it into the Parthenon completed in 438 BC and other temples he designed. It was also incorporated, together with Pi, into the designs of the great medieval cathedrals, and today it is copied in many every day to day items such as doors, windows, luxury cars, postcards, playing cards and credit cards. Of Biblical significance, it appears in the dimensions of the Ark of the Covenant given to Moses (Exodus 25:10).

5.5 Perfection in Music

The piano and organ keyboards are directly related to the Fibonacci numbers. The black keys are in groups of 2 and 3 known as the pentatonic scale whilst the octave is composed of 8 white keys, the diatonic scale, there are only 12 "notes" in the scale. Without a root and octave - a start and an end - there are no means of calculating the gradations in between, so this 13th note making up the octave is essential to computing the frequencies of the other notes. The 8 white and 5 black keys comprising 13 altogether, make up the chromatic scale. In a scale, the dominant note is the 5th note of the major scale; this is also the 8th note of all 13 notes that comprise the octave. Two, three, five and eight are all Fibonacci numbers (Figure 5.3).

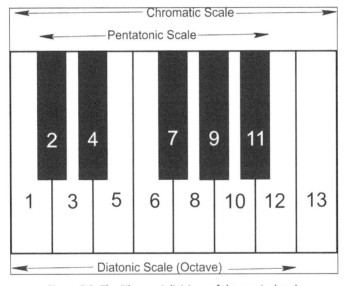

Figure 5.3: The Fibonacci divisions of the musical scale

The major sixth (C and A) and the minor sixth (E and higher C) are regarded as the most beautiful chords in music. Notes in the scale of music are based on natural harmonics created by ratios of frequencies. Ratios found in the first seven numbers of the Fibonacci series (0, 1, 1, 2, 3, 5, 8) are related to key frequencies of musical notes. The major sixth has 264 and 440 vibrations per second, a ratio of 3:5. The minor sixth has vibrations of 330 and 528 per second, a ratio of 5:8. Both of these are Fibonacci ratios (Missler 1999). Mozart and other composers have incorporated the Fibonacci series into many of their compositions. Mozart would introduce a theme followed by a sequence developing and repeating the theme with approximately 1.618 times more bars of music. The golden proportion is also present in the physical (length to width) dimensions of the violin and cello families (~2.618).

5.6 The Fibonacci spiral

The Golden Rectangle has an exceptional property; if a square is removed from one end the remaining rectangle is still a golden rectangle and the ratios remain the same. Conversely by connecting the corners of successive squares and continually adding squares with the dimension of the preceding long side we generate an expanding sequence of golden rectangles into which a "Golden Spiral" fits perfectly. It is the only spiral that does not alter its shape as it grows. The one below uses squares of sizes 1, 1, 2, 3, 5, 8, 13, 21, and 34:

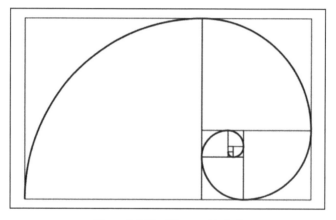

Figure 5.4: The Fibonacci Spiral

In nature Fibonacci numbers are recognised in features as diverse as the dimensions of chicken's eggs to the branching of veins in tree leaves. Spiral forms approaching the series are present throughout Creation in shapes as diverse as hurricanes, waves breaking on the seashore, whirlpools and comets winding a course about the Sun. Fibonacci spirals are present in animals, for example, in rams' horns and elephant tusks, mammal ears and the cochlea inside the human ear. We see them in ancient and modern shells such as ammonites, nautiloides and snails

(Figure 5.5) as well as in features constructed by the insect kingdom such as spider's webs.

Figure 5.5: The Fibonacci Spiral expressed in modern (nautilus) and ancient (ammonite) shells showing the repeated expression of the golden rectangle

5.7 Perfection in the world of Flora

The Fibonacci Series is strikingly present throughout nature in the floral world of flowers, seeds and cones (Figure 5.6). The seeds of the sunflower are an exceptionally intricate example; they are configured into a collection of spirals in both clockwise and counter clockwise ways the number of spirals in each direction comprise adjacent Fibonacci numbers:

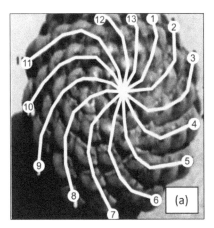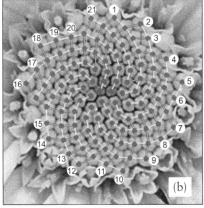

Figure 5.6: The Fibonacci Spiral in plants: (a) the 13-fold spiral in a Pine; (b) the 21-fold double spirals in a Sunflower; (c) 5-fold spiral in a Flowering Artichoke; (d) Sequential leaf growth in a plant: each leaf is exactly 0.618 (phi = 1/Phi) of a clockwise turn from the previous one.

The leaves of plants are ordered in a spiral arrangement around the stem of the plant in a way that is a function of the leaf shape but always conforms to the Fibonacci Series; this is true for all the 416 families of angiosperms (flowering plants) and the ~1000 families of gymnosperms (seed-producing plants). It optimizes the exposure of the leaves to sunlight and air without shading or crowding leaves from the same stem above and below. The rotational angle from leaf to leaf in a repeating spiral is represented by a fraction of a full rotation around the stem; incorporating Phi is the only way that repeated rotation can prevent sunflower seeds for example, degenerating into a series of spokes. When just two opposite leaves are present the angle is 1/2 of a full rotation. In beech and hazel the angle is 1/3, in oak and apricot it is 2/5, in sunflowers, poplar and pear, it is 3/8, and in willow and almond the angle is 5/13.

In each of these examples the numbers are a Fibonacci number and its second successor. This property of the leaves is repeated in the property of the flower petals: a lily and iris have 3 petals, yellow violet, buttercup and larkspur have 5, delphinium has 8, mayweed, corn marigold and ragwort have 13, aster, chicory and doronicum have 21, pyrethrum has 34, helenium has 55 and the michaelmas daisy has 89 (Missler 1999). The numbers are always Fibonacci numbers. In the sunflower there are two families of spiral patterns: one winding clockwise and the other counterclockwise (Figure 5.6). The number of spirals in each family are always two consecutive Fibonacci numbers and the effect is the result of closely packing points separated by 137.5° in tight spirals. The golden proportion allows both for optimal sun exposure and for maximum packing in a horizontal space.

5.8 Perfection in the Solar System

In the Solar System the successive ratios of planetary revolutions around the Sun prove to be very close to the Fibonacci sequence. Starting with the outmost defined planet Neptune where the rotation times in days are Observed/*Theoretical adjusted* (i.e. adjusted to an ideal elliptical orbit according to Kepler's Law) 60.193/*62,000* days. The following planets with the ratio to the preceding planetary figure moving inwards and shown in bold are: Uranus: 30,688/*31,000*/**1.2**, Saturn: 10,670/*10,333*/**1.3**, Jupiter: 4,332/*4,133*/**2.5**, Asteroids: 1,200-2,000/*1,500*/**3.8**, Mars: 687/*596*/**5.13**, Earth: 365/*366*/**8.2**, Venus: 225/*277*/**8.2** and Mercury 8.8/*8.7*/**13.3**. The successive ratios increase in conformity with numbers in the Fibonacci sequence, and for planets with more than one moon there is a Fibonacci correlation in the distances of the moons to the host planet. Whilst these numbers do not of course, precisely match the Fibonacci sequence, by integrating individual orbits with the dynamic relationships between planet pairs as recorded in the frequencies of their synodic conjunctions, and including two dwarf planets (Juno and Pluto), Roger Tattersall has achieved a close match between the Fibonacci series and the dynamic relationships between all the planets in the Solar System with less than 2.75% error (https://tallbloke.wordpress.com/2013/02/20/).

This ordering of the planets in our Solar System currently defies a physical explanation. According to the conventional Nebular Hypothesis the planets should have originated from a stream of ejected material from which they subsequently accreted and cooled. This predicts that the most massive planets should be closer to the Sun when in fact Jupiter, Saturn, Mercury and Uranus are furthest away; as discussed in Chapter 4.3.7, this is essential to preserving life on Earth from cosmic destruction. Furthermore the planets would all be expected to have similar spin

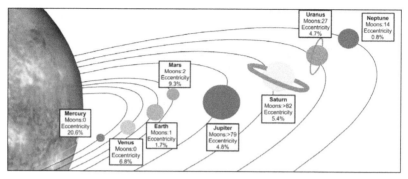

Figure 5.7: The Planets of the Solar System. This system appears to be unusual by its size, possessing a single sun, having rocky planets closer than gas giants, and exhibiting groupings of planets with similar rotational properties but contrasting with other groups. Regardless of these differences, the orbits conform closely to Fibonacci properties. Eccentricity is expressed as the percentage difference between the maximum and minimum orbits. Note that Earth is not only sited at an optimum distance from the Sun but has a nearly-circular orbit stabilized by a single large moon (Chapter 4.3.4).

directions and rates. Instead several different rates are found: Earth and Mars spin at similar rates with day-lengths of about 24 hours, Jupiter and Saturn have very rapid spins with day-lengths of about 10 hours, Neptune and Uranus make a combined rotation of 17 hours, whilst Mercury rotates every 59 days and Venus takes longer to make a single turn than it takes to circle the Sun. There is also no harmony between the planets and the rotations of their respective moons. The Sun which contains about 99.87% of the mass of the Solar System should also conserve almost all the angular momentum of a nebular system when in reality it possesses less than 4% and almost all the angular momentum is concentrated in the angular momentum of the planets (Missler 2016). These observations show that the planets did not originate with nebular material that created our Sun. Instead they seem to have been captured individually or in pairs making their collective placement within the Solar System according to the Fibonacci Series all the more remarkable.

5.9 Perfection in the Universe

Our Solar System is just one of a vast number of solar-planetary systems comprising the Milky Way Galaxy. This is more than 100,000 light years in diameter, contains several hundred billion stars, and probably a vastly greater numbers of planets. It is usually considered to have formed as gas and dust came together to form stars. These then became gravitationally attracted to each other to create clusters of stars shrouded with gas spinning around a common center of mass. The rotations cause the cluster to squash into a flat disk only about 1,000 light-years thick but with a bulge in the centre. Chapter *4.3.4* notes the optimum position of our Solar System within the Milky Way so we view the turbulent centre of this galaxy from one of the outer arms as a broad band of light spanning the sky. The density of material in the galactic bulge is so full of gas, dust, and stars that we cannot see through it to the other side. At the very centre is a black hole. Although this cannot be viewed directly, its effect is detected by its influence on the paths of stars close by.

The Milky Way comprises four spiral arms with at least two smaller arms or spurs including the Orion-Cygnus spur containing our Solar System. Where gas and dust crowd together and move more slowly in the arms they are compressed so that new star formation is an ongoing process. The time taken for each part of the galaxy to rotate is a function of the distance from the centre and is described by a rotation curve (velocity of rotation as a function of distance from the centre of the galaxy). From our position some 25,000 light years from the galactic centre, the Solar System moves in an ellipse completing a revolution once every 250-225 million years. Although this proves to be remarkably close to the duration of Genesis Day 6 (see Chapter 9.7), any link currently remains speculative. However the Milky Way galaxy is surrounded by an enormous rotating halo of hot gases and dust hundreds of thousands of light-years in diameter, and it is to be expected that our Solar System will from time to time move through clouds much denser than the space we are currently passing through. The consequences would include a drastic dimming of the Sun and intense bombardment of the Earth by cosmic rays detrimental to life. There is therefore the potential for these cosmic collisions to be the cause of the major extinctions which have punctuated geological history (Chapter 9). Such a collision might also be related to prolonged periods of global cooling such as the "Snowball Earth" in Late

Precambrian times (see Ice Ages in Chapter 6.10). We now know that there are more than 200 billion galaxies in the observable Universe and remarkably they all have a common spin rate of once every billion years regardless of size or mass - the largest scale example of God's supreme creation (http://www.astronomy.com/news/2018/03/all-galaxies-rotate-once-every-billion-years).

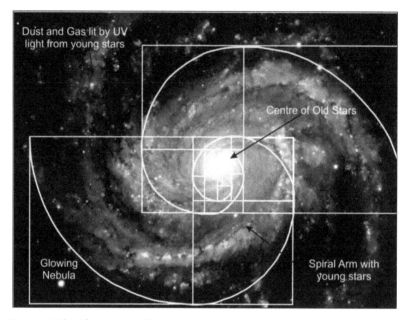

Figure 5.8: The Fibonacci Spiral superimposed onto a Hubble image of a spiral galaxy with major features of the galaxy image noted.

Spiral galaxies include gas, dust and stars all rotating around a centre, and our Milky Way has several spiral arms. As we observe them from Earth the denser spirals adopt the logarithmic shape conforming closely to the Fibonacci spiral (Figure 5.8). Since most of the matter within galaxies is concentrated near the centre, it is anticipated that the inner stars will move much faster than the stars on the outer rim: the rotation curve should then decrease with distance. According to classical Newtonian physics the angular speed of rotation of the galactic disk should vary with distance in a way that makes the radial arms wind in on themselves as the galaxy rotates. However, the rotation curve shows that the outer stars are actually found to move about as fast as the inner stars. This implies that the outer parts appear to move as fast as the cores to preserve the Fibonacci spiral. The popular solution to this conundrum is that unseen "dark matter" adds to the gravitational force holding the galaxies together. *(https://www.sciencedirect.com/topics/ physics-and-astronomy/galaxy-rotation-curves).* Up to 95% of the mass of a galaxies may comprise this unseen material. The assignment of the word "dark" implies ignorance and although the observational case is weak due to the inability to observe it directly, it relates to the parallel concept of "dark energy" invoked to explain the way that the Universe is expanding. This is discussed in Chapter 8.5 where we also note a likely Biblical reference to the creation of this dark concept.

The arguments so far documented in this Chapter recognize a common link between the microscopic, the macroscopic and the near-infinite symmetry and ordering recorded in items as diverse as DNA, plants, animals, planets and galaxies. It is surely reasonable to see this as the signature of a Single Creator who delights in order and beauty.

5.10 The Fibonacci Spiral of Time

Just as the Fibonacci Series and the corresponding spiral prove to be the ordering property of the three dimensions of space, they also prove to be the inherent property of our fourth dimension, time. This is a key to the calculation of the durations of the Six Days of Genesis Chapter One. A few simple equations that concisely express the Fibonacci Spiral can be shown in either Cartesian or polar coordinates. In the former system we express the position of any point in space in terms of its distance from the origin along the x and then vertically by $y,$ the distance above the origin. However in the case of the continuously-expanding spiral it is most convenient to express any position on the curve in polar coordinates. In this system the position of any point on the curve is located by its distance from the origin and by the angle from the reference direction (taken as the x axis of the Cartesian system). These two systems are illustrated in the figure below:

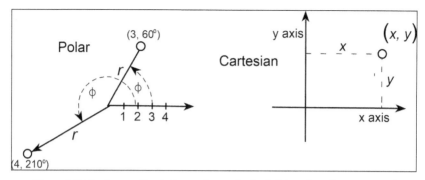

Figure 5.9: The two methods for mathematically defining the Fibonacci Spiral

The equation for the Fibonacci spiral was first derived by Jacob Bernoulli (1655-1705). It is a function of *e,* the base of natural logarithms which proves to be the third key irrational number found in Creation. The spiral is expressed as a polar equation in the form of the power of the angle θ, where θ is the angle from the horizontal axis position:

$$r = e^{b\Theta} \quad ....(\text{Equation } 5.1)$$

The value r is the distance from the x-y intersection (the origin, 0) to the point on the curve. The angle θ, is the angle from the x axis to this point and b is a constant. A natural logarithm is a logarithm to the base of the mathematical constant *e,* where *e* is the exponential growth constant known as Euler's Constant. It is approximately equal to 2.718 and is the limiting value of the simple formula $(1 + 1/n)^n$, the Compound Interest formula. It defines the curve where the change per instant of time is a function of the time value at that point, so the familiar logarithmic curve climbs more and more steeply as it migrates away from the origin. Euler's Constant, **e**, is basic to the description of all spirals whilst the circle defined by π is the special case where the rate of growth is zero. This form of the curve expands outwards to infinity. The same equation with a negative exponent (i.e. $r = e^{-b\Theta}$) spirals in towards the origin as a swirling vortex with no end, and always moving closer but never actually reaching the origin. Although the size grows or contracts exponentially, the shape does not change as the pattern gets larger or smaller as is seen in some of the figures above. The time spiral can also be expressed in Cartesian x-y coordinates and it is in this form that Schroeder (1997) applied the expansion of the Fibonacci Spiral to estimate durations for the Six Days of Genesis in our perspective of cosmic days. We examine this further in Chapters 8 and 9.

5.11 Pi (π) and Euler's Constant (e): the other Irrational Numbers of Creation embedded in the Bible

Pi (π) is the ratio between the diameter and the circumference of a circle; it is found as a constant in many formulae in diverse branches of science and engineering. It is the most familiar of the three key irrational constants expressed in Creation and is curiously related to Phi by the equation $\pi - \phi^2 = 0.5326$, where 0.5326 is the dimension of the ancient unit of measurement, the cubit, in metres. Missler (1999) discovered that the unique value of π is found in two places in the Bible. The first is in the Book of 1 Kings 7:23 and concerns the casting of a large bronze basin *"ten cubits from the one brim to the other...the height was five cubits and a line of thirty cubits did compass it round about"*. At first reading this seems to be an error because the circumference of a circle is not three times the diameter, but the diameter times Pi. In the original Hebrew text the word for circumference when written correctly would have a numeric value of 100. However at this point in the Scriptures it has two extra Hebrew letters added one superimposed above the other, namely *vav* with a numeric value 6, and *hay*, with a numeric value of 5 indicating an adjustment according to the ratio 111/106 which revises the ratio to 3.1415, close to the correct value of Pi. This derivation of Pi as present in the Tanakh is discussed in more detail by Shore (2007).

Missler (2016) has also noted two remarkable definitions of the irrational numbers Pi and *e* in the two Biblical verses describing Creation in the Old and New Testaments respectively in the form of a Remez (Chapter 2.3). The extraordinary properties of the seven words comprising the verse 1 of Genesis have already been alluded to in Chapters 2 and 3. When the numerical values of each of the **Hebrew** letters and the numeric value of the words are entered into the ratio below we derive the value of Pi to the power of the exponent 17, i.e. 3.1416×10^{17}; 17 is the Biblical number of eternal security (Table 5.1),:

(The number of letters) x (The product of the letters)/ (The number of words) x (The product of the words)

The equivalent New Testament verse defining God as Creator is the first verse of John's Gospel: ***"In the beginning was the Word and the Word was with God and the Word was God".*** The same calculation is now made by inserting the numbers in the ratio, this time from the **Greek** original:

(The number of letters) x (The product of the letters)/(The number of words) x (The product of the words)

This calculation yields the value of 2.7183×10^{40}. This is *e*, **Euler's irrational number,** and 40 is the Biblical number of probation, purification and testing.

The three irrational numbers at the root of Creation, *Pi*, *Phi* and *e*, by definition expand into an infinite series of decimal numbers. The successive groups of numbers in these series have numerous links to the gematria of the Biblical words in the Old Testament and the Greek of the New Testament with the former explored by Dr Haim Shore in his book *Coincidences in the Bible and in Biblical Hebrew* (2007).

5.12 The Trinity in Creation

The Trinity is the fundamental tenant of Christian belief - three co-equal persons in one God. Hebrew has a threefold use of the singular, the dual, and the plural, with plural words ending in *him* expressing three or more. Right from the first verse of the Bible where ***Elohim*** (אֱלֹהִים) the word for "Lord" appears, it occurs as a plural word, but is used in a contradictory way in a singular context (e.g. Genesis 1:26) to preclude any implication of polytheism (multiple gods). Other Hebrew plural words can also have a Biblical significance. The word for "Jerusalem",

Yerushaláyim, is plural: there are three Jerusalem's: the City of King David, the present city name restored during the era of Byzantium, and the Heavenly Jerusalem (Revelation 21:2). Whilst the word for "death", *"mavet"*, is singular, the word for "life" is the plural *"chayim";* for the believer there are three lives: before and after the commitment to belief, and then the eternal destiny.

The Trinity is expressed in **Triangle Numbers** ordered into a perfect equilateral triangle (Figure 5.10). The first five triangle numbers are 1, 3, 6, 10 and 15 but as the number base expands they become very rare. Only 4% of numbers up to 1000 have this property.

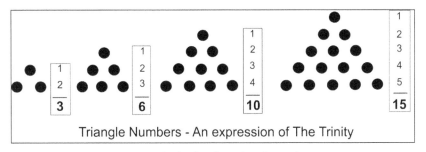

Triangle Numbers - An expression of The Trinity

Figure 5.10: The first four triangle numbers

The triangles are equilateral - contained by sides of equal length implying equality and unity of purpose, and expressed by the word "godhead" - a word that occurs just three times in the Scriptures. The distinction is also made in the Scriptures between the Hebrew word אחך (*Echad*) referring to a Compound Unity and חיך (*Yacheed*) referring to an Absolute Unity, an Only One. The verse usually taken to refer to "one God" actually uses the compound form: ***"Hear, O Israel; the Lord our God is One (Echad) Lord"*** (Deuteronomy 6:4). There are only twelve places where the singular *Yacheed* is used in the Bible and the meaning is always unequivocally in the context of one solitary person. It is implicit in the Tanakh, the Old Testament, that one of three parts of the Godhead would take the human form of the "Son of God", notably six times in the Psalms (especially Psalm 2) and the key verse concerned with the Creation in the Book of Proverbs (30:4).

The number three pervades the Scriptures. It occurs for example, with groups of people such as *Shem, Ham* and *Japheth*; *Peter, James* and *John*; *Matthew, Mark* and *Luke* - the synoptic gospels. It is present in the testimony of the Old Testament (*Law, Prophets* and *Psalms*). The number three characterizes the fall of humankind (Chapter 8.1) where the temptations comprise the *lust of the flesh*, the *lust of the eyes* and *the pride of life* (1 John 2:16). The enemies of our relationship with God are *the World, the Flesh* and *the Devil.* Man corrupts the Word of God by *taking from, adding to,* and *altering it.* We are advised to "walk worthily" of *our vocation* (Ephesians 4:1), *of the Lord* (Colossians 1:10) and *of God* (1 Thessalonians 2:12). Jesus' ministry lasted three years during which He raised three people from the dead; He is described as *Prophet, Priest* and *King* and as *the way, the truth and the life.* The three inscriptions on the cross show the completeness of His rejection by man. Three men were crucified, and Jesus is acknowledged as the *"Good Shepherd"* in death (John 10:14), the *"Great Shepherd"* in resurrection (Hebrews 13:20) and the *"Chief Shepherd"* in glory (1 Peter 5:4). The Hebrew language comprises 22 letters with five extra letters having a different form if they occur as the last letter of a word (see Chapter 2); this creates 27 letters (3 x 3 x 3) altogether. The time interval *"three days"* occurs frequently throughout the Old Testament. It is represented for example, by the pause before entering the Promised Land (Joshua 3:2) and is key to the Book of Jonah; it has its ultimate fulfillment in the death and resurrection of the Lord Jesus Christ. It occurs extensively in ways that would seem trivial without the recognition that these are actually all points of interpretation embraced by Midrash (Chapter 2.4).

The number three also pervades the description of Creation and the composition of the material world. The Creation comprises three parts: firstly, there is *mass* which can neither be created nor destroyed, only converted into energy. Secondly there is *space*. Thirdly there is *time.* The natural world comprises *animal, vegetable and mineral.* Our perception of time is *past, present* and *future.* Humankind occupies the third planet. There are three types of mitochondrial DNA. There are three dimensions to space and at the atomic level there is a trinity of *electrons, protons* and *neutrons*. Study of the sub-atomic level of matter recognizes four families of particles referred to as "bosons" with each one comprising three smaller elementary particles (i.e. particles which cannot be subdivided) called "quarks". These likely featured as an exclusive phase at the earliest stage following the Big Bang (see Chapter 8.5). There are considered to be 36 different kinds of quarks featuring the forces required to hold matter together and falling into 12 groups of threes such as "up quarks", "down quarks", "charmed quarks" etc. These are the building blocks of the larger particles including **Gluons** comprising members referred to as *up*, *charm* and *top*, and **photons** comprising *down*, *strange* and *bottom* members. Z **bosons** comprise *electrons*, *muons* and *tau,* and **w bosons** comprising *electron neutrinos*, *muon neutrinos* and *tau neutrinos* - always preserving the three-fold nature of matter. CERN is currently spending vast resources exploring what is holding matter together - it is reaching to another boundary between the physical and spiritual realms. Colossians Chapter 1:16-17 tells us that it is the Creator, the "Word" (Chapter *2.6.1*), declared in Genesis Chapter one and repeated in Chapter One of John's Gospel.

5.13 Why Six Days in Genesis Chapter One?

This is a legitimate question. Why did God use six steps to transform chaos into order? These days are not the completed part of the Heptadic Seven. Instead we are only told that the completed creation after six days was "very good" (Genesis 1:31) and that God *"rested"* on the 7th day and *"sanctified"* it (Genesis 2:2-3). The meaning of the latter word, relevant to the era we are living in now, can embrace "blessed", "ordained", "authorized" and "permitted"; it can also mean that this seventh day is "redeemed" and "purified". Six days were transformative but six is not a member of the Fibonacci Series. However, this number does reflect the perfect and triune nature of God. Six is the ***third triangle number***. But it has another key property - it is the ***first perfect number.*** Perfect numbers are quantities equal to the sum of all the different numbers that divide into them exactly so we have: $6 = 1 + 2 + 3$. The second perfect number is 28 which happens to be the number of days that the Moon takes to circle the Earth, and is correspondingly used to define the lunar month in ancient calendars. The next perfect number is much larger (496); this is the gematria value of *malchat*, the Hebrew word for our earthly physical home. Only 32 perfect numbers have so far been discovered of which the largest has the enormous value of 455,663 digits.

God relates the number six to man and the sinfulness of man throughout the Scriptures. The usage of this number and certain other numbers is entirely consistent throughout the Old and New Testament Hebrew and Greek texts respectively. The properties of these numbers are summarized in the Table 5.1 below. Much more information on the Biblical properties and usage of these numbers can be found in Bullinger's book *"Number in Scripture"*, James Harrison's *"The Pattern and the Prophecy"* and Michael Hoggard's *"By Divine Order"* as well as on a number of websites. A comprehensive record of the many Biblical prophecies which have already been fulfilled according to these numbers is summarized by Johnson (2010).

Table 5.1: The Biblical use of Numbers

	Biblical Meaning
1^1	Unity and Primacy
2	Second member of the Trinity, Divine and human, Minimum testimony (2 or 3)
3	The Trinity
4^2	Creation, the world, worldliness
5^3	Grace, the numeric value of the 5th Hebrew letter (ה 'hay')
6^4	Man, the sinfulness of man
7^5	Divine completeness, wholeness of a cycle
8	Resurrection, new beginnings, gematria of "Jesus" in the Greek is 888
9^6	Finality, judgment
10	Divine order, law and testimony, the cycle of completion, 4th Triangle number
11^7	Disorder and confusion, imperfection and disintegration
12	Governmental perfection; the Patriarchs, Apostles, Tribes etc.
13^8	Rebellion and depravity, Satan's number
17^9	Eternal Security, the seventh prime number (2, 3, 5, 7, 11, 13, **17**)
18^{10}	The sinfulness of man.

22^{11}	Revelation and Spiritual Knowledge; number of letters in the Hebrew alphabet
24^{12}	Priesthood, Heavenly Government
30	TrinityxDivine Order, the age at which priesthood/government authority begins
37^{13}	The Wisdom of God, Trinity-Divine Completeness
40^{14}	In days or years, the interval of Probation and Testing, Purification
42	(7 x 6) = The conflict between God and Man and their ultimate restoration
49	(7 x 7) = Compounded Perfection, preparing for the Jubilee (50)
50^{15}	In years, the Jubilee interval, the year of restoration to the original owner
70	7 x 10, appears in the context of Divinely-ordained order
153^{16}	The redemption of mankind (1 + 2 + 3 +......+17 = 153), 17th Triangle number, (John 21:13)
490^{17}	In years, the Old Testament Covenant Periods and Daniel's 70 weeks
666^{18}	Antichrist, the most intense expression of a man
2520^{19}	The judgment and restoration of Israel in prophetic Biblical years of 360 days

Footnotes

[1] Whilst there are a number of words implying deception (lies, deceit etc.) there is only one word for "truth". **Jesus** said: ***"I am the way, the truth and the life"*** (John 14:6) and ***"The truth shall make you free"*** (John 8:32) The word for "truth is תמא This word is embraced by the first (א Aleph) and last (ת Tav) letters of the Hebrew alphabet. The aleph was written in primitive Hebrew like the head of an ox to imply "first" and is symbolically taken as implying to the One Almighty God; if we remove the Aleph we have the Hebrew word for "death" תמ

[2] Many examples include *The Fourth day which* saw the *material creation finished; the four elements: earth, fire, air and water.* There are *four seasons* and *four divisions of the Earth: north, south, east and west,* whilst the divisions of humankind are *lands, tongues, families and nations* (Genesis 10).

[3] Phrases containing the word "Grace" occur in numbers which are multiples of 5 in the Scriptures. The 5th letter of the Hebrew Alphabet, "hay", ה, is shaped like an enclosure implying security. It was added to the names of Abram and Sara when they found grace in the eyes of God.

[4] This number, 5 + 1, negates God's grace by man's addition, whilst 7 − 1 falls short of God's perfection.

[5] Sevenfold cycles pervade the Scriptures and words containing "seven" always occur in multiples of 7.

[6] Nine is not only the last digit but the digits forming its multiples are always multiples of 9: e.g. 4 x 9 = 36 and 3 + 6 = 9, 5 x 9 = 45, 4 + 5 = 9, 8 x 9 = 72 and 7 + 2 = 9. It is related to 6, the number of man since 6 is the sum of its factors (3 x 3 = 9 and 3 + 3 = 6) and is also a factor of 666 (= 9 x 74).

[7] This number undoes the perfection of Divine Order (10) but falls short of Divine Governmental Perfection (12)

[8] All 10 names given to Satan in the Scriptures (serpent in Hebrew, serpent in Greek, Son of the morning, tempter, Belial, dragon, Devil, Beelzebub, murderer and Lucifer) have gematrias which are multiples of 13; this also applies to phrases with "Antichrist". The dangerous significance of this number to the secular world is clearly well–founded.

[9] This number is 7 + 10 or spiritual plus ordinal perfection. On the 17th day of the first month (Nisan) Jesus rose from the dead, Noah's Ark touched the ground and the Jewish people were delivered from the wrath of Haman in the time of Esther. Romans 8:35-39 gives 17 entities that are unable ***"to separate us from the love of God which is in Christ Jesus our lord: Tribulation, distress…………...height, nor depth, nor any other creature".*** Psalm 91, often considered to be the psalm of blessed assurance to the believer under trial and distress, contains double 17 messages assuring the redeemed person that God is there and will shield them in adversity.

[10] The number adds to our eternal security (17 + 1 = 18) to get the number of antichrist: 6 + 6 + 6 = 18. Chapter _13_, verse _18_ of the Book of Revelation implies that he will dominate the Earth during the Great Tribulation (the 70th week of Daniel Chapter 9).

[11] Words implying the search for knowledge, "seek", "mystery", "sight", "reveal" etc. occur in multiples of 22 times in the Scriptures.

The Bible comprises 22 x 3 books with the final book, Revelation, revealing the end of history comprising 22 chapters.

[12] This is the number of Courses of the Temple Earthly priesthood and appears again in the context of the Redeemed as Heavenly Priests in Chapter 4 of the Book of Revelation.

[13] This number pair (Trinity-Completion) appears extensively in the gematria of the Scriptures as documented by Bullinger and Harrison and see Chapter *2.6.1* of this book.

[14] There are 25 examples of this time interval in days or years referring to periods of testing or waiting in the Bible (https://www.exposingsatanism.org/biblical-numerology/biblical-numerology-part-2/). The Second Temple was destroyed and the Jewish nation scattered in 70 AD; this was 40 years after the earlier part of the Ministry of the Lord Jesus Christ when He had already demonstrated the miracles to confirm that He was the Messiah, but still found Himself rejected and called "Beelzebub" by the Rabbinic establishment (Matthew Chapter 12), probably in 30 AD (See Chapter *8.9.1*). Jewish nationhood was finally extinguished by the siege of Masada beginning on April 15th 73 AD, 40 years after the crucifixion of the Lord Jesus Christ.

[15] The Jubilee theme of restoration to the original owner is considered by students of prophecy to constrain the time line of history (see 2014 book *"God's Final Jubilee" by Dan Goodwin, 174pp*). It is expressed in recent times in the restoration of Israel: First settlement (1847), to Zionist Conference (1897) to UN approval of Nationhood (1947); offset and advanced by 20 years we also have Jerusalem delivered from the infidel (1917), Jerusalem restored to the Jews (1967) and Jerusalem first recognised as the Capital of Israel by a gentile nation (2017).

[16] This number has extraordinary properties. The "Trinity Function" multiplies each component number by three times e.g. <u>888</u> (Jesus) = 8^3 + 8^3 + 8^3 = 512 + 512 + 512 = 1536. Applying this function *six times,* the gematria of Jesus is transformed into 153: i.e. **888** → 1536 → 369 → 972 → 1080 → 513 → **153** (Harrison 1995). Continuing to apply the Trinity Function 153 *does not change*: i.e. 153 → 153 → 153 → 153..: 153 proves to be the terminal number of *one third of all numbers* (Harrison 1995). The gematria of "Sons of God" in the

Hebrew is exactly 153 and the expression "Sons of God" occurs 7 times in the Scriptures.

[17] According to Bullinger the history of ancient Israel falls into four 490 (7 x 70) year intervals comprising; (i) from Abraham to the Exodus, (iii) from Exodus to the dedication of the First Temple, (iii) from the First King (Saul) to the Babylonian Captivity and (iv) from King David to the Decree of Artaxerxes. This latter decree initiates the 5th example, a new dispensation embracing the 70 weeks of years (70 x 7 = 490 years) given to Daniel (Chapter 9:24-27) during the exile in Babylon. The interval began with the decree by the Persian Emperor Artaxerxes to rebuild the walls of Jerusalem in the month of Nisan during the 20th year of his reign. The decree is an event accurately recorded in history as March 14th 444 BC. Daniel's prophetic vision of 70 weeks of years comprises 69 weeks until the "cutting off of the Messiah". These 69 weeks of years expired with the entry of Jesus into Jerusalem on 10th Nisan accompanied by four days teaching in the Temple and followed by His Crucifixion on 14th Nisan (Thursday 10th, April 32 AD); these days correspond exactly to Jewish tradition where the sacrificial lamb is selected on the 10th, observed to ensure perfection for four days, and then sacrificed on the 14th. We are currently in a gap period of unknown duration - the Church Age - with the last 7th week of years of the prophecy, conventionally interpreted by Biblical scholars as the Great Tribulation, still awaiting fulfilment.

[18] This number is the most intense expression of man: 6 x 6 = 36 and 666= 1+2+3+..+36

[19] This number is 7 x 360, God's number of perfect completion x the days in the Biblical prophetic year. It is also the product of four Divine numbers: 3 – the Trinity, 7 – the number of completions of a cycle, 10 - the number of Ordinal perfection and 12 – the number of Governmental perfection. Because of His promise to King David, God would not destroy the Jews but was forced to punish them for their sin. The duration of this punishment was given to the Prophet Ezekiel as 430 years (Ezekiel 4:3-6). The desolation of the nation took place in two phases: the *servitude* of the nation by Nebuchadnezzar occurred in 606 BC and led to the exile of much of the nobility including Daniel; rebellion was followed by a siege in 589 BC leading to replacement of the vassal ruler. When he

too, rebelled Nebuchadnezzar returned to destroy the nation; this led to the *desolation of Jerusalem* and the destruction of Solomon's Temple in 587-586 BC. Seventy years of exile were served in Babylon. These are often considered to make up for the seventh part of 490 years when the people had neglected to keep the ordained Sabbath rest of the land. Only a small number of Jews bothered to return to Jerusalem at the end of the 70 years of exile, and then largely in unbelief. This caused the remaining 360 years of punishment to be multiplied by 7 times according to Leviticus 26:18. The 2520 years of punishment span two periods, the first being the *servitude* of the nation and the second the *desolation of Jerusalem*; in prophetic years of 360 days this amounts to a total of 907,200 days. This is the exact interval between July 23rd 537 BC and May 14th 1948 when Israel recovered nationhood and *servitude* ended (although it should be noted that the exact day in 537 BC when the first 70 years of punishment ended is not recorded). It is also the exact interval between 70 years after the destruction of the Temple on August 16th 518 BC and the recovery of Jerusalem by Israel on June 7th 1967; symbolically this was the ending of the punishment and the ending of the *desolation* of Jerusalem.

References:

Bullinger, E W., 2009. *Number in Scripture: Its Supernatural Design and Spiritual Significance,* Kregel Publications, Grand Rapids, Michigan, U.S.A., 303pp.

Harrison, James, 1995. *The Pattern and the Prophecy*, Isaiah Publications, Peterborough, Ontario, Canada, 399pp.

Hoggard, Michael. 1999. *By Divine Order*, Prophetic Research Ministries, Festus, MO 63028, USA.

Johnson, Kenneth, 2010. *Ancient Prophecies Revealed: 500 prophecies listed in Order of when they were Fulfilled*, ISBN 143825346X, 174 pp.

Missler, Chuck, 1999. *Cosmic Codes: Hidden Messages from the Edge of Eternity*, Koinonia House Publications, Coeur d'Alene, Idaho, U.S.A., 535pp.

Missler, Chuck, 2016. *Beyond Newton*, Koinonia House Publications, Coeur d'Alene, Idaho, U.S.A., 115pp.

Missler, Chuck, 2016. *Beyond Time and Space*, Koinonia House Publications, Coeur d'Alene, Idaho, U.S.A., 105pp.

Schroeder, Gerald, 1997. *The Science of God: the Convergence of Scientific and Biblical Wisdom*, Broadway Books, New York, 226 pp.

Shore, Haim, 2007. *Coincidences in the Bible and in Biblical Hebrew*, iUniverse Publishers, New York, 319pp.

Chapter 6

Constraining Time: The Determination of Age

6.1 Introduction

There are two contrasting explanations of Biblical time, and specifically the time durations implied of Genesis Chapter One. These are succinctly defined as **Young Earth Creationism (YEC),** which regards the Earth as just 6,000 years old and the six days of Genesis 1 as literal present 24 hour days, and **Old Earth Creationism (OEC)** which regards these days as representing much longer periods of time and generally acknowledges the presence of a large gap between the first and second verses of Genesis Chapter One. People holding these opposing views are henceforth referred to as YEC's (Young Earth Creationists) and OEC's (Old Earth Creationists).

Most of the great preachers of the vibrant age of evangelism during the 19th and early 20th Century were Old Earth Creationists in so far as they embraced the GAP, a concept explained in Chapter 7. These men were fundamentalist in belief and notably included men such as John Nelson Darby, C.I. Schofield, G.H. Pember, Dwight L. Moody and Harry A. Ironsides. They all acknowledged the significance of a long but indeterminate time gap between the verses of Genesis 1:1 and Genesis 1:3. Since we see the veracity and effectiveness of their preaching by their fruits, we have to reject the view that these men were deceived. Rather we recognize that the multitudes who came to faith by the preaching of these, and others holding comparable views of Genesis, over the past two centuries contrasts with the relative poverty of church mission and the level of apostasy in the west today. Sadly, we have to note that it is during these last few decades that the promotion of the YEC case has become most prominent.

Young Earth Creationism has been actively promoted mainly since the middle of the last century by ministries such as *Creation Research* and *Answers in Genesis*. It rejects the GAP and insists on present 24 hour durations for the six days of Genesis Chapter One with 6000 years for the total time span of Creation. This has created a crisis of testimony and belief because general knowledge cannot hide the fact that astronomic and geological ages have been very long: light from the distant universe takes millions of light years to reach us and the sedimentary rocks lie on great volumes of metamorphic rocks which have undergone multiple cycles of cooling very slowly from high temperatures. As we show here, the YEC case requires a gross distortion, and in some cases ignorance, of scientific observations about the determination of the ages of the Universe, Planets, Earth and the rocks. We take no pleasure in correcting these errors because we acknowledge that Young Earth Creationists are, like ourselves, believers in the absolute truth of the Bible. Our aim is rather to support those who have been open to taking the examination of Intelligent Design further, and especially new Christians, who have suffered the damage of false testimony and have been put off addressing the claims of the Bible by the obvious abrogation of the scientific age evidence.

Regrettably the promotion of the YEC case has been forceful even to the point of claiming the exclusive right to Biblical interpretation and questioning the Salvation of those holding to the OEC position (Sarfati 2014). This is surely unwise because even ardent atheists of the likes of Richard Dawkins will not be consigned to Hell for promoting their interpretation of scientific evidence. The only sin that will send anyone to perdition is the choice of rejecting the manifestation of God's unconditional gift - His grace. *"For God is not willing that any should perish, but that all should **come to repentance**"* (Peter 3:9). *"For God so loved the World that He gave His only begotten Son that **whosoever believes in Him** should not perish but have everlasting life"* (John 3:16). Only by rejecting this provision, which we can do nothing by our own abilities to earn, will we reject a heavenly destiny.

The primary mindset of the YEC advocates is that if we accept the long periods of astronomic and geologic time then evolution becomes a possibility (Wise 2002). Within this mindset the following concepts are inseparable:

YOUNG EARTH = CREATIONISM
OLD EARTH = EVOLUTION

The case proving that Evolution is false has been explored in Chapter 3. However there are two general points showing that the advocates of the YEC case need to abandon the above mantra:

(i) If Evolution is impossible (as we have aimed to show in Chapter 3), *it is impossible on any timescale.*

(ii) By any reckoning the chances of the supremely organized building blocks of life being formed by chance are many times beyond the age of the Earth and even the Universe. Ultimately, they have to be acknowledged as impossible because the Universal Laws of Physics do not allow for order to be created out of chaos without a creator. *The Universe is very old but Evolution remains impossible.*

➤ **The cardinal error of Young Earth Creationism is the assumption that time is a constant, our present twenty-four-hour day has always been that.** The Law of General Relativity has shown that this assumption is simply untrue. Time is a variable dimension. In simple terms: as space expands time contracts, and it is this observation that provides the concise explanation of the Six Days recorded in Genesis Chapter One as we explore in Chapters 8 and 9 of this book.

In the remaining narrative of this chapter we outline the various methods used to determine the age of rocks, the Earth and the Universe emphasizing their collective reliability, and noting that the evidence they provide cannot be sensibly denied or obfuscated. *In the following we highlight the errors of the YEC arguments with the italicized text.*

Possibly because of the difficulties reconciling the chronologies in Genesis Chapter One with their minuscule timeframe, the YEC case has usually concentrated attention on Noah's Flood with the aim of demonstrating that this brief event can explain the whole sedimentary rock succession. There are five key issues demonstrating that this interpretation is untenable:

(i) Noah's Flood occurred after Day 6. It was apparently a feature of Day 7. We are told that Day 6 had come to an end with the culminating act of God - the creation of Adam and Eve. Several generations of men had come and gone after this and before the time of the Flood. We are not told that Day 7 has ended; by the time of the Flood the perfected order completed on Day 6 was already running down from order towards the ultimate chaos of "universal heat death" (Chapter 8). We are told that God was now sanctifying His work of creation with the Sabbath rest (Genesis 2:2 and Chapter 9).

(ii) The sedimentary rock column includes substantial volumes of rock formed in terrestrial (land) environments as well as numerous advances and retreats of the sea. In no way can it be construed to record a single flood event.

(iii) The Pre-Flood history of Genesis is described in the context of a landscape close to that at the present day. The world of the Garden of Eden in Genesis 2 was structured around the four rivers Pishon, Gihon, Tigris and Euphrates that Moses would have connected with real locations in his own time; also mentioned are Cush and Ashur. These names still refer to real places: the present Tigris and Euphrates lie on the top of a sedimentary rock pile more than six kilometers in thickness, whilst the rivers Pishon and Gihon refer either to now-dried up watercourses crossing Arabia or to the rivers Halys and Araxes which now rise in Eastern Turkey and drain into the Black Sea (Pearce 1993).

(iv) Sedimentary rocks the world over lie on much greater volumes of metamorphic basement ignored by proponents of the YEC position. These rocks have undergone multiple cycles of heating (sometimes to temperatures in excess of 800°C) and accompanied, or followed by, deformation and subsequent cooling. Silicate rocks are very poor conductors of heat and these cycles have indisputably been very long.

(v) The YEC position requires an outright rejection of the Stratigraphic Column of time periods embraced by the Palaeozoic, Mesozoic and Cenozoic eras. The stratigraphic record is the foremost achievement of the Earth Sciences. It has been established by the careful work of multitudes of investigators (including Bible believers) over two centuries. These investigators did not deliberately set out to contend with the YEC position, indeed most of them would hardly have given it a second thought. By and large they conducted their studies for altruistic reasons with a desire for recognition for the quality of their research. To reject such an enormous body of scientific evidence is surely lacking in wisdom.

Young Earth Creationism originated in 1902 with George MacReady's book "Outlines of Modern Christianity and Modern Science" (Numbers 1992, Heaton 2009) in which he aimed to constrain Earth history as it was then understood into a single flood event. Further developed by Price (1916, 1935), the theory of "Flood Geology" has since been widely promoted particularly by the work of Henry Morris, (1972, 1974). It has the advantage for the YECs in bringing together all the complexities of the geological record (or at least the sedimentary component) into a single, supposedly catastrophic, event lasting less than a year. As noted in the Introduction, the widespread adoption of the YEC case was primarily a knee-jerk reaction to the widespread teaching of Evolution. Since the early 1960s three major YEC organizations have come to dominate evangelical outreach with this interpretation of time. **The Institute for Creation Research** (ICR) was founded in 1972 by Morris and now run by his son John. The larger international ministry **Answers in Genesis** (AiG) was founded by the Australian Ken Ham in 1994 after he had worked with Morris at ICR. A third ministry, **Creation Ministries International** (CMI) based in Australia, was founded in 2006 following a controversial split with AiG. Since the 1960's the Flood History embraced by these ministries has gained a wide caucus of followers with a comprehensive overview provided by Heaton (2009).

The YEC position holds that the Earth is only ~6000 years old as an article of faith and the proponents have broadly taken two approaches to argue for such a youthful chronology. Firstly, they have used their own methods invoking natural clocks to document a short history for the Earth and Universe, but with their interpretation always constrained by a brief ~6000 years time frame. Secondly, they have aimed to discredit the old ages produced by other methods. Because their approach to scientific knowledge has often been cavalier, and the YECs frequently disagree with one another on central issues, the points of evidence used to support their case vary somewhat from advocate to advocate. However, the following headings embrace the subjects that require the need to clarify the truth. In developing this section, we have made liberal use of the information in Brent Dalrymple's 2004 seminal book *"Ancient Earth, Ancient Skies"* and the comprehensive Christian perspective on age dating by Rogers Wiens (2002) as well as a diverse range of web sites, particularly those posted by Professor Timothy Heaton accompanying his broad study of the developing YEC literature.

6.2 Radiometric Age dating

Radiometric (radioactive) dating methods determine the absolute ages of rocks using the decay rates of radioactive isotopes. The abundances of naturally-occurring radioactive isotopes are compared with the abundances of their decay products. The matter comprising the Universe, the elements, are often present as different isotopes, with each isotope differing in the number of neutrons in the nucleus. A particular isotope of an element is called a *nuclide*. The nuclides useful for radiometric dating are inherently unstable. An atom of an unstable nuclide will undergo radioactive decay and transform spontaneously into another nuclide. The transformation is accomplished in a number of ways including alpha decay (emission of alpha particles) and beta decay (electron emission, positron emission, or electron capture); a further possibility is spontaneous fission into two or more nuclides. Although the moment in time at which a particular nucleus will decay is unpredictable, a collection of radioactive nuclides always decays exponentially (i.e. the rate of decay becomes slower and slower as time passes) with a rate of instability defined by a *half-life*. When one half-life has elapsed, one half of the atoms of the nuclide will have decayed into a decay product called the "daughter" nuclide and one half of the parent nuclides will remain. The daughter nuclide may itself be radioactive; decay will then continue through a chain of event which will only end up with the formation of a nonradioactive stable daughter nuclide. Each step in this chain of decay is characterized by a distinct half-life.

For most radioactive nuclides, the half-life depends solely on nuclear properties: it is a constant which has proved to be unaffected by factors such as temperature, pressure, chemical environment, or even magnetic and electric fields. The exceptions are nuclides that decay by the process of electron capture, such as beryllium-7, strontium-85, and zirconium-89 where the decay rates may be influenced by local electron density. For all other nuclides, the proportion of the original nuclide to its decay products changes in a predictable way as the original nuclide decays; the relative abundances of the related nuclides can then be used to measure the time that has elapsed between the time the original nuclides were incorporated into the rock (usually during formation), and the present day.

To provide a reliable age determination radiometric dating requires that neither the parent nuclide nor the daughter product can enter or leave the rock after its formation or cooling. It is therefore essential to have as much information as possible about the material being dated and to check for any signs of alteration and isotope escape. Precision is enhanced when measurements are taken on multiple samples from different locations of the rock body, or on different minerals from the same rock sample. Correlation between different isotopic dating methods is then able to confirm the absolute age of a sample. Accurate radiometric dating of old material is achieved when the parent has a long enough half-life to ensure that it is still present in significant amounts; enough daughter product must have been produced to be accurately measured and distinguished from any daughter initially present in the material. Very precise and accurate procedures involving isotope-ratio mass spectrometry are used nowadays to isolate and analyze parent and daughter nuclides.

The main limitation of radiometric dating occurs when the initial amounts of the parent-daughter isotope pairs are difficult to determine because daughter atoms were already present before the decay process began. *Isochron dating* surmounts this problem when there are elements with both radiogenic and non-radiogenic (stable) isotopes. As time goes by some of the parent isotope will decay to the radiogenic isotope of the daughter. The ratio of the daughter to the non-radiogenic isotope becomes larger with time and the parent to daughter becomes smaller. Mass spectrometers directly measure the ratios of isotope concentrations comprising the radiogenic isotope to the daughter, and the parent to the non-radiogenic daughter. These ratios are plotted on an isochron diagram to reveal a sloping line. Applying an appropriate equation, the slope of the line is used to derive the age of the rock and the intercept on the axis gives the original ratio of the daughter to the non-daughter isotope in the sample (Dalrymple 2004). The isochron method is used for dating the cooling of igneous rocks, the times of metamorphism, the ages of grains in sedimentary rocks and shock events such as asteroid impacts.

If a rock is subjected to heating the daughter nuclides diffuse away and the isotopic "clock" is reset to zero. The temperature at which this occurs is known as the "closure" or "blocking" temperature. Below this temperature the mineral becomes a closed system to isotope migration. Metamorphic and igneous rocks which have cooled slowly will not begin to exhibit radioactive decay until they cool below this temperature. This becomes a valuable way of measuring the cooling history of rocks which have been heated and then cooled from high temperatures.

The methods most commonly used to date rocks and other ancient materials are:

The Radiocarbon-14 dating method

Carbon-14 is the radioactive isotope of carbon which decays into ^{14}N (nitrogen-14) through the process of Beta decay with a half-life of 5,730 years. It is formed in the upper atmosphere as cosmic rays from the Sun hit atoms and release neutrons; these can then be absorbed by ^{14}N atoms which lose a proton in the process and become ^{14}C. Carbon-14 ends up as a trace component in atmospheric carbon dioxide which plants absorb by the process of photosynthesis. Along with the much more abundant ^{12}C and ^{13}C, it is incorporated into animals as they eat the plants and it ultimately moves through the food chain. Every living thing absorbs ^{14}C in a measurable ratio to ^{12}C and ^{13}C. However, the relative amount of ^{14}C is extremely small; ^{12}C, the most common isotope makes up just under 99% and ^{13}C about 1% of all carbon. When a plant or animal dies, carbon ceases to be absorbed into its tissue and the ^{14}C begins to decay from this initial ratio of carbon isotopes; the proportion of ^{14}C remaining in the organism is then a measure of the time that has elapsed since death. This method is ideal for dating organic remains but has a useful time limit of around 60,000 years beyond which little measureable ^{14}C is left.

Cosmic ray flux from the Sun has varied over time and needs to be understood to precisely resolve the significance of ^{14}C determinations. By cross-checking with techniques such as tree ring dating and coral ring analysis, these variations have now been reliably calibrated and can be accounted for back to several tens of thousands of years.

The ^{14}C dating method has figured most prominently in the YEC literature because the age determinations are closest to the time frame required for a young Earth. However, since the oldest reliably-determined ages are approximately ten times the 6000-year time frame they need for Creation, it is proposed that older ages are inflated by approximately ten times because modern ratios of ^{14}C to ^{12}C do not reflect the ratios in the pre-Flood world (Baumgardner 2005). However, a valid criticism proposed by the YEC literature concerns the detection of very small amounts of ^{14}C in apparently-ancient coal beds and diamonds which should have no measurable ^{14}C remaining. The significance of this finding has not yet been comprehensively researched but cannot be attributed to a young Earth. As noted below, the accelerated decay rates required by the YEC's to discredit old age determinations would have expelled any residual ^{14}C in rocks. Assuming that the possibility of contamination is excluded, it is likely to be due either to alpha-particle emissions from trace amounts of uranium and thorium converting ^{14}N into ^{14}C, or to ^{13}C converting to ^{14}C when it interacts with thermal neutrons.

The Uranium–thorium dating method

A second dating technique applicable to young materials is based on the decay of uranium-234 into thorium-230, an isotope with a half-life of about 80,000 years. Uranium-235 decays into protactinium-231 with a half-life of 32,760 years. The thorium and protactinium are insoluble and are precipitated into ocean-floor sediments. Their ratios can then be measured to yield an age determination for materials up to several hundred thousand years old. The related ionium–thorium dating method is also used to date ocean sediments by measuring the ratio of ionium (thorium-230) to thorium-232.

The Samarium–neodymium dating method

This measures the alpha particle decay of ^{147}Sm to ^{143}Nd with a half-life of 1,060 million years. Accuracy levels of <20 million years (Ma) for ages of ~2500 Ma can be achieved with this method.

The Potassium–argon dating method

This method is based on the electron capture, or positron decay, of potassium, K^{40} to Argon, Ar^{40}; since K^{40} has a half-life of 1,300 million years the method can be applied effectively to the oldest Earth rocks. K^{40} is common in minerals such as micas, feldspars and hornblendes. However, since the argon daughter product is a gas, it can escape above the closure temperature which ranges from 350°C in micas to 500°C in hornblende. The age determined by this method is therefore only retained when the temperature falls below these closure temperatures; in this context it proves to be a useful method for dating the very slow cooling of metamorphic rocks and large igneous intrusions.

The Uranium–lead dating method

Uranium (U) – lead (Pb) dating employs two radioactive isotopes of uranium, U^{235} and U^{238}. Rocks can therefore potentially provide two clocks, one based on U^{235} decay to Pb^{207} with a half-life of 700 million years (Ma), and the other based on U238 decay to Pb^{206} with a half-life of 4.5 billion years. This dual scheme has been refined to the point where error margins of less than two million years in 2,500 Ma are achievable. U-Pb dating is often performed on the mineral zircon ($ZrSiO_4$) because it has a very high closure temperature, is resistant to mechanical weathering, and is chemically inert. It often also grows in layers during metamorphic episodes so that each layer can record the age of a distinct geological event. As a typical example of the achievements of this method, the age of the very ancient highly metamorphosed Amitsôq gneisses from western Greenland has been determined as $3,600 \pm 50$ Ma from U-Pb dating and also as $3,560 \pm 100$ Ma from the Pb-Pb method noted below.

The Rubidium–strontium dating method

This is based on the beta decay of rubidium-87 to strontium-87, with a half-life of 50 billion years. This scheme is used to date old igneous and metamorphic rocks, and has also been used to date lunar samples. Closure temperatures are so high that they are not a concern. Rubidium-strontium dating is not as precise as the U-Pb method and errors of 30 to 50 Ma for a ~3,000 Ma rock would be typical.

6.3 Integrated Age Dating - Perfecting the evidence

The efficacy of radiometric dating is endorsed by the wide range of half-lives present in naturally-occurring isotopes available for study. This enables the entire time frame of the history of the Earth and meteorites to be unraveled without serious ambiguity. The results are endorsed when a variety of different methods are used to date the same material and yield accordant results. In addition to the methods noted above, there is now a broad range of other methods with variable half-lives that can also be used to collectively confirm age determinations. These include: argon–argon (Ar–Ar), iodine–xenon (I–Xe), lanthanum–barium (La–Ba), lead–lead (Pb–Pb), lutetium–hafnium (Lu–Hf), potassium–calcium (K–Ca), rhenium–osmium (Re–Os), uranium–lead–helium (U–Pb–He), uranium–uranium (U–U), krypton–krypton (Kr–Kr), beryllium (^{10}Be–^9Be), Chlorine-36 (half-life ~300,000 years) and Luminescence methods. The integrity of the multiple results from so many diverse methods confirms the efficacy of age dating and indirectly endorses the OEC position (Wiens 2002).

6.4 Lead Isotopes and the Age of the Earth

As well as their use for dating rocks, lead isotopes provide some of the best evidence for the age of the Earth. In order to be used as a natural clock to calculate this age the processes generating the lead isotopes need to meet four conditions: (i) the decay has been irreversible, (ii) it has occurred at a uniform rate, (iii) the initial condition, and (iv) the final condition can be established. Dalrymple (2004) cites examples of lead isotope dating that give an age for the Earth of ~4,500 million years. Lead is important because two different isotopes (^{207}Pb and ^{206}Pb) are produced from their separate decay series from uranium isotopes ^{235}U and ^{238}U. Both decay series contain a unique set of intermediate radioactive isotopes, each with its own half-life, enabling them to produce independent but consistent age determinations.

The presence of a stable lead isotope that is not the product of any decay series (^{204}Pb) allows lead isotopes to be normalized on a "concordia-discordia" isochron diagram and define highly accurate age determinations. Two other characteristics of Pb isotope measurements make this superior to other methods. Firstly, measuring the isotope ratio of a single element can be done more precisely than measuring isotope ratios of two different elements. Secondly, when two isotopes of the same element are used the results are not influenced by any disturbance that may have happened since the formation of the rock (Dalrymple 2004). The original age of Earth came from radiometric dating of lunar rocks and meteorites. It was derived from a model using mineral ores on Earth assuming that their Pb composition is representative of meteorites and the rocky planets. This original result of 4,500 ± 300 million years is close to the value accepted today and has since been refined by many other studies. The presence of three Pb isotopes, with two of them radioactive, provides a valuable integrated tool for establishing the age of the Earth and excellent evidence linking the formation of the Earth to the meteorites and other bodies in the Solar System (Dalrymple 2004). A precise maximum age for the Solar

System of 4,568 Ma has since been derived from isotopic studies of chrondritic meteorites; these have more varied chemical compositions than iron meteorites and include calcium and aluminum silicates (Burckhardt et al. 2008).

6.5 The Ages of the Stars

The luminosity and temperature of a star are an expression of the nuclear forces operating within the interior. Luminosity is defined as the brightness of a star relative to the brightness of our Sun, and the age of a star can be determined by measuring luminosity together with the color spectrum. This in turn, provides a measure of the surface temperature and the rate at which the star is burning its nuclear fuel. Stars originate as clouds of gas collapse by gravitational attraction. At early stages of formation temperatures are too low for hydrogen fusion. Instead nascent stars are powered by release of huge amounts of gravitational energy producing hot gases and a massive solar wind. This initial stage of star formation is known as the "T Tauri" phase (Chapter 4.3.4); the star is then highly luminous due to its large radius. As the gravitational energy disperses, the star contracts to join the main star sequence (Figure 6.1) and the large internal heat release causes the hydrogen gas within the cloud to burn and produce helium by nuclear fusion. Nuclear fusion reactions then generate the heat and light responsible for the subsequent luminosity and high temperatures throughout the subsequent active life of the star.

Luminosity and surface temperature are used to estimate the lifespan of a star although they cannot determine its absolute age. The lifespan of a star depends on the amount of nuclear fuel available and the rate at which that fuel is burning up. Larger, hotter stars contain more fuel than smaller, colder stars, but burn their fuel at higher rates and burn out more quickly; they exist for much shorter periods of time. The burning of nuclear fuel defines the lifespan, and therefore the stellar evolution, of the star as we measure it from Earth in terms of the luminosity and surface temperature.

To calculate luminosity the distance from Earth to the star must be known and is calculated for the closer stars using two measurements with some simple algebra. The observer measures the position of the star against the background of more distant stars twice at intervals several months apart. The apparent shift of the star is known as the parallax and is used together with the known diameter of the Earth's orbit to measure the distance between Earth and the star. The apparent brightness of a star diminishes as the square of the distance so the radiation emitted can be combined with this distance measurement to yield the luminosity. Stellar luminosities are found to range from as little as 0.1 times, to as large as 60,000 times, the luminosity of our Sun. The color of a star is directly related to the wavelength of the radiation it emits, and the temperature is calculated from an equation developed by the physicist Max Planck linking the radiation emitted by a hot body to its temperature. Values range from 3,000°K for the colder red stars up to 40,000° K for the hottest blue-white stars.

The relative age of a star is evaluated by determining an age for the globular cluster of stars to which it belongs. Globular clusters of stars are gravitationally-attracted groups formed at the same time with numbers ranging from tens to more than a million. Using the luminosity and surface temperature within a single cluster, scientists establish the apparent age of the cluster from a Hertzsprung-Russell (H-R) diagram where luminosity is plotted as a function of temperature. On this diagram the star plots are clustered along a continuous line sloping diagonally from the upper left to the lower right portion of the plot (Figure 6.1). The upper right part of the population comprises the most massive, hottest, and brightest burning stars, whilst the lower right portion comprises the less massive, cooler, and least luminous stars.

As a star grows older, it will eventually exhaust all of its hydrogen fuel. It then undergoes a dramatic expansion in size. It rapidly decreases in luminosity to become a "red giant". As this transformation occurs, the star leaves the main sequence and moves toward the upper right corner of the H-R diagram. The part of the graph below this turning point is the record of the burning up of the stars and is used to estimate the age of the star cluster. It shows a characteristic migration with age illustrated below (Figure 6.2).

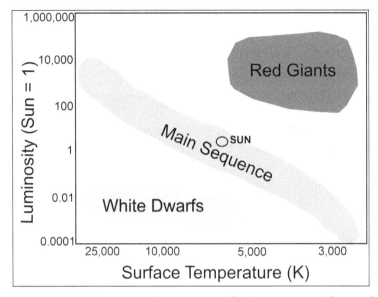

Figure 6.1: The Hertzsprung-Russell Diagram used for determining the lifespan of the stars. Note the position of our Sun near the centre of the Main Sequence

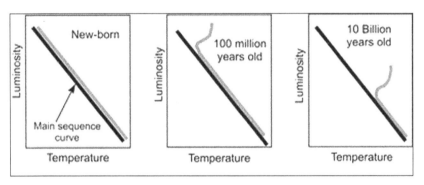

Figure 6.2: Migration of Luminosity versus Temperature of a star cluster as it ages

Large, bright stars in the upper part of the main sequence burn their fuel more quickly and transform into red giants sooner than the smaller stars of the lower main sequence. In a younger star cluster, the turnover point will form at the top of the main sequence, where the more massive stars are beginning to transform into red giants. As a cluster becomes older, less massive stars will deplete their hydrogen fuel; the turnover point then moves down along the main sequence (Figure 6.2). Eventually, the turnover point will be near the bottom right of the main sequence in the oldest clusters. The initial condition of the cluster is where all the stars in a galaxy reside on the main sequence. The turning points down the main sequence are controlled by the volume of nuclear fuel and the rate at which this fuel is being consumed. The migration of the turnover point can thus be used to monitor the passage of time within a galaxy cluster. Plots of the luminosity and temperature values of stars on H-R diagrams yield age estimates in the range 11,500,000 to 14,000,000 years for globular clusters of stars in the Milky Way galaxy. Since globular clusters reside near the center of a galaxy and all formed at about the same time, their age is representative of the age of the galaxy as a whole (Dalrymple 2004).

Ultimately red giant stars expel their outermost material to create a planetary nebula and leave a hot core known as a white dwarf. White dwarfs are extremely dense. Since the nuclear fuel has been used up, they can only run on the residual heat from their previous life. Due to this constraint their heat and light signatures rapidly decline. The initial condition of a dwarf can be compared with its current brightness (and therefore its temperature) to estimate the rate of cooling and then determine an age. Hubble Space Telescope observations on the M4 globular cluster of the Milky Way galaxy have yielded an age estimate of 12,700,000 ± 700,000 Ma. This approximate age for the galaxy is in good agreement with ages estimated from the H-R diagram and agreement between the two methods indicates that the age of the stars in the Milky Way galaxy is likely greater than 11,000,000 Ma but clearly less that the ~13.9 billion year time of the "Big Bang" (Chapter 8.5 and 8.6).

6.6 The Ages of the Elements

Only the two elements with the smallest atomic sizes, namely hydrogen and helium, were created following the Big Bang. These elements have been fused in the stars to create successively larger nuclei by nuclear burning. Firstly the hydrogen fuel is all used up by fusing into helium, then the helium fuel is used up to produce carbon, then oxygen and so on towards larger atomic sizes and ultimately up to iron (element number 26). Star formation cannot produce heavier elements by the process of nuclear fusion alone; instead the heavier elements are produced by processes of slow and rapid neutron capture described below. The elements composing the Earth, beyond hydrogen and helium (and including carbon the building block of life), have all been generated within former stars. Once a star has consumed its hydrogen and helium fuel by fusing into heavier elements, the entire mass of the stars collapses in on itself. This releases an immense burst of energy and the star explodes into a supernovae sending the newly-formed elements out into space. Here they will ultimately be incorporated into new solar systems and the cycle will be repeated as more and heavier elements are produced. The 92 elements that comprise our present Earth tell us that we are composed of the products of a lengthy history of recycling, likely through several now-extinct stellar systems, all predating the ~4.55 billion-year age of our Solar System.

The heavy elements are created most effectively in large, short-lived stars where they can be recycled back into space to be incorporated into new stars and planets within the ~13,900 - ~4,500 Ma interval between the formation of the earliest planets and our Solar System. The formation of elements heavier than iron results from neutron capture. Lighter elements can capture passing neutrons by a mechanism known as the *s-process* as these neutrons are captured; isotopes with a higher mass are then produced until a point is reached where a radioactive isotope is formed and decays as quickly as it forms. This blocks the generation of heavier isotopes. The s-process cannot therefore generate all the elements we have on Earth; it would be confined to red giants where neutrons are not abundant enough to result in a second process known as rapid neutron capture, ***the r-process.*** In this case neutrons are being captured faster than any unstable isotopes can decay and elements of progressively higher and higher mass are produced until production and decay of the radioactive nuclides are in equilibrium. When equilibrium has been achieved the r-process ceases. The r-process is essential for producing the heavier elements beyond iron but it can only occur in areas of exceptional neutron production such as supernovae. Supernovae explosions are also the most effective mechanism for dispersing the new elements and thus allowing them to be incorporated into new planets such as Earth.

The ages of elements can be determined when they include pairs of long-lived radioactive nuclei provided that one is stable and the other is radioactive. In these "chronometer pairs" the ratio of the two changes over time as one decays and the other stays constant. The ^{232}Th/^{238}U ratio where the former decays only to Pb^{208} and the latter to Pb^{206} provides a chronometer pair which has been applied to observations on meteorites, lunar rocks and terrestrial samples, and used to estimate the age of the Milky Way Galaxy. The production history is ongoing and both nuclides are produced solely through the r-process which defines a single rate of production. Use of this chronometer pair yields age estimates of 12,000 to 13,000 ± 3,000 Ma for heavier elements in the Milky Way galaxy (Dalrymple 2004). Evidently some of these heavier elements were already being formed in massive stars relatively soon after the Big Bang.

Only thirty-four of the known radioactive nuclides have half-lives over one million years and only twenty-three are found in nature, with just five continually produced through natural processes. The remaining seventeen all have half-lives greater than 82 million years. Assuming that the eleven radioactive nuclides which are no longer found have completely decayed to extinction, it is inferred that the Solar System is older than 4,500 Ma but less than 10,000 Ma in age. This follows because a younger solar system should include the missing nuclides whereas an older age would have effectively eliminated any radioactive nuclide with a half-life greater than this 82 Ma figure (Dalrymple 2004).

Although the elements incorporating radioactive nuclides provide a natural clock, they are only able to provide a range of ages for the materials making up the stars and planets. Nevertheless, the broad conclusions that the Solar System is between 4,500 and 10,000 Ma old, and that the Milky Way Galaxy is between 9,500 and 14,000 Ma old constrain the great antiquity of the Earth and Universe. Earth evidently formed at a relatively late stage in the evolution of the galaxy; this is confirmed by its varied element composition which includes a wide range of heavier elements essential for humankind to live and prosper.

6.7 Dating the beginning of Creation - The Big Bang

The Earth, the stars and the elements are all the record of multiple cycles of transformative processes from primeval hydrogen and helium from God's initial act of Creation. This is now widely acknowledged to be the Big Bang assigned to the record of Genesis Day One in Chapter 9. To date the initial act of the creation of matter we need to seek the earliest signature of this event. This is key to defining the beginning of time as we know it and is explored in Chapter 8 (8.5-8.8).

6.8 The YEC Case confounded

The proponents of the YEC viewpoint either have to ignore or dismiss the results yielding all but the very youngest ages for rocks and the origin of the Earth and Universe (Morris 1972, 1976), or otherwise find an explanation for the vast canon of ancient age determinations. The latter was the motivation of the RATE project (Radioisotopes and the Age of The Earth). Although providing the most scientifically-based YEC investigation to date, this project can hardly be regarded as objective because the RATE group was formed with the preconceived purpose of discrediting radioisotope dating. Nevertheless, it remains the most important attempt by the YEC fraternity to refute the results of isotopic dating (Vardiman et al. 2005). The team acknowledge that radioactive decay has actually been occurring and can be measured accurately, and that it would require thousands of millions of years at present rates to account for the current condition of the Earth. Their primary conclusion is therefore that radioactive decay was much more rapid at the time of the Noah's Flood. Before the publication of the RATE report YECs widely concluded that according to Genesis it is theologically possible for rocks to have been created with an appearance of age; radiohaloes where high-energy alpha-particles have damaged surrounding crystal grains for example, were used to suggest this (Snelling 2000, 2005) although this evidence has other interpretations (Wiens 2002). The ancient appearance of the Earth is then a manifestation of God's divine will: He created it in such a way that it appears to be much older. This is impossible to disprove and bypasses science altogether. It makes attempts to learn more about the world around us futile.

A young Earth appearing as an old Earth then becomes an item of blind faith, but more seriously it gives the impression that God is a deceiver. This violates the essence of His character because He has never relied on blind faith for us to believe in Him (Ross 2004). It has always been the unique tenant of Christianity that it is the one faith with foundational scriptures in the Bible provable from recorded history, fulfilled prophecy and transformed lives. We rely on the constancy of God's laws to live out our daily lives - the uniform passage of time, the constancy of the forces of gravity and magnetism etc. Why should God violate these laws just to make a young Earth appear old?

The key conclusion of the RATE report, namely that radioactive decay was much faster in the past, nevertheless deserves consideration. The evidence presented to support this conclusion has focused on four items of observation namely, helium accumulated in zircon crystals, the presence of polonium halos, isotope discordance, and the presence of ^{14}C in diamonds. In each case the evidence avoids the absolute time scales and is ambiguous; it could equally well be compatible with an old Earth (Wiens 2002, Heaton 2009). More seriously for this conclusion, the radioactivity produced by accelerated decay during just six days would have produced catastrophic environmental effects and killed everything on the planet. Heat acceleration during the Flood alone would likely have released enough energy to heat the Earth to a temperature of more than 22,000°C, or roughly four times the temperature at the surface of the Sun (DeYoung 2005). This would have vaporized the entire planet and simply obliterated the geologic evidence cited by RATE in support of rapid acceleration of radioactive decay in the past.

The alpha and beta decay rates of natural radioisotopes have been shown experimentally to be highly resistant to extremes of temperature and pressure, chemical alteration, and to magnetic and electrical fields

(Dalrymple 2004). Furthermore, there are several independent checks for any change in decay rates. Supernovae for example, produce large amounts of radioactive isotopes which in turn produce gamma rays with frequencies and fading rates predictable from present decay rates. These predictions have been confirmed for supernova SN1987A, 169,000 light-years away, and for supernova SN1991T 60,000,000 light-years away. Radioactive decay rates were evidently not signifi-cantly different during these great time periods (Isaak 2003). Since present decay rates are consistent with observations on gamma rays and fading rates of such ancient galaxies, we have no reason to doubt that they are valid on geological time scales. In summary, the conclusions of the RATE report deny the findings of rational science (Henke 2005).

The renowned Bible teacher Chuck Missler (1934-2018) was also an accomplished scientist and engineer. Although not well versed in the Earth Sciences, he achieved a broad knowledge of the physical sciences that he put to extensive use over his long career. An issue he noted concern over was the possibility that the unit we normally regard as immutable, namely the velocity of light, c, was not actually a constant. Whilst c appears to show no sign of variability in a high vacuum, it must be acknowledged that a true vacuum is unattainable and this test is compromised by the possible presence of dark matter. Small varia-tions in the speed of light have indeed been routinely observed thousands of times by laboratories around the world evidently caused by the distortion of space by gravity. Gravity not only bends light, it bends the space through which light travels. This appears to explain why large masses such as stars, black holes and planets, create a "lensing effect" that bends the light of stars travelling near those masses as the light makes its way towards Earth. This is why stars appear to shift around the perimeter of the Sun when observed during a total eclipse.

Changes in c would influence the absolute values of ages determined by the radiometric methods and have been invoked by the YECs to reduce the great ages of the Earth and Universe down to their own time scale. However, whilst variations in c can be recognized on a cosmic scale, several lines of evidence show that they have not significantly affected our understanding of the history of what has happened on Earth. Firstly, *if the speed of light were increased by the amounts required to reduce the age estimates down to the values required by the YECs, the vastly more rapid release of heat would have catastrophic consequences. On Earth the oceans would evaporate and crust would likely melt; the amount of energy released by the nuclear fusion in the Sun would be increased by the square accordingly to Einstein's Equation and utterly destroy the inner planets including Earth. Secondly, according to Carlip (2005) the supernova evidence would not be affected by change in the speed of light and influence the recognition of rapid cosmic expansion. Thirdly, Stassen (2005) observes that numerous other phenomena would manifest if decay rates had changed; these include the radius of planets, the orbit of Earth and the Moon, and the absorption lines of quasars. Lastly, a practical indication that the value of c has not changed significantly on Earth comes from the Oklo natural fission reactor in Gabon. Uranium is only soluble in the presence of oxygen. Uranium-rich mineral deposits could only begin to form when oxygen-saturated ground waters appeared by ~2.0 Byr ago to produce a natural environment in which uranium can be mobilized (see the Great Oxygenation Event defining Genesis Day 4 in Chapter 9.6). This enabled uranium to move and act as a neutron moderator for natural atomic reactions. Study of isotopes from the Oklo reactor indicate that the fine structure constant, α, which also controls universal parameters such as the speed of light, has not changed significantly since ~1.8Byr (Isaak 2003, Carlip 2005).*

6.9 The Stratigraphic Time Scale and the Geological Column

This section refers specifically to the history of the Earth, not to the Cosmos. The Stratigraphic Time Scale is the time sequence of intervals recorded by the rock record throughout Earth history, whilst a geological column is the succession of rock layers in a particular region. Because environments vary from place to place over the globe and change with time as the continents move, the geological column recorded in one place will differ from the column in another place: some locations will have been sited at placid subsiding continental margins, whilst others would have lain at active margins characterized by earthquakes, volcanic activity and rapid sedimentation; yet others would be in quiescent continental interiors where sediment may accumulate by river, rain, wind or even ice activities. However, each column always records segments of the same Stratigraphic Time Scale (Figure 6.3) defined by key items of floral and faunal content as well as radiometric ages. The primary divisions of the earlier *Precambrian* segment of the time scale (~3900 Ma to 541 Ma) are the *Hadean*, the *Archean* and the *Proterozoic* eons. Whilst the latter two are represented by substantial thicknesses of sediments, the underlying basement metamorphic terranes, which record profound thermal-tectonic events, represent the larger component of this older rock record. The latest metamorphic events are the best preserved because the record of the older events is obscured to varying degrees by the partial overprinting by the younger events.

Traces of organic carbon and single-celled fossils of bacteria are found in the oldest ~3.800 Ma Precambrian sedimentary rocks together with the first recorded appearance of liquid water essential for the survival of life. These single-celled organisms remain the only record of life until the Ediacaran Period at ~635 Ma ago shortly before the end of Precambrian times. There is then a dramatic appearance of multitudes of complex soft-bodied multi-cellular creatures with globular and tubular shapes. These are preserved as impressions in sedimentary rocks that were formerly soft mud and mostly had a static life style. Equally dramatically, this fauna had disappeared by the beginning of the Cambrian Period (~541 Ma) when abundant multi-cellular organisms representative of all the present-day phyla appeared. This history in described in the context of the Genesis record in Chapter 9.6.

The "Cambrian Explosion" was likely concentrated within less than 5 Ma and it begins the latest stratigraphic record of geological history comprising the *Phanerozoic* eon divided into the *Palaeozoic*, the *Mesozoic* and the *Cenozoic* eras. In very general terms these three divisions record long intervals dominated successively by invertebrates, reptiles and then mammals. The eras are in turn, subdivided successively into *periods*, *epochs* and *ages* on the basis of their faunal and floral contents. Organisms appearing for short time intervals are most useful for defining these subdivisions. In the stratigraphic record they appear and disappear abruptly; they may modify their morphologies in response to environmental changes, but remained the same species.

Whilst the geological columns vary from place to place over the globe typically embracing rocks formed in a wide variety of different environments including deep to shallow submarine, coastal, terrestrial (river, desert, equatorial to temperate and glacial), they invariably include long-time gaps recorded by *disconformities* or *unconformities*. The latter are recognized as angular differences between successive rock layers and show that tectonic deformation occurred during the unrepresented time interval in between. Since rocks which are highly brittle at the surface, can only deform into folds very slowly under conditions of elevated temperature and pressure, the presence of unconformities is always indicative of very long intervals of time.

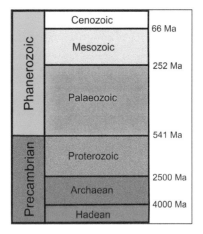

Figure 6.3 (a) Summary of the main divisions of Phanerozoic Eon (543 Ma to the present). (b) The major divisions of Geological Time from the Hadean (~3900 Ma ago to the present).

The divisions of the Stratigraphic time Scale are now defined absolutely by multiple radiometric age determinations on rock units occurring at defined points throughout the scale using the range of methods summarized in Section 6.1. There will always be an estimated error on each determination with the magnitude of the error in years increasing with the age; the younger ages are now very well defined, whilst advances in the quality and quantity of age dating have ensured that even uncertainties on the older age boundaries are now small.

The Stratigraphic Time Scale, the greatest single achievement of the Earth Sciences, is an embarrassment to the YEC position and essentially has to be ignored or explained away in terms of complex successive inundations by Noah's Flood. Since there are multiple changes in the climatic record, and alternations between marine and land environments present in the geological columns in all the continents, there is however, no way that they could record a single flooding event. Successive fossil organisms used to define the Periods and Stages obviously do not occur together as required by the Flood Model; others such as Lingula and Nautilus, which are of no value for stratigraphic subdivision, are present throughout. Whilst the YEC proponents could claim that absolute definition of the Stratigraphic Time Scale is dependent on radiometric dating, the reliability of the age determinations has been endorsed by the multiple independent lines of evidence discussed in the preceding section. The YECs make the cardinal error of highlighting examples of rapid sedimentation such as the output from the St Helens volcano or sediments rapidly burying single tree trunks, and then assume that this applies to all sediments. These are typically either the products of a catastrophic volcanic eruption, or the breaching and rapid lateral migration of a river system in a flood plain. More commonly the bulk of the sedimentary column was deposited continuously and very slowly over long periods of time. The Cretaceous chalk, the Cambrian laminated mudstones of North Wales and the fine spring-neap tidal laminae in the Windermere Supergroup of the Lake District are typical examples from Britain of deposits formed very slowly over long periods of time.

Furthermore, there are other more qualitative indications to show that the time periods involved are indeed very long. We can for example, gain an approximate indication of how long it takes sediments to be deposited from the study of modern sedimentation in seas and rivers. The concept of Uniformitarianism invoked by James Hutton and Charles Lyell (1797-1875) is no longer strictly applicable because geological history has been found to be punctuated by numerous catastrophic events. However, it is now possible to recognize the products of these events, such as tsunami-triggered turbulent turbidity current deposits, catastrophic slumps and cataclysmic volcanic eruptions, by their signatures in the rock record. The products of these incidental events contrast with vast thicknesses of, for example, fine grained mudstones deposited as clay in prolonged tranquil environments. Furthermore, many of these sediments contain annual or seasonal growth rhythms which can be counted to show that they embrace very long periods of time. In a comparable way the annual Spring melt varve cycles deposited in lakes bordering the ice sheets during the Pleistocene glaciations record time periods vastly longer than the duration of Noah's Flood.

The YECs also fail to address the long periods of time required to transform the soft sediments that we see forming in rivers and coastlands today into hard rock. Two processes are involved. The first is called "lithification"; as the soft sediment undergoes compaction and expulsion of the water between the grains, cementing films of minerals such as calcite and quartz in the spaces to bond the grains together. The second process is "diagenesis"; this involves the chemical alteration of the unstable mineral grains into more stable minerals and the maturation of organic material such as algae trapped in between the grains, ultimately to form oil and gas which is either trapped within the rock or escapes to the surface. These two processes have been profoundly studied over many decades, notably by the hydrocarbon industry, and have been shown to take many thousands of years to achieve the hard-brittle rocks that comprise the geological column.

6.10 The Ice Ages

Glaciations are defined as periods when freeze-over conditions and also ice sheets, which are characteristically polar in origin, occasionally extended into latitudes that we now regard as temperate, or even in a few cases into tropical latitudes. At least three and possibly up to seven glaciations are recognized in the geological record. These comprise the Pleistocene (<2.5 Ma and likely continuing at the present time), the Permo-Carboniferous (~360-260 Ma), the Ordovician-Silurian (Andean-Saharan, 460-430 Ma), the Ediacaran (Gaskiers at ~590 Ma and the Baykonurian at ~547-542 Ma), the Cryogenian (comprising the

Sturtian at ~720-660 Ma and the Marinoan at ~650-635 Ma), the Huronian (~2400-2200 Ma) and the Pongola (~2900 Ma). Whilst some of these may have had more limited impact than the latest Pleistocene Glaciation, some such as the Cryogenian, were likely more extensive and how far they extended into present low latitudes is still a subject of active debate (the "Snowball" or "Slushball" Earth). This latter event need not have been characterized by extensive ice cover because freeze-over conditions may have precluded the atmospheric circulation required to generate snowfall. The significance of the Precambrian glaciations is now being actively questioned from isotopic studies because carbon dioxide levels, and therefore greenhouse conditions, persisted during most of this era (Robinson 2017). The Phanerozoic glaciations were also apparently not consistently cold intervals. The Pleistocene for example, has been characterized be advances and retreats of the ice with the latest advance beginning about 110,000 years ago and the retreat beginning about 15,000 years ago. Some of the interglacial periods may have approached "greenhouse" conditions, and this alternation between warm and frigid conditions was likely a feature of the earlier glaciations. The impact of these ancient glaciations is well seen in remarkable rock exposures in many parts of the world. Figures 6.4 and 6.5 show the record of the Late Precambrian (Cryogenian) Glaciation in the Canadian Rockies where an ancient boulder bed is found well below the base of the Cambrian:

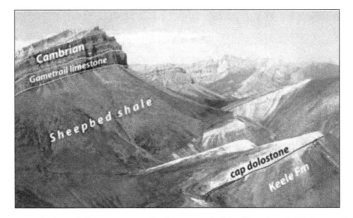

Figure 6.4: Thick rock formations including a probable glacial rock (dolostone) lying far beneath the Cambrian in the Rocky Mountains of Western Canada

Figure 6.5: Close up photograph of Late Precambrian sediments showing evidence for rapid climate change as a boulder bed with possible glacial debris is overlain by cream-coloured warm water limestones, Western Canada. Photographs after Hoffman and Schrag (2002)

YEC adherents are usually ready to acknowledge the existence of a Pleistocene Glaciation but insist that it was the only glaciation (Whitcomb and Morris 1961). Unfortunately, they compound this rejection of all the other glaciations in the geological record by insisting that it occurred after Noah's Flood, although neither the Bible nor other historic writings describe any such event. We consider the evidence for the Flood in Chapter 10 but note here that since the Biblical chronology places the Flood at ~2300-2400 BC, it occurred well after the last retreat of the glaciers between ~15,000 and 9,000 BC. In contrast, sediments of river and marine origin datable to, or shortly after this latter interval, are found extensively above glacial rocks deposited during the last glaciation. Figure 6.6 shows rock successions illustrating this point from south west Wales and the Yenissei Basin of northern Siberia. Both examples show great thicknesses of sand deposited above the last glacial horizon, whilst the former shows more than one advance of the ice sheet separated by interglacial intervals.

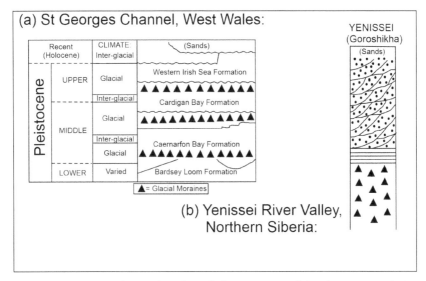

Figure 6.6: Stratigraphic sections through the upper part of the Pleistocene rocks in the St Georges Channel of western Wales and in the Yenissei River of northern Siberia. They demonstrate that Pleistocene to Recent times included several episodes of glaciation, with the last succeeded by later deposition of thick sands.

6.11 The Earth's Magnetic Field

The Earth's magnetic field is mainly sourced in the liquid Outer Core of the Earth where convection of a self-exciting dynamo responsible for a dipole field closely aligned with the rotation axis of the Earth. It generates a *magnetosphere* in the space around the Earth protecting us from harmful cosmic rays (Chapter *4.3.3*). The magnetic field has been subject to substantial fluctuations in intensity as well as frequent reversals in polarity. When these reversals occur the intensity of the dipole field collapses and only a residual field (which does not behave like a dipole) remains; this comprises just ~10-20% of the typical dipole field. Reversal events at specific time levels are identified throughout the world and dated by reference to the Stratigraphic Time Scale. The chronology of reversals is known as the *Geomagnetic Polarity Time Scale*. The process of reversing lasts a few thousand years with the last reversal event to the present "normal" polarity state of the field accurately dated to 720,000 years ago. Although in the short-term reversal events appear to occur at random time intervals, in the long term they occupy intervals building up from long periods when they were absent to times of frequent reversal. The Cretaceous Normal "Superchron" (121-83 Ma) was the last long interval when reversals were absent; subsequently the frequency of reversals has increased to a maximum about 10 Ma ago since when the reversal rate has been declining.

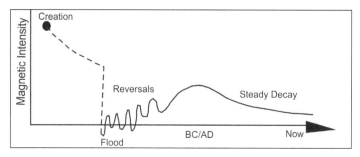

Figure 6.7: The false YEC version of the history of Earth's Magnetic Field

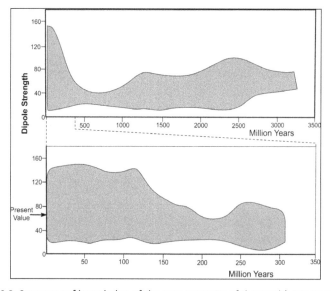

Figure 6.8: Summary of knowledge of the past Intensity of the Earth's Magnetic Field. (a) The shaded field embraces the results from Precambrian times. (b) The expanded range of numerous data covering Phanerozoic times (545 Ma to the present). Note that there is no systematic decline in the strength of the field into recent times. The vertical axis show units of Dipole Moment which is directly related to the Intensity of the Field. After Biggin et al. (2012).

A supposed decay of the Earth's magnetic field has been used by YECs to support their case with an argument based on the assertion that the magnetic field has been decaying at an exponential rate since the beginning of creation (Matson 2002). A claim that the magnetic field was approximately 40 percent stronger in 1000 A.D. than today leads, by backwards extrapolation, to the conclusion that the Earth is no older than 10,000 years otherwise the strength of the magnetic field would supposedly cause the Earth to melt (Sarfati 1998). Knowledge that the magnetic field has fluctuated and reversed in polarity over time, has further prompted some YECs to propose that plunging of tectonic plates toward the Earth's core, supposedly at the time of Noah's Flood, would cause sudden cooling of the outer core; they speculate that this would cause convection currents to flow within the core generating numerous reversals of the magnetic field over the course of thousands of years (Humphreys 1986, 1990 and Figure 6.7). Although it is true that the intensity of the field has been declining over the past few hundred years, it still remains well above the values found during reversals of the field. Since the last reversal occurred long before the time of Noah or Adam, any attempt to link rapid reversals to accelerated Plate Tectonics during the Flood is simply untenable. The study of the ancient intensity of the magnetic field (palaeointensity) has found that the strength of the field during Recent times has actually been considerably higher than during most of previous geological times (Figure 6.8). There is no case for postulating a progressive decline in the magnetic field as required by YEC proponents.

6.12 Plate Tectonics

Due to ongoing release of radioactive heat from the interior, Earth is a mobile planet with a present-day behavior described by *Plate Tectonics*. This paradigm developed in the late 1960's from the integration of two lines of investigation. The study of magnetism of rocks (palaeomagnetism) on the continental crust during the 1950's onwards was able to demonstrate that the continents have been continuously migrating over the surface of the globe; these movements were found to conform with the movement of the crust through climatic zones as shown by the equatorial to polar climatic signatures in the rock record. This is

Continental Drift. Parallel investigations of the deep oceans over the same time period were able to demonstrate that the ocean crust has been growing outwards from the volcanically-active *mid-ocean ridges* and consumed into *subduction zones* mainly focused around the margin of the Pacific Ocean. This process is referred to as *Sea Floor Spreading.* As a result of this mutual creation and consumption of the ocean crust the surface area of the globe stays constant.

Plate Tectonics show that most of the heat energy produced within the Earth is presently expended on the surface at the margins of an inter-locking system of seven large and many smaller rigid plates. There are three kinds of margins: the plates grow by the addition of volcanic rocks at *constructive margins* comprising the mid-ocean ridges; they are consumed back into the mantle of the Earth by the process of subduction at *destructive margins*, or they may slip past one another at *conservative margins* along major faults in the crust of which the San Andreas Fault in California is the best-known example (Figure 6.9).

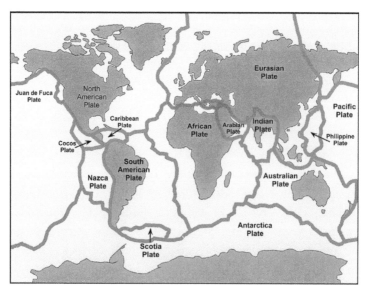

Figure 6.9: Mercator projection of the globe showing the distribution of the crustal plates at the present day. The contacts between them shown by the thick red lines are constructive along the mid-ocean ridges, destructive (mostly around the margins of the Pacific Ocean) and conservative where they slip past one another

The rates of Plate Tectonic movement are of the orders of centimeters per year. The consistency of these rates is confirmed by several independent methods. (i) Direct laser ranging enables us to measure the present-day rates of movement of both continental and oceanic crusts. (ii) Past rates of growth and spreading of the ocean crust are dated by correlating the positive (normal polarity) and negative (reversed polarity) magnetic fields over the oceans with the Geomagnetic Polarity Time Scale of reversals. (iii) The sediments accumulating on the abyssal ocean floor as the crust spreads away from the mid ocean ridges have been extensively cored and dated from their faunal contents by comparison with the Stratigraphic Time Scale, and by certain radiometric methods noted in Section 1; the younger sediments can also be dated by the uranium-thorium method. (iv) The volcanic basements beneath the sediments have also now been extensively cored and directly dated by isotopic dating. (v) The growth and destruction of the ocean crust is complemented by the translation of the continents; palaeomagnetic study of the continental rocks resolves rates of movement of the order of centimeters per year, in this case over much longer time intervals of hundreds of millions of years. The movements of the continents through latitudes and climatic zones are dated by comparison with the Stratigraphic Time Scale of Figure 6.3. This record of continental movement goes back way beyond the history of the oldest ocean crust (~190 Ma) and shows that movements of the continents have always been slow. These diverse methods for determining the rate at which Plate Tectonics is occurring all accord with figures of a few centimeters a year.

Most YECs now generally accept that Plate Tectonics has occurred (Reed et al. 2000) but incorporate it into their short time scale by postulating the theory of Catastrophic Plate Tectonics (Austin et al. 1994, Froede 2000, Baumgardner 2003). This concentrates all long-term effects of Plate Tectonics into the short time frame of Noah's Flood. The details differ from proponent to proponent as discussed by Heaton (2009). The theory however, fails completely from two observations: (i) the range of independent methods used to determine rates at which sea floors are spreading and continents are drifting, both in the past and continuing to the present day, all show rates of centimeters per year; the fastest recorded rate of spreading, which has only rarely been reached, is no more than ~25 cm/year. (ii) The supposed rapid generation of the ocean crust by volcanic activity after the Flood would have generated catastrophic amounts of heat and dust in a short time and have led to wholesale destruction of life, as well as the Earth itself.

6.13 The Metamorphic Foundations

The geological columns all over the continental crust lie with unconformity on vast volumes of basement of older metamorphic rocks. These have been heated to temperatures of hundreds of degrees and transformed by re-crystallization into new minerals. They typically form hard resilient terranes which come to the surface in the *Precambrian shields* such as the Canadian Shield and the Baltic Shield. They are composed of metamorphic minerals with well-established physical properties showing that they crystallized over temperatures up to ~800°C, and at pressures equivalent to great depths in the continental crust. Metamorphic rocks classified according to their temperature and pressure scales as *low (~200-400°C)*, *medium (~400-550°C)* and *high (~550-800°C)* grades. Since rocks are poor conductors of heat, cooling that followed the heating and compression requires many millions of years. Metamorphism is sometimes "static" but more commonly it occurs under powerful stress fields responsible for deforming the rocks into complicated fold patterns whilst still in a plastic condition. Examples of this are illustrated in the figures 6.10 and 6.11.

The presence of the metamorphic rocks of the continental shields is devastating to the YEC position. In fact, we can only be surprised at the scale of obfuscation that has ignored such an obvious refutation of a ~6000-year-old Earth. There seems to be no serious discussion of the significance of the metamorphic basements in the YEC literature and thermal arguments (without even considering the radiometric evidence) inevitably encounter time periods of many millions of years which simply cannot be accommodated by belief in a young Earth.

Figure 6.10: Banded metamorphic rocks recrystallized and deformed plastically at high temperatures. After cooling down they were cut by a brittle fracture filled in by the white quartz vein.

Figure 6.11: Metamorphic basement in the Canadian Shield. These rocks have been heated to high temperatures, sometimes several times, plastically deformed and re-crystallized into new minerals only stable at high temperatures and pressures.

6.14 The Dinosaurs and Man

The subject of dinosaurs is popular with Young Earth Creationists due to their appeal to the young. They are supposed to have walked Earth with the generations of men prior to Noah only to be destroyed by the Flood. However, dinosaur bones are never found with human bones. Although many large mammals, sometimes of extraordinary appearance, have existed in Pleistocene to Recent times, the dinosaurs were a characteristic fauna of the much earlier Mesozoic era between 252 and 66 Ma ago. Their extinction at the Mesozoic-Cenozoic boundary is attributed to a meteorite impact (Chapter 9.7) with a devastating environmental impact.

The YEC position seemed to be supported for a while by the supposed footprints of both dinosaurs and man in the Paluxy River rocks of Texas. The Paluxy River exposure is known for a large number of dinosaur footprints but more careful examination has shown that many of the supposed human tracks are in fact "natural irregularities and erosion features of the substrate....elongate, metatarsal dinosaur tracks...made by dinosaurs that impressed their soles and heels as they walked" (Kuban 1992). Often the toe marks of the dinosaur tracks are partially in filled to resemble very large human footprints. When the filling sediment is removed the tracks are clearly made by a three-toed dinosaur. Kuban goes on to write that "Recent claims that some of these tracks have human prints within them have been shown to be as baseless as the original claims". Investigations both by creationists (Neufeld 1975) and evolutionists (Milne and Schafersman 1983) have confirmed that the so-called human tracks are a combination of dinosaur tracks, random erosion marks and carvings made during the Great Depression.

The proposal that the dinosaurs were drowned by the Flood of Noah is also baseless: the dinosaur bone beds of Texas for example, occur at the top of up to fifty thousand feet of sediment extending into the Gulf of Mexico, and not at the base where they should be found if they were drowned in a single flood event.

6.12 Failed Clocks

A number of methods for dating the age of the Earth and oceans have been proposed in the past and deserve passing mention here although we now know that they have demonstrably failed.

6.12.1 Moon Dust

In an unpublished proposal in the 1950's Hans Petterssen suggested that accumulation of dust on the lunar surface could potentially have reached 35 ft over a ~4,000 million-year life span. This has formerly been used by YECs to suggest that the Moon is actually much younger (Wise 1990). However, Petterssen rooted his calculations in Earth observations on the assumption that no nickel existed on the Earth before it began to accumulate by meteorite impacts. In fact the Earth has always had primary nickel and when this is taken into account there is a dramatic decrease in the estimated dust accumulation on the Moon. Studies of lunar material have since shown that the Moon formed 4.51 billion years ago, just ~60 million years after the formation of the Solar System. As early as 1965 it was clear that only minimal dust accumulation was present on the lunar surface, a point confirmed by the lunar landing in 1969.

6.12.2 Comet Disintegration

Comets range in size from 1 to 15 kilometers in diameter and consist of ice, dust and rock reckoned to have been orbiting the stars since the formation of the Solar System (Stern 2003). The comets visible from Earth are those that pass close to the Sun, although it is only the tail, and not the nucleus, that is visible. Since they lose a large percentage of their material every time they pass near the Sun, once captured into a solar orbit their average lifetime is short. Comets with a short orbital period pass close to the Sun more frequently and therefore disintegrate more quickly than long period ones. The lifespan of Halley's Comet for example, is estimated to be approximately 10,000 years although smaller comets may have life spans of only ~2,000 years (Ross 2004). They cannot be used as evidence for a young Universe however, because enormous potential reservoirs of comets, probably left over from the formation of the Solar System, exist at distances from the Sun mostly beyond the planetary system. The *Kuiper Belt* is a comet-rich area beginning near the orbit of Neptune and continuing beyond Pluto where gravitational perturbations will send comets into orbits around the Sun from time to time. The *Oort Cloud* is considered to consist of a billion, billion comets occupying an immense space at the very edge of the Solar System, somewhere between 1,000 and 100,000 A.U. (Stern 2003; an astronomical unit (A.U.) is the distance from the Earth to the Sun). It is too far away for direct observation although ground-based observations have confirmed the existence of both the Kuiper belt (Stern 2003) and the Oort Cloud (Irion 2004). The Oort Cloud is so far away from the Sun that it becomes susceptible to the gravitational pull of passing stars from other planetary systems. From time to time comets are dislodged and sent towards the inner Solar System to provide a continuous source of new comets as old ones disintegrate.

6.12.3 Lunar Recession

George Darwin, the son of Charles Darwin, originally proposed that the Moon broke away from the Earth and calculated that it would have taken at least 56 million years for the Moon to reach its current distance from the Earth. The Moon is indeed slowly receding from the Earth as an exchange of angular momentum occurs between them. This is caused mostly by the friction of tides across shallow seas around the continents. It has been responsible for reducing the number of days in the year over geological time, a reduction that can be determined from growth rings in fossils such as corals. Lunar recession is currently occurring at a measureable rate of 3.8 cm/year as determined by beaming laser rays from reflector arrays positioned on the Moon. Extrapolated backwards in time this rate predicts a Moon catastrophically close to the Earth in Late Precambrian times ~1,000 million years ago. However, the effect of tidal braking has varied enormously over geological time. It was high during the Cretaceous Period when most of the continents were covered by shallow seas but was very low before the Cambrian Period when the continental crust was aggregated into a quasi-rigid supercontinent and shallow seas were much more limited than they are today (Piper 2013). It now seems likely that the Moon was never catastrophically close to the Earth during the ~3,900 million-year history of the continental crust acknowledged by Old Earth Creationism.

Remarkably, it is only during the time of the creation of humankind that the lunar disc has shrunk to a size identical to the size of the solar disc as we see it from Earth. As a result, this is the only time in the history of the planet that that we have been able to observe total eclipses and corona during eclipses. This has enabled development of the science of spectroscopy applied to study of the composition of light from the stars and galaxies. The results of these investigations have enabled the determination of the temperatures, velocities, masses and compositions of the stars - it is as though this point in the lunar recession was designed for us to discover the properties of our Universe.

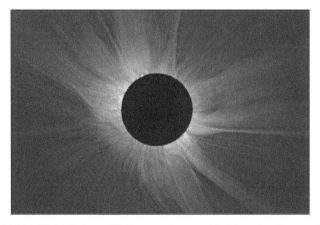

Figure 6.12: Total Solar Eclipse with Corona. Because the Moon has been continuously retreating from the Earth it has only been possible to see this during the recent and brief lifetime of humankind.

6.12.4 Salinity of the Seas

This method for dating the age of the oceans was originally proposed more than 300 years ago. It seemed potentially a simple matter to measure salt in the oceans due to its abundance: when one cubic foot of sea water is evaporated it yields approximately 2.2 pounds of salt. The eminent astronomer Edmund Halley first addressed this method of testing the ocean's salinity in 1715 by observing that oceans and lakes were fed by rivers and therefore constantly receiving more salt. He could not test his theories because he needed to know the salt content of the oceans earlier in time to calculate a rate of accumulation. In 1876 T.

Mellard Reade called this process "chemical denudation", and calculated that it would take 25 million years for calcium and magnesium sulfates to reach their present concentrations in the oceans. The physicist John Joly calculated an age of 99.4 million years in 1899, 10 years later revising his equations to estimate an age for the oceans of between 80 and 150 million years.

However, to use salt as an indicator of the age of the oceans it is necessary to assume that they started with 0% salinity, and also that when the salt is dissolved it stays there permanently. In fact, salt is continuously recycled by the dynamic processes of Plate Tectonics. Sea water enters and alters the volcanic rocks of the ocean floor as it moves away from the mid-ocean ridges by Plate Tectonics. This water, together with the water in the sediments accumulated above, is consumed back into the Upper Mantle of the Earth as the crust is subducted at the destructive plate margins. Salt water is also drawn and evaporated into porous sediments along arid seashores; they are now found as massive salt deposits of marine origin found at intervals through the geological columns. These deposits generally correlate with times when the continental crust was migrating through zones of warm temperate climates. *In spite of this obvious flaw the website Answers in Genesis continues to use the salt clock as a valid measuring device (Sarfati 2005).*

6.12.5 Cooling of the Earth

Lord Kelvin sought to apply knowledge of the physics of heat conduction to the problem of dating the Earth. Given that temperature increases with depth below the surface, Kelvin concluded that the planet was slowly cooling. He aimed to calculate the time required to cool and solidify from an initially molten state. Kelvin needed to know: (i) the temperature at Earth's core, then thought to be entirely solid rock, (ii) the temperature gradient with depth below the surface, and (iii) the thermal conductivity of rocks. The first figure had to be below the temperature at which lavas solidified at the surface. Kelvin then made his own measurements of conductivity and used a temperature gradient of 1°F per 50 feet determined in deep mines. In 1862 he derived an age of 100 million years whilst acknowledging uncertainties requiring broad upper and lower age limits of 400 and 20 Ma. Based on new measurements of the melting point of rocks, Kelvin adjusted his estimate down to 20 million years (Burchfield 1975). Although sometimes favorably reported by YEC's because of his attacks on Darwin, Kelvin was clear that the Earth had to be very old. Once it was discovered that radioactive isotopes are abundant in rocks and that radioactive decay releases tremendous amounts of heat, Kelvin's assumption of a closed system and dwindling initial heat proved to be demonstrably false.

6.13 The preservation of soft tissue in ancient rocks

Until recently the single remaining item of evidence in the armory of the YEC position appeared to be the preservation of soft tissue in Mesozoic dinosaur fossils and the long-term survival of DNA - items which should have long ago decayed in an oxygen-rich atmosphere. Beginning in 1994 with study of the thigh bone of a *Tyrannosaurus* dated ~68 Ma, Schweitzer and co-workers (1994) identified blood vessels of the type seen in bone and marrow containing red blood cells with nuclei typical of reptiles and birds. The vessels appeared to be lined with specialized endothelial cells found in all blood vessels and containing the protein collagen, the building block of all connective tissue. A further issue concerns the recognition of DNA in Neanderthal bones, insects in amber, and other dinosaur fossils of Mesozoic age. It was considered that DNA should not exist in natural environments for longer than 10,000 years and bacteria have now been revived with no DNA damage from fossils much older than this. It has since been found that iron, which is abundant in the blood, is the agent which appears to preserve this ancient tissue. Iron is present in both ferrous and ferric forms and highly reactive; when released upon death it breaks down into fine particles that generate radicals which in turn, transform and act as a preservative to effectively seal and preserve soft tissue (Schweitzer et al. 2014). The importance of the iron from the blood is shown by the growth of the iron carbonate, siderite, around the bones (Ullman et al. 2019).

6.14 Conclusions

As described in outline here, the wide range of methods available for dating the origin of the Earth and the subsequent geological record all

consistently show that the planetary history is of great antiquity. Since the Flood Model was initially proposed over 100 years ago many YECs have made genuine attempts to incorporate current scientific knowledge into the very brief time period that they have to work with. However, since their 6,000-year limit is sacrosanct and non-negotiable, they have repeatedly to invoke scientifically-untestable supernatural events to constrain the evidence to their model, some of which would catastrophically-destroy the very evidence they are trying to use.

Science works by evaluating testable hypotheses. Miracles are excluded in scientific investigation because they violate known laws by appealing to something unknown. Miracles are exceptional events which defy science and are beyond its ability to investigate; to believe in them is an article of faith. Nevertheless, it is our contention that miracles have indeed taken place. The preceding chapters 2 to 5, as well as this chapter, note repeated examples where God is clearly present in the design and continuity of Creation and humankind. Ultimately only Divine intervention could have been responsible for a most remarkable miracle of all - the creation of life (Chapter 3). When honestly investigated the life, death and resurrection of the Lord Jesus Christ then proves to be amongst the most comprehensively-recorded and best-established events of ancient history (Chapters 1 and 2), with resurrection from death to life being surely the most remarkable miracle and one that defies rational science.

The difficulty with the multiple miracles required by the YEC position is that they rely on interventions that conflict with the nature of God. They defy His unchangeable nature, a property which is specifically claimed in the Scriptures. Unlike the miracles recorded in the Bible, the miracles invoked by the YECs have no relevance to the story of humankind's redemption and are introduced purely to satisfy the mantra that the Earth is 6000 years old. As shown in Chapters 8 and 9, when relativity is acknowledged it concisely explains the chronology of the Six Days in Genesis. To attribute the Geological Column to a downpour lasting just 40 days and an ensuing flood lasting just 150 days, without even allowing time for soft sediments to lithify into hard rock, is inviting ridicule and has proved a significant barrier to Christian testimony for at least 70 years. Whilst the full sequence of processes that might operate to preserve ancient tissue have yet to be fully researched, there is little point in YECs clinging to the preservation of soft tissue as a point of disputed significance. The overwhelming case for an old Earth is beyond obfuscation or counter-argument: the multi-facetted evidence confirms the long durations of cosmic and geological time to yield a case that is likely unassailable. Following this conclusion the Biblical and Scientific knowledge embracing the OEC position is addressed in the remaining chapters of this book.

References and further reading:

Austin, S.A., Baumgardner, J.R., Humphreys, D.R., Snelling, A.A., Vardiman, L., Wise, K.P. 1994. Catastrophic plate tectonics: a global Flood model of Earth history. *In: Walsh, R.E. (ed.) Proceedings of the third international conference on creationism.* Creation Science Fellowship, Pittsburgh, 609–621.

Baumgardner, J.R., 2003. Catastrophic plate tectonics: the physics behind the Genesis Flood. In: Ivey, R.L. Jr. (ed.) *Proceedings of the 5th international conference on creationism.* Creation Science Fellowship, Pittsburgh, 113–126.

Baumgardner, J.R., 2005. 14C evidence for a recent global Flood and a young Earth. In: Vardiman, L., Snelling, A.A., Chaffin, E.F. (eds.) *Radioisotopes and the age of the Earth, vol II: results of a young-earth creationist research initiative.* Institute for Creation Research, El Cajon, 587–630.

Biggin, A.J., Strik, G.H.M.S. and Langeris, C., 2009. The intensity of the geomagnetic field in the late-Archaean: new measurements and an analysis of the updated IAGA palaeointensity database, Earth Planets Space, 61, 9–22.

Burchfield, J. D. 1975. *Lord Kelvin and the age of the Earth,* Science History Publications, New York, 260 pp.

Carlip, S., 2005. Have physical constants changed with time? Usenet Physics FAQ. http://math.ucr.edu/home/baez/physics/ParticleAnd Nuclear/constants.html

Dalrymple, G. B., 2004. *Ancient Earth, Ancient Skies: The Age of the Earth and Its Cosmic Surroundings.* Stanford University Press, Stanford, California.

DeYoung, D., 2005. *Thousands... not billions: challenging an icon of evolution, questioning the age of the Earth.* Master Books, Forest Green, Arkansas.

Froede, C.R. Jr., 2000. Questions regarding the Wilson cycle in plate tectonics and catastrophic plate tectonics. In: Reed, J.K. (ed.) *Plate tectonics: a different view.* Creation Research Society, St. Joseph, 147–160.

God and Science. Not Enough Dust on the Earth or Moon Prove the Earth is Young. http://www.godandscience.org/youngearth/dust.html

Heaton, T.H., 2009. Recent Developments in Young-Earth Creationist Geology, Science & Education 18(10):1341-1358.

Henke, K., 2005. "RATE's Ratty Results: Helium Diffusion Doesn't Support Young-Earth Creationism." http://www.talkorigins.org/faqs/helium/zircons.html.

Hoffman, P.F. and Schrag, D.P., 2002. The snowball Earth hypothesis: testing the limits of global change. Terra Nova 14, 129-155

Humphreys, D.R., 1986. Reversals of the Earth's magnetic Field during the Genesis Flood. In: Walsh, R.E., Brooks, C.L., Crowell, R.S. (eds.) *Proceedings of the First international conference on creationism, vol. 2.* Creation Science Fellowship, Pittsburgh, pp 113–126.

Humphreys, D.R., 1990. Physical mechanism for reversals of the Earth's magnetic Field during the Flood. In: Walsh, R.E., Brooks, C.L. (eds.) *Proceedings of the second International conference on creationism, vol. 2.* Creation Science Fellowship, Pittsburgh, 130–137.

Irion, R. 2004. Far Out Ice World. Science. 303, 5665. 1743-1743

Isaak, M., 2003. CF210: Origins, http://www.talkorigins.org/indexcc/CF/CF210.html

Kuban, G. J., 1992. Man Tracks? A Summary of the Paluxy "Man Track" Controversy. http://talkorigins.org/faqs/paluxy/mantrack.html.

Matson, D., 2002. Young-Earth "proof" #11: Since the Earth's magnetic field is decaying at an exponential rate, its strength would have been unrealistically high 25,000 years ago. (http://www.infidels.org/library/modern/dave_matson /youngearth/specific_arguments/ magnetic_field).

Milne, D.H. and Schafersman, S.D. (1983). Dinosaur tracks, erosion marks and midnight chisel work (but no human footprints) in the Cretaceous limestone of the Paluxy River bed, Texas. Journal of Geological Education, 31(2):111-123.

Morris, H.M., 1972. *The remarkable birth of planet Earth.* Creation-Life Publishers, San Diego.

Morris, H.M., 1974. *Scientific creationism.* Creation-Life Publishers, San Diego.

Neufeld, B. (1975). Dinosaur tracks and giant men. Origins (Geoscience Research Institute) 2(2):64-76

Numbers, R.L., 1992. *The Creationists: The Evolution of Scientific Creationism.* Alfred A. Knopf, Inc., New York.

Pearce, E.K.V., 1993. *Evidence for Truth: Science*, Evidence Programs, Eastbourne, Sussex.

Piper, J.D.A., 2013. A planetary perspective of Earth evolution: Lid Tectonics before Plate Tectonics, Tectonophysics, 589, 44-56.

Price, G.M., 1916. *Back to the Bible or the New Protestantism.* Review and Herald Pub, Washington, DC.

Price, G.M., 1935. *The modern Flood theory of geology.* Fleming H. Revell, New York

Reed, J.K., Bennett, C.B., Froede, C.R. Jr, Oard, M.J., Woodmorappe, J., 2000. *An introduction to plate tectonics and catastrophic plate tectonics.* In: Reed, J.K. (ed.) Plate tectonics: a different view. Creation Research Society, St. Joseph, 11–21.

Robinson, S.J., 2017. *Marine carbon isotopes, carbonate mineralogy and indices of chemical weathering during the Tonian and Cryogenian periods: examples from North and South China,* Ph.D. thesis, University College London. https://discovery.ucl.ac.uk/id/eprint/1547543/1/Robinson_combinepdf.pdf

Ross, H., 2004. *A Matter of Days*. NavPress.

Sarfati, J., 1998. "The Earth's magnetic field: evidence that the Earth is young" Answers in Genesis. http://www.answersingenesis.org/creation/v20/i2/magnetic.asp.

Sarfati, J., 26 October 2005. "Salty Seas - Evidence for a Young Earth." Answers in Genesis. http://www.answersingenesis.org/creation/v21/i1/seas.asp.

Sarfati, J., 2014. *Refuting Compromise*, Creation Book Publishers, 514pp.

Schweitzer, M.H., Wenxia, Z., Cano, R.J. and Horner, J.R., 1994. Multiple lines of evidence for the preservation of collagen and other biomolecules in undermineralized bone from Tyrannosaurus Rex, Journal of Paleontology, 14:45A.

Schweitzer, M.H., Wenxia, Z., Cleland, T.P., Godwin, M.B., Boatman, E., Theil, E., Marcus, M.A. and Fakra, S.C., 2014. A role for iron and oxygen chemistry in preserving soft tissues, cells and molecules from deep time, Proceeding of the Royal Society of London, B, 281.

Snelling, A.A. 2000. "Radiohalos." In: L. Vardiman, A., A. Snelling, and E.F. Chaffin (eds.) *Radioisotopes and the Age of the Earth, Volume II: Results of a Young-Earth Creationist Research Initiative*, Institute for Creation Research, El Cajon, California.

Snelling, A.A. 2005. Radiohalos in granites: Evidence for accelerated nuclear decay. Chapter 3. In: L. Vardiman, A., A. Snelling, and E.F. Chaffin (eds.) *Radioisotopes and the Age of the Earth, Volume II: Results of a Young-Earth Creationist Research Initiative*, Institute for Creation Research, El Cajon, California.

Stassen, C., 2005. The age of the Earth, Origins Archive. http://www.talkorigins.org/faqs/faq-age-of-earth.html#constant.

Stern, A.S. 2003. The Evolution of Comets in the Oort Cloud and Kuiper Belt. Nature, 424, 6949, 639-643.

Ullmann, P. V., S. H. Pandya, and R. Nellermoe, 2019. Patterns of soft tissue and cellular preservation in relation to fossil bone tissue structure and overburden depth at the Standing Rock Hadrosaur Site, Maastrichtian Hell Creek Formation, South Dakota, USA. Cretaceous Research. 99, 1-13.

Vardiman, L., Austin, S.A., Baumgardner, J.R., Boyd, S.W., Chaffin, E.F., DeYoung, D.B. et al. (2005) Summary of evidence for a young Earth from the RATE project. In:

Vardiman, L., Snelling, A.A., Chaffin, E.F. (eds.) *Radio-isotopes and the age of the Earth, vol II: results of a young-Earth creationist research initiative.* Institute for Creation Research, El Cajon, 735–772.

Whitcomb, J.C., Morris, H.M., 1961. *The Genesis Flood: the biblical record and its scientific implications.* Presbyterian and Reformed Publishing Co, Philadelphia.

Wiens, Roger, 2002. Radiometric Dating: A Christian Perspective. Available at: http://www.asa3.org/ASA/resources/Wiens2002.pdf

Wise, D., 1990. Moon Dust. Last Update: Feb 1, 2003. Accessed: Oct 18, 2005. http://members.aol.com/dwise1/cre_ev/moondust.html.

Wise, Kurt. 2002. *Faith, Form, and Time.* Broadman & Holdman Publishers, Nashville, Tennessee.

Chapter 7

The GAP Explained

This chapter deals with an aspect of the Biblical narrative that will likely seem strange, even incredible, to the person who has not experienced a scriptural education because it is focused on a spiritual realm outside of our dimensional physical understanding (Chapter 8.3). Nevertheless, if the Bible is the holistic truth of Divine testimony - a view we believe is established by the foregoing chapters of this book - this is an issue requiring informed treatment. It also sources the origin of evil - the biggest conundrum of the secular world that would ultimately go on to infect humankind (Genesis 3:1-7). It commences right at the beginning of the text in the second verse of Genesis Chapter One with a principle referred to as "The GAP" and introducing the concept of a Satanic realm. A comprehensive interpretation of the Biblical narrative builds on the testimonies of the Book of Isaiah chapters 14 and 24, Ezekiel 28, Jude 1:6 and Revelation 12:9 as well as the words of the Lord Jesus Christ himself. In Luke 10:18 He highlighted the significance of an angelic insurrection. It implies that a third of the population of created angelic beings rebelled against God at the behest of a leading angel called Lucifer who through pride desired to be like God. Banished to the Earth, he became Satan or the serpent. As a created being, he is not omnipresent like God but is described in both Old and New testaments as "walking to and fro across the Earth". He first appears corrupting God's creation of humankind with Adam and Eve (see Chapter 8.1). As they succumb to his lies and seek the knowledge of good and evil, the ruler ship of the Earth passes from Adam to him. He then becomes the leading motivator of attempts to frustrate God's purposes for redeeming humankind through subsequent generations, and most specifically by attacking the Jewish people to frustrate God's ultimate purposes through them. The demonic realm of fallen angels is considered to operate at his bequest. As a result, Jesus did not question that Satan had the right to offer Him the kingdoms of the world (Luke 4:8). Since the time of Abraham, God's purposes for humankind's redemption have centered on a chosen people, the Jews, intended to be His light to the world through first and second comings of Jesus Christ. These foundational concepts are necessary to expand the significance of the GAP.

The GAP concept has a long pedigree beginning with the Jewish sages and Early Church Fathers. It formed a key component of interpretation supported by a wide range of Bible scholars throughout the Church Age well before the scientific study of geology had begun, or Darwin had proposed evolution (Langford 2011). It has tended to fall out of favor during the past few decades as a consequence of the ardent promotion of Young Earth Creationism. However, careful textural analysis building on a long history of linguistic study has shown that it is more than a theory and is currently being restored to its rightful position in the analysis of Biblical time. The outline that follow is based mainly on Langford's book *"The Gap is not a Theory"*, the web resource *www.kjvbible.org/genesisgap/*, and teachings of Dr Chuck Missler. However, the GAP is nowadays not sufficient by itself to accommodate the record of Earth and Planetary history because it concerns an event with no stated time frame which is primarily spiritual in nature: it does not address the moves that God took to transform His creation into order; the latter are purely physical events that follow through the Six Days described in the remainder of Genesis Chapter One. These are addressed in Chapters 8 and 9.

The GAP Case begins with a perfect Creation:

In the beginning God created the heaven and the Earth. (Genesis 1:1)

God's intention is: ***"For thus saith the LORD that created the heavens; God himself that formed the Earth and made it; He hath established it, <u>He created it not in vain</u>, He formed it to be inhabited"*** (Isaiah 45:18).

In the Book of Job, likely the oldest book in the Bible and recorded in the most ancient form of Hebrew, God addresses Job:

Then the Lord answered Job out of the whirlwind and said "Who is this who darkens counsel by words without knowledge? Now prepare yourself like a man; I will question you, and you shall answer Me: Where were you when I laid the foundations of the Earth? Tell Me, if you have understanding. Who determined its measurements? Surely you know! Or who stretched the line upon it? (Job 38:1-5)

As a work of God it would have been perfect (Psalm 18:30) and Job is told that the angelic hosts, already created and referred to as "the sons of God", rejoiced:

To what were its foundations fastened? Or who laid its cornerstone when the morning stars sang together, and all the sons of God shouted for Joy? (Job 38:6-7)

The metaphor of the stars singing together is repeated in other places in the Old Testament Scriptures:

"Praise ye Him, all His angels: Praise ye Him, all His hosts, Praise ye Him, SUN and MOON: Praise Him all ye STARS of light" (Psalm 148:2-3)

"Sing O ye heavens for the Lord hath done it; shout, ye lower parts of the Earth" (Isaiah 44:23)

"The heavens declare the glory of God and the firmament sheweth His handiwork. Day unto day uttereth speech, night unto night sheweth knowledge. There is no speech nor language where their voice is not heard" (Psalm 19:1-3.)

But the Creation then became waste and empty, in Hebrew *tohu wa-bohu*:

And the Earth was without form, and void; and darkness was upon the face of the deep. And the Spirit of God moved upon the face of the waters. (Genesis 1:2)

As quoted above, the sense of this verse in incomplete. Textural issues require amplification as underlined below:

<u>And</u> the earth <u>was</u> without <u>form,</u> and <u>void</u>; and <u>darkness</u> was upon the face of the <u>deep</u>. And the Spirit of God <u>moved</u> upon the face of the waters.

"And" is adversative and more correctly translated as "<u>But</u>".

"Was" is a transient (pluperfect form) verb *"hayat"* requiring action and better translated "<u>had become</u>"; it can imply a time gap.

"Without form" or *"tohu"* - "<u>confusion</u>", "<u>pattern-less</u>".

"Void" or *"bohu"* - "<u>void</u>", "<u>empty waste</u>", "<u>wrecked</u>"

"Darkness" or *"choshek"* is an "<u>unnatural darkness</u>"

"Deep" refers to *"tehown"* - "<u>abussos</u>", "<u>abyss</u>", "<u>home of demons</u>".

"Moved" or *"merahefet"* - "<u>to hover above</u>", "<u>brood</u>", "<u>vibrate</u>".

Note that "bohu" also implies filled with the building blocks of matter (Schroeder 1997).

Revising Genesis 1:2 with these amplifications we have:

> *But the earth had become confused and an empty waste; and an unnatural darkness was over the abyss, <u>the home of demons</u>. And the Spirit of God brooded over the face of the waters.*

The terms *"tohu wa-bohu"* are used in two other places in the Scriptures and both occur in the context of Divine judgment:

"But the cormorant and the bittern shall possess it; the owl also and the raven shall dwell in it: and he shall stretch out upon it the line of confusion (kav-tohu), and the stones of emptiness (avnei-bohu)". (Isaiah 34:11) The implication of the amplified words here is failure to meet the Biblical yardstick (*kav*) and bricks which have become broken down (*avnei*).

"I beheld the earth, and, lo, it was waste (tohu), and void (bohu). And the heavens, and they had no light. I beheld the mountains, and lo, they trembled, and all the hills moved lightly. I beheld, and lo, there was no man, and all the birds of the heavens were fled". (Jeremiah 4:23-26). The significance of these verses is amplified by what follows: *"For thus says the Lord, the whole land shall be desolate. Yet I will not make a full end"* (Jeremiah 4:27). This is a record of judgment specifically on the sinful nation of Judah in 587-586 BC, whereas the implication of Genesis 1:2 is the record of a cosmic judgment affecting the whole of the new creation. The sense of Genesis 1:2, specifically the reference to *"dark"* and *"the abyss",* shows that this was actually a spiritual event with physical consequences. The verbs derived from these two words provide additional insight with **tahah** meaning "was astonished", "amazed" and **bahah** similarly meaning "to be surprised", "amazed".

No time frame is given for Genesis 1:2. Bible scholars link the spiritual implications of this verse to the fall of the Satanic realm described by two key prophecies in the Books of Ezekiel and Isaiah:

Ezekiel 28: 12-15: *"Son of man, take up a lamentation upon the king of Tyre, and say unto him, Thus saith the Lord God; Thou sealest up the sum, full of wisdom, and perfect in beauty. Thou hast been in Eden the garden of God; every precious stone was thy covering, the sardis, topaz, and the diamond, the beryl, the onyx, and the jasper, the sapphire, the emerald, and the carbuncle, and gold: the workmanship of thy tabrets and of thy pipes was prepared in thee in the day that thou wast created. Thou art the anointed cherub that covereth; and I have set thee so: thou wast upon the holy mountain of God; thou hast walked up and down in the midst of the stones of fire. Thou wast perfect in thy ways from the day that thou wast created, <u>until iniquity was found in thee</u>".*

In the context of the inclusion of "Eden" and "cherub", the "King of Tyre" is considered to be used metaphorically here for Satan, because it refers to an angelic being created perfect in God's heavenly realm but fell when iniquity was found in him due to his pride (unlike the King of

Tyre who was not in Eden, was Earth-bound and would have had antecedents).

Ezekiel's extraordinary prophecy continues (verses 16-19) with a description of the violent consequence of Satan's fall and his ultimate judgment:

"By the abundance of your trading you became filled with violence within, and you sinned: therefore I will cast you as profane out of the mountain of God: and I will destroy you, O covering cherub, from the midst of the stones of fire. Your heart was lifted up because of your beauty, you corrupted your wisdom by reason of you splendor: I will cast you to the ground, I will lay you before kings, that they may behold you. You defiled your sanctuaries by the multitude of your iniquities, by the iniquity of your trading. Therefore I brought fire from your midst; it devoured you, and I turned you to ashes upon the Earth in the sight of all who saw you. All who knew you among the peoples are astonished at you; you have become a horror and shall be no more forever."

The second reference comes from the Book of Isaiah and is the only place where Satan is referred to as "Lucifer" - the Light Bearer, the name before his fall. It notes the material consequence of his fall - the weakening of the nations. Also his ultimate destiny is the pit, or the *abyss*, the same term recorded in Genesis 1:2.

Isaiah 14:12-15: *How art thou fallen from heaven, O Lucifer, son of the morning! how art thou cut down to the ground, which didst weaken the nations! For thou hast said in thine heart, I will ascend into heaven, I will exalt my throne above the stars of God: I will sit also upon the mount of the congregation, in the sides of the north: I will ascend above the heights of the clouds; I will be like the most High. Yet thou shalt be brought down to hell, to the sides of the pit.*

These are deep theological issues which are widely explored elsewhere. The remit of this study is concerned primarily with the time frame. We observe that it occurred at a time not directly related to the following

Genesis record of the Six Days which talk only of physical restoration, although there are indications noted below implying that it had occurred by Day 3.

YECs have often claimed that Dr Thomas Chalmers of the Church of Scotland was the first person to promote the GAP in 1814. They justify this from his writings which included addressing the new discoveries of James Hutton on the great antiquity of the Earth and the statement that "The writings of Moses do not fix the antiquity of the globe". To the YEC viewpoint this is tantamount to allowing time for evolution. However, in view of the solid Biblical foundation, it is unfortunate that the YECs have dismissed the GAP all for the sake of preserving a 6000-year mantra. Furthermore, an antecedence long predating Dr Chalmers or any serious understanding of geology is recorded in the historical background of Arthur C. Custance in his book *Without Form and Void* (1970). The concept of the GAP was evident to Bible scholars long before they had any significant understanding of geology (Langford 2011).

Following Genesis 1:1-2 the text of Genesis continues with the description of how God moved across His creation to transform chaos into order in six steps for Earth to become a perfect habitation for humankind. These are the only known instances where the Universal Laws of Thermodynamics are reversed. The Six "Days" are introduced from Genesis 1:3 without introduction. In each case they are initiated by God speaking order into chaos. Genesis 1:3 is the first recorded utterance of God's voice and the steps of ordering are framed the same way in each case:

(v3.) "Then God said....there was evening and there was morning" - Day One (v.5)

(v6.) "Then God said....there was evening and there was morning" - Day Two (v.8)

(v9.) "Then God said....there was evening and there was morning" - Day Three (v.13) (v14.) "Then God said....there was evening and there was morning" - Day Four (v.19)

(v.20) "Then God said....there was evening and there was morning" - Day Five (v.23)

(v.24) "Then God said....there was evening and there was morning" - Day Six (v.31)

These steps are physical, not spiritual, in nature. We are provided with no indication how these steps between "evening" and "morning" follow the extraordinary event of Genesis 1:2. We can however, infer that the Genesis 1:1-2 event had occurred by Day 3 because it is specifically applied to the Earth. Isaiah 45:18 affirms that the Earth *"was not created in vain"* - it was created to be inhabited. Also, with the introduction of the plant and animal kingdoms in Day 3, death had become a feature of life. The consequences of the "violence" and "weakening of the nations" that accompanied the fall of Satan apply to humankind and were to come into effect after Day 6 when God had completed His six steps of ordering from chaos. By Genesis Chapter Three Satan is seen symbolically as a serpent operating on the Earth in the world prepared for Adam (Chapter 8.9.2). When Adam falls by seeking knowledge of good and evil, Satan has succeeded in becoming the corrupter of humankind. Adam's lordship of the Earth becomes transferred to him and this necessitates the redemptive plan initiated by God in Genesis 3:15.

Hebrew is an economical language and Biblical Hebrew comprises only about 8000 words. Single words can have multiple meanings and root meanings. Thus, the steps between "evening" and "morning" do not have to record literal present days. The Hebrew word for "evening" "twilight", "sunset", is *erev* with the root meaning also including "disorder", "mixture" and "chaos", "approaching darkness", "connoting danger and hence dread". The Hebrew word for "morning" is *boker* also with the root meaning "break of day", "dawn", "approach of day", "orderly", "able to be discerned" and "connoting security and joy". The implication is that six steps transitioning chaos into order are recorded here without specified time frames. *However, it is crucial that "evening" occurs before "morning" in the six statements above - if the order had been reversed the whole chaos to order implication of the Six Days would have been lost.* Evening is also symbolic of disorder because once the Sun has gone down darkness pervades and no order is apparent; when the Sun rises there is light and order can be discerned. As if to reflect this, the Hebrew day continues to begin with the night at 6pm in the evening followed by the dawn at 6am the following morning.

The word *yom* (יום) translated as "day" in Genesis Chapter One can have eight possible meanings according to Wikipedia: (i) a period of light contrasting with a period of darkness, (ii) a general term for time, (iii) a point of time, (iv), sunrise to sunset, (v) sunset to the next sunset, (vi) a year (as used in the plural in 1 Samuel 27:7, Exodus 13:10 etc.), (vii) a time period of unspecified length and (viii) a long, but finite period of time embracing an age, an epoch or a season. Whilst this word is translated to mean a literal 24-hour day in the majority of cases where it occurs in the Septuagint text of the Bible, this assignation is not exclusive and there are important alternative Biblical uses such as "the Day of the Lord" (Zechariah 14:1) which is taken to refer to the time of the Great Tribulation, an era specifically described in the Book of Daniel in Chapter 9 as his 70th week of years, and also in the Book of Revelation. Nevertheless, the use of the Hebrew in Genesis One and all the ancient Jewish commentaries affirm that the six days refer to six literal 24 hour days (Schroeder 1997). We concur with this perceived wisdom in the present analysis, and following Dr Schroeder's explanation, in Chapters 8 and 9 we examine how the Six Days translating chaos into order can preserve this property when the changing space-time frames back to Creation at the Big Bang are considered.

Reference:

Custance, A.C., 1970. *Without Form and Void*, Doorway Papers (Classic Reprint Press, 2008), 292pp.

Langford, J.W., 2011. *The GAP is not a theory*, Xlibris Publications, 252pp.

Schroeder, G.L., 1997. *The Science of God*, Broadway Books, New York, 226pp.

Chapter 8

The Beginnings of Time

8.1 Introduction

This chapter heading deliberately uses the word "beginnings" in the plural because there are two specific times initiated by the Biblical account in Genesis Chapter One. The first is the creation of the Universe, now widely acknowledged to be the Big Bang event; the second starts with the creation of humankind beginning with Adam, the first man created in the image of God with body, soul and spirit, and therefore able to communicate with Him. The name "Adam" relates to the Hebrew noun *"ha adamah"* meaning "the ground" or "earth" and the verses concerning Adam (Genesis 1:26-27) are the first to use both the words "made" and "created". The word "image" does not imply a physical likeness because we are told that God is spirit; the second person of the Trinity only adopted a physical form as the Lord Jesus Christ in order to redeem humankind from its fallen nature. It is the soul and spirit which sets this unique creation apart from the remainder of life as indicated in Genesis 2:7 which reads: *"the LORD God formed man of the dust of the ground, and breathed into his nostrils the breath (neshama) of life; and man (Adam) became a living soul"*. This gift added to his soul - his consciousness - a spirit to enable him to become aware of his Creator and is the first mention of the word "soul" in the Bible. The soul is usually taken to refer to the mental ability and perception of a living and breathing being. In this sense the properties of a soul were not exclusive to Adam because the animal kingdom was created able to respond to its surroundings. However, in his case the original Hebrew has an additional letter reading: *"Adam became to (ל) a living soul"*. Yod ,ל, is the tenth letter of the Hebrew alphabet symbolic of ordinal perfection, and it is also the first letter in the

Hebrew name of God. It is the tenth and last "and God said" command in Genesis 1:28 in which dominion of the Earth is given to humankind. The implication is that Adam was God's final creative deed and elevated him with an additional property that the earlier living creation did not possess.

The Hebrew gematria of the name "Adam", אָדָם is **45**. This is the same as the number of chromosomes that the male and the female have in common. The name *ah-dahm* is made up of two parts: the letter א *Aleph*, the first letter of the Hebrew alphabet with the value of one. Like all Jewish letters it is derived from a picture, in this case an ox's head, and it has the meaning of "first", "strength" and "leader"; it always has the symbolic meaning of God (Chapter 2), who provides the spiritual soul. The remaining two letters spell דם - *dahm* (gematria value of **44**) meaning "blood". The Book of Leviticus (17:11) notes: ***"the life of the flesh is in the blood"*** and the words for father, *av*, and mother, *em*, have a combined gematria value of **44**; added to the number one for *aleph*, this completes the gematria of **45**. The Hebrew gematria of Adam's name combines the word for "blood" with the first letter of the alphabet symbolic of the one Almighty God in whose three-fold likeness he was created. A mysterious property of the Biblical Hebrew Name assignments is recognized when the names of Biblical characters are written in reverse and an aspect of their character is revealed (Shore 2007). Thus, Laban who cheated on Jacob becomes *naval*, or "villain", Moses, who was promised that he would be a prophet like God (Deuteronomy 18:15), becomes *Hashem*, or one of the names of God, and Noah, the Patriarch who was saved, becomes *chen* meaning "grace" or "favour". When the Hebrew word for "Adam", אָדָם, is written in reverse the three letters read "*mah-ohd*", מאד, the word for "more", again implying that Adam was elevated above the rest of living creation. This is further implied by the Hebrew for "in His own image", *Betzelem Elohim,* which carries the sense of the ability to talk. The unique Divine creative aspect of the Hebrew word for "image" applied to Adam is seen in the gematria: this is *Beth* (2)-*Tsaddi* (90)-*Lamed* (30)-*Mem* (40) = 162 or 100 x **Phi** - the golden proportion and the widespread signature of God's Creation as explored in Chapter 5.

The episode described in the Garden of Eden is symbolic of the rebellion of humankind, rejecting God's perfect provision and aiming to be like Him, a god or *elohim*. This was the temptation of Satan in the guise of the serpent (Genesis 3.5), and is repeated again in the later post-Flood episode of the Tower of Babel where they declare *"build **us** a city" and "make **us** a name"* Genesis 11:4). The word for "us" in Hebrew (לנו), has a gematria of 39, the same as the word "elohim" and it becomes a signature of rebellion. In Genesis 11:5-9, the Hebrew records that it was YHWH and not Elohim who came down to Babel (Babylon), confounded the languages and scattered the people (see section 8.12 of this Chapter). As discussed in Chapter 2.3, "**Elohim**" is used to refer to God in His capacity as creator and ruler of the Universe, whereas "**Yahweh**" **is** the personal name by which He introduced himself to Moses **(Exodus 3:13-15)** and where He desires to be in relationship with humanity.

8.2 Interpreting the Six Days

The Book of Genesis distinguishes two sets of generations, the first applying to the Heavens and the Earth, and the second to the generations from Adam:

These are the ***generations*** of the ***heavens and of the earth*** when they were created, in the day that the LORD God ***made the earth and the heavens*** (Genesis 2:4).

This is the book of the ***generations of Adam. In the day that God created man,*** in the likeness of God made he him (Genesis 5:1).

The Hebrew word to create from nothing is ***bara*** and is used only five times and three contexts in the narrative of the Six Days: firstly the initial creation of ***matter***, secondly the creation of ***life -*** fish and fowl in Genesis 1:21, and thirdly the spiritual nature of ***man*** in Genesis 1:27. Both the phrases above are however, used in the context of days where their usage implies that they refer to the literal present 24 hour days of the time frame that we have experienced since Adam was created (Chapter 7 and Schroeder 1997). There appears to be no case for regarding these days as epochs, or even intervals of "a thousand years" (2 Peter 3:8) where these latter days are actually "with the Lord" and not with us. The interpretation of the Six Days of Genesis applied here is accordingly constrained to this 24-hour day view - we need to explain why the history of the Earth and Universe can appear as 6 present days in one time frame and ~13.9 billion years in another time frame.

8.3 The Significance of Dimensionality

Our universe does not just comprise the three physical dimensions of space. One of the great achievements of the Laws of Relativity was to show that time is a physical dimension. We are constrained to a four dimensional framework comprising the three dimensions of space and one of time. However, the fields of particle and theoretical physics have now formalized a *string theory* in which the point particles of particle physics are replaced by dimensional objects called "strings" and a theory has developed telling us that at least 10 dimensions are possible. The brilliant Jewish sage Moses ben Nachman (Nachmanides) of Genoa born in 1194, had already inferred that our Universe has ten dimensions from analysis of the Hebrew of Genesis Chapter One, including the four which we know and six which are beyond our ability to know. Two passages in the Scriptures tell us that space can be "rolled up" (Isaiah 34:4 and Revelation 6:14) - since there must be additional space for the four dimensions of space-time to roll up into, more than our four dimensions are implied in verses such as these.

There are multiple examples in the Bible narrative implying dimensions that are beyond our appreciation. Spiritual beings appear and disappear from the reality of the observer a number of times in the Old Testament. Some, such as the appearance of the "I Am" at the burning bush (Exodus 3:2), the warrior to Joshua (Joshua 5:13) and the fourth man in the furnace with Shadrach, Meshach and Abednego (Daniel 3:24) are usually interpreted by Bible commentators as *theophonies* - pre-incarnate appearances of the Lord Jesus Christ. In Luke Chapter 16 Jesus explains that *Sheol* (or *Hades* in Greek), the holding place of the souls of the dead, is divided into two parts, evidently different dimensions, visible to each other but impossible to move between. In the concluding passages of each of the gospels we find that Jesus in His resurrection body was able to move into and out of the Apostle's dimension at will *"in another form"* (Mark 16:12). The Bible has no conflict with the existence of dimensions beyond the four that our world is confined to.

8.4 Understanding Energy and Radiation: a few essential Principles

It was James Clark Maxwell (1831-1871) who first drew together the separate equations for electricity and magnetism into a unified theory in 1865 to demonstrate that they comprise a symmetrical wave with a velocity equal to the measured velocity of light. He was able to conclude that light was an electromagnetic (EM) radiation. However the light that our eyes are sensitive to is just a small spectrum of waves within an infinite range of EM frequencies comprising synchronized oscillations of electric and magnetic fields. All these waves move through space with a constant velocity denoted by c equal to 299.8 kilometers per second. The energy carried by the waves is a function of the frequency - high frequencies are high energy, low frequencies are low energy; alternatively we can state this as energy is inversely proportional to the wavelength. Whilst we classically understand electromagnetism as waves, quantum physics tells us that paradoxically waves can also behave as particles and their energy is actually released as discrete units or *quanta*. These quanta are described as elementary particles called "photons". They carry the force of the radiation at the velocity of light (c) with an energy given by the simple equation $E = h\nu$ where E is the energy of the photon, ν is the frequency and h is a constant known as Plank's Constant. Photons only have a finite mass when they are in motion and their energy is then given by Einstein's equation $E = mc^2$: c is the speed of light in a vacuum; it is normally considered that nothing can travel faster than c although as we note in Chapter 6.8, this need not always apply.

The properties of space and time, and how we view events within our dimensions of space and time, were articulated by Albert Einstein

(1879-1955) as Special Relativity (first published in 1905) and General Relativity (1915). Both have been confirmed by multiple experiments. Special Relativity describes how observers are influenced by movement at constant velocity, whilst General Relativity focuses on observers who are experiencing acceleration. In Special Relativity all the laws of physics are the same in all inertial frames. Space and time are a unified system of four dimensions and events considered simultaneous by one observer will not be simultaneous to another observer moving relative to the first. In Special Relativity only flat space-time is dealt with and, combined with the laws of physics, it anticipates that mass and energy are equal according to the famous equation $E=mc^2$. The General Theory of Relativity incorporates the effect of gravity: as observation frames move farther apart or closer together there is a change in the attraction between them. The added effect of gravity causes mass and energy to distort or warp space-time; it is illustrated where we observe light being bent around massive objects. Basically Special Relativity is simple but breaks down when applied to the large volumes of space whereas General Relativity can be applied to large spaces like the Universe; it is comprehensive but complex.

8.5 The Start of Cosmic Time - The Big Bang

The prevailing view that Creation began at a point in time, now referred to as the "Big Bang", is another example where the Biblical narrative was ahead of scientific understanding. Prior to the observation that the galaxies were drifting apart at an accelerating rate, the prevailing secular view extending back at least as far as the Greek philosophers Aristotle and Plato, was that time was uniform and eternal. The same theme is held by Eastern religions. The equivalent modern concept, the Steady State Theory, did not survive scientific scrutiny beyond the early 1960's. Edwin Hubble (1889-1953) observed that all the galaxies we see are shifted slightly towards reddish in color due to the Doppler Effect called the "redshift". He reported in 1929 that the galaxies and clusters of galaxies are flying apart from each other at great speed, and that the universe is growing in size: the farther away a galaxy is, the faster it is receding. This relationship, known as Hubble's Law, has since been repeatedly verified and implies that the Universe had a finite origin - the Big Bang. Evidence supporting this concept, both theoretical and experimental, continued to accumulate through the twentieth century and has notably included the discovery of a microwave echo of the Big Bang event at the edge of space. More recent accurate measurements of the redshifts of supernovae have also confirmed that the expansion of the universe is accelerating. This acceleration is most commonly attributed to the repulsive effect of dark matter and dark energy (Chapters 4.2 and 5.9). These are inaccessible to us and cannot be directly detected, although dark matter may make up ~95% of all the matter, and dark energy 68% of the total energy in the observable Universe. We are limited to only directly observing the remainder although there are a number of indirect methods for exploring dark matter and energy; these can be investigated on Wikipedia.

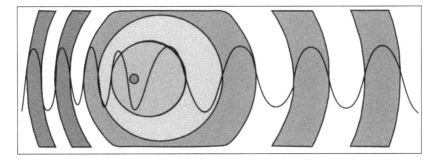

Figure 8.1: The Doppler Effect

God's act of Creation was awesome - totally beyond our comprehension. Time as we understand it is viewed as beginning at a *singularity*, a point of infinite mass and temperature. At this point General Relativity is unable to explain the Laws of Physics and cannot operate before a point ending the so-called *Plank Era* at ~10^{-43} seconds. Before this, time as we understand it has no meaning. Between ~10^{-43} and 10^{-36} seconds the force of gravity began to operate and the first elementary particles were created. Rapid expansion *("cosmic inflation")* followed so that by ~10^{-12} seconds the next (strong nuclear) force could separate from the remaining two forces (electromagnetism and gravity) and interactions could occur to create large numbers of particles. As the Universe grew exponentially, gravity produced density variations which initiated "ripples" to produce the large-scale and highly inhomogeneous universe that we see today. Before matter as we know it, there was an extremely brief time when only quarks were present; this is the "quark confinement". Quarks are subatomic particles - the fundamental constituents of matter. They combine to form protons and neutrons, the nucleus of the atom; they have never been directly observed but theoretical predictions based on their existence have been confirmed experimentally. Then the pure energy of Creation would go on to transform the quark medium into the matter which now makes up at least 100 billion galaxies in the Universe.

Thus beginning at $\sim 10^{-12}$ seconds the four fundamental forces (see Chapter 4.2) assumed their present form; inflation paused and a reheating occurred which enabled the universe to reach a temperature required for the production of a quark–gluon plasma (an ionized gas consisting of positive ions and free electrons), as well as all the other elementary particles. At this point the temperature would have been enormously high, about 5.5 trillion degrees Celsius. The unstable plasma was impossible to contain and decayed radioactively to produce massive amounts of radiation. This *Quark Era* is reckoned to have lasted for just a few microseconds ($\sim 10^{-12}$-10^{-6}), after which the Universe would have cooled to a trillion degrees Celsius and allowed quarks and gluons to combine and form protons and neutrons, the building blocks of matter. Then after a few minutes the temperature would have fallen to a billion degrees and allowed atomic nuclei to begin to form hydrogen; nucleosynthesis could follow and produce the first simple atomic nuclei such as helium and lithium.

The issues surrounding the Big Bang continue to challenge the greatest brains in the field of cosmology. The most important is the subject of entropy. The earliest stage would be a chaotic sea of particles, including matter, antimatter, gluons, neutrinos and photons - namely one of disorder (high entropy). This was transformed into one of very low entropy as particles organized into atoms. Since then the Arrow of Time has been taking the Universe into progressively higher entropy as energy and matter are dispersed. The Biblical explanation of the sequence: high entropy - low entropy - high entropy, which confounds rational discussion, is explained by Genesis Chapter One in terms of God stepping into His creation in Six steps (Days) to convert chaos into order. Here we have verse 3-5 description of Day 1 (Chapter 9.1). According to the famous calculation of Sir Roger Penrose the initial high entropy state at the Big Bang would have been tuned to a fine order of 10^{10} and then to a hyperpower of 123 to produce our Universe (https://evolutionnews. org/2010/04/roger_penrose_on_cosmic_finetu/). This unimaginably vast number is enormously greater than all the particles in the Universe.

After about 300,000 years radiation is reckoned to have decoupled from matter as the temperature fell to around 3,000 degrees. The ionized hydrogen and helium atoms could then capture electrons to bind them into atoms and neutralise their electric charge. Only at this point would the universe have become transparent with light passing through space largely unimpeded. This is Genesis 1:3: ***"let there be light"***. The signature of radiation is the *Cosmic Background Radiation* (CBR) discovered by Arno Penzias and Robert Wilson in 1964. This is the earliest possible epoch that we can observe today and provides us with a visible vestigial signature of the Big Bang event. Enormous energy, which began as intensely high frequency radiation at unimaginably high temperatures (estimated to be $\sim 10^{34}$ °C), has by now dispersed to very long frequency, very low energy, waves that can only be detected as a faint signature by radio telescopes. At the same time the temperature of space has collapsed and is now just 2.35°C above absolute zero (-273°C). The latter is the temperature at which there will be no energy left and all motion right down to the atomic level will cease. Although the CBR has a remarkably uniform temperature it is not absolutely uniform (Figure 8.2) and satellite studies show that there are tiny differences of the order of one part in 100,000. The differences record concentrations of material that have moved together by gravity to form galaxies and stars. Because of the time it takes the light to reach us we are seeing the CBR signature as it was ~13.9 billion years ago. It is by now reckoned to have moved more than 46 billion light years away far beyond what we can see. Similarly, we are viewing galaxies as they were long ago and they may by now have drifted far beyond our ability to see or (because of the time needed for a signal to get to us) even to detect.

No stars would have been formed by the time of the CBR event. The Universe would have been literally dark until the first quasars started to form between ~150 and 1000 million years after the Big Bang. Their intense radiation would then ionize clouds of cosmic gas which would, in turn, start to collapse under their own gravity, trigger nuclear fusion reactions between hydrogen atoms, and create the very first stars. These are predicted to have gradually clustered into galaxies from 300-500 billion years onwards with denser parts of the Universe moving to form stars, galaxies and quasars. After about a billion years galaxy clusters and superclusters would have been established.

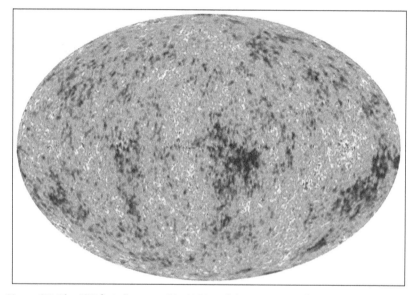

Figure 8.2: The CBR first discovered in 1964 and shown on a Mollweide map projection of the whole sky. This map has been compiled from years of radio telescope data. Small temperature variations are shown between colder (blue) and hotter (red) colours. (Wikipedia and Google images).

As we view space today we see the Universe composed of massive super clusters of galaxies with vast voids in between. Where the gravitational forces are weak, the relict clouds of hydrogen gas formed just a few minutes after the Big Bang comprise the primordial gas clouds. The nature of the forces controlling these processes is bound up with the mysterious concept of the influence of dark matter. The

Universe is now expanding outwards everywhere with the expansion accelerating as it inflates. Isaiah 42:5 refers to God as *"He who created the heavens and stretched them out"*, whilst other passages from the books of Isaiah and Job also refer to "the stretcher of the heavens" and imply this ongoing expansion. Also, the Hebrew of Genesis Chapter One indicates that "darkness" is not simply the absence of "light" (Schroeder 1990); instead it is also something created. This is implied by the Book of Isaiah 45:7 where we read *"I form the light, and <u>create</u> darkness"*, a likely allusion to dark matter.

The future of the Universe is usually seen in terms of a continuing and accelerating expansion accompanying a fall in temperature to absolute zero after ~10^{-14} years. The universe then enters "heat death" or the "big chill" when thermal equilibrium has been reached. This is the point of infinite entropy when there will then be no useable energy left and all motion right down to the atomic level will cease. The Universe will then be a near vacuum and all that remains will be dispersed burnt-out stars, cold dead planets and black holes. As noted above, temperature has already declined close to absolute zero. When this point is reached the order that God created from chaos, as described in Genesis Chapter One, will have collapsed back into a state of infinite entropy and zero order.

8.6 The Time of the Big Bang

Determining when the Creation began with the Big Bang starts with the determination of the Hubble Constant. This is used to determine the present rate at which the Universe is currently expanding and is given by the recessional velocity, $v = H_0D$, where H_0 is the Hubble constant and D is the distance to the galaxy under observation. H_0 is presently estimated to be about 72 km/sec/million light years. It is not actually a constant because the expansion of the Universe is accelerating. To determine when the Big Bang occurred we have to model how we think H has changed with time and then integrate this change over the history of the Universe. The most reliable "clock" employs the Doppler Effect causing the red shift plus the basic theory derived from the physical model outlined in the previous section. Although there are some variations in the estimates of the constants used in these calculations, they all yield an age for the Big Bang of about 13.9 billion years (Byr); although with an estimated uncertainty of only about 120 million years, values as low as 13.7 Byr are still quoted in the literature. A general uncertainty surrounding these figures is that they are confined to our observable Universe; we do not know how much universe, if any, lies outside of this.

A second method for determining the time of the Big Bang comes from analysis of the warmer and cooler spots in the cosmic microwave background. Sound waves from the Big Bang left an imprint on the microwave radiation in the form of slightly warmer and cooler spots (Figure 8.2) corresponding to regions where the radiation is being compressed or expanded. The size of these spots is uniform throughout the Universe, and the older the Universe is, the farther apart these spots should be and the smaller they should appear. Analysis of these warmer and cooler spots of background radiation gives the present estimate of 14 ± 0.5 billion years for the age of the Universe.

These estimates are broadly confirmed by the ages of the oldest stars as outlined in Chapter 6.5 and 6.6. When stars reach the end of their lives they become supernovae as the star becomes a white dwarf; the outer layers erupt off this core and fly out into space as a huge explosion. The white dwarf left behind glows at first, and it then cools as it ages and the residual heat is used up. When white dwarves are really cool the time required to reach such low temperatures can be estimated to determine their age. The ages of the oldest white dwarfs emerge with values of around 12.7-13.2 billion years; ages older than this are unknown. When we observe very distant galaxies ~14 billion light-years away we are viewing galaxies which now have a recession speed faster than the speed of light. This arises because light that is emitted today from these galaxies is way beyond our event horizon. We see the light that these galaxies emitted in the past but because of the high rate of expansion, it is possible for the distance between these objects and Earth to be greater than the value calculated by multiplying the speed of light by the age of the Universe.

8.7 Relativity and the variable nature of Time

Relativity is a further concept embedded in the Scriptures. Albert Einstein, who famously said *"I shall never believe God plays dice with the world"* and *"when the question is simple, God is answering"*, acknowledged that his famous formula actually occurred in the text of the Bible. He once told a group of rabbis in New York City that he had done a rabbinical study of רים *ohr*, the Hebrew word for "light" in Genesis 1:3 and צשמיר *maohr*, for "light" in Genesis 1:14, and arrived at his conclusions about relativity. He noted that the two terms are not alike. The light in verse 3 appears to be the Divine source, while the light in verse 14 is of a different order: *Maohr* means "from light" and thus has a source emanating from the *ohr*. Rabbis consider the *ohr* to be the primeval light – the shekinah glory of God. Einstein took the word for light (maohr) and by a complex series of grammatical divisions and substitutions, arrived at the words for mass צש *ma*, light רים ohr, speed צשישר mahar, raised רוצ rum and squared רקנשי rebah. This led the Jewish genius to discover that **E** "energy" could be derived from **M** "mass" multiplied by the **C²** "square of the constant" (the mathematical "constant" assumed to be the speed of light). Albert Einstein discovered his groundbreaking formula using an age-old and proven rabbinical method for interpreting the depths of the Biblical Hebrew. He not only proved that the formula works, but also that the original author of the formula placed it in the opening chapter of the Bible describing His creative acts *(www.prophecyinthenews.j.r.church/ archives)*.

When Einstein published his groundbreaking discovery as his General Theory in 1915 he was able to show that the rate at which time passes varies from place to place: changes in gravity (**G**) and velocity (**V**) of travel change the rate at which time passes. Our experience is not just controlled by the three dimensions of space, but also by the fourth dimension of time. Thus, any event that we experience occurs at a point of space and time. The "proper time" between any two events depends not just on the events themselves, but also on the motion of the clock between them. This relativity of time is not normally apparent to us. It is only observed when we compare our frame with another frame with very different **G** and **V**. An exception is the Global Positioning System (GPS) used for navigation since it uses orbiting satellites that experience significantly less gravity than the Earth's surface; they are also moving very fast and this results in a time distortion of about 38 microseconds a day that has to be repeatedly corrected for.

When General Relativity was first proposed it was necessarily classed as a theory but it has now been tested and verified so many times that it is confidently described as The *Law* of General Relativity. It demonstrates the apparently illogical reality that *energy* in its condensed form is *matter*, and it expands to our understanding from modern physics that radiation such as light can be both a wave and a particle. As we seek to explain the Six Days of Genesis we just need to recognize that we see time from the restriction of our four dimensions as an *Arrow of Time* beginning with the Big Bang. God is infinite and not restricted to our reference frame. The Six Days of Genesis Chapter One as viewed from our dimension are not present days of 24 hours. They are not even of equal time duration. However, the Jewish mathematician and applied theologian Gerald Schroeder has provided an explanation for the enormous difference between the Biblical and Scientific perspectives of time. By acknowledging the implications of General Relativity, he developed this concept in his first book *"Genesis and the Big Bang"* published in 1990 and subsequently reported calculations in his second book *"The Science of God"* published in 1997. These were able to estimate limits to each of the Six Days of Genesis which appeared to correlate well with the ages of critical geological and cosmological events. In the next section of this Chapter we adopt Schroeder's approach to show how the overall time frame of the Six Days correlates with the time since the Big Bang. In the following Chapter 9 we use his analysis of the suggested time intervals occupied by each of the Six Days to evaluate their correlation with the scientific record of Cosmological and Geological history.

8.8 The Biblical Framework of Cosmic Time

All galaxies are moving away from a common centre of the Universe, although we do not know where we are relative to this centre. Because the expansion is accelerating, the galaxies further away are moving faster than those nearer the centre. General Relativity tells us that time is dependent on Gravity (**G**) and Velocity (**V**): the flow of time at a location with high **G** or high **V** is slower than at another location with lower **G** and lower **V**. These differences in the passage of time are known as *time dilation* and this means that there are any number of ages within the universe - each one correct for the location at which the measurement is made. It follows that there are any number of locations where a clock can record ~13.9 billion years since the Big Bang and other places where the same clock would record just 6 days. God is outside of our timeframe. This is reflected in the version of His name *Yehovah* (Jehovah). Although often viewed as a Christian replacement for the Hebrew names of God, Yahweh-Elohim, this word has a solid etymological basis in the Hebrew: it is the composite of three tenses namely *hayah* (He was), *oveh* (He is) and *yehihey* (He will be); together these compose the Divine name to become *yeh* (future) + *ov* (present) + *ah* (past) (Shore 2007). In Genesis Chapter One God appears to be dictating to Moses the creation as He views it before He created Adam: what He sees as six days outside of His creation, we see as billions of years from inside the creation - the issue is one of relativity. To compare Moses' view of time with God's view we need to identify the universal perspective of the Bible's space-time reference frame. The CBR forms the basis for measuring *cosmic proper time* since it dates from that earliest time when plasma converted into fundamental particles to form atoms, the material from which the Universe is built. At this point the material creation would no longer have been able to absorb the radiation and the Universe would effectively have become transparent.

The stretching of space as the universe expands stretches the wavelength of the radiation, and the increase in the wavelength of the radiation slows the perceived passage of time - the waves of radiation propagated into space since the creation have been expanded in the same proportion that the universe has expanded. This is expressed by the Expansion Factor given by the ratio:

<u>Stretched radiation</u>
Unstretched radiation

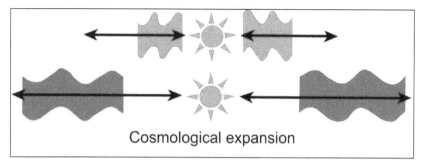

Figure 8.3: Diagrammatic illustration of the stretching of radiation accompanying the cosmic expansion: as a pulse of radiation moves out it lengthens and the wavelength broadens.

The Big Bang produced unimaginably hot radiant energy of such a high level that matter was unable to form from the energy as expressed by Einstein's equation. However, soon after the Big Bang the energy levels (i.e. the ambient temperature) would have fallen below a minimum level allowing energy to change into matter (at the *quark confinement* noted above) ~0.00001 seconds after the Big Bang. The temperature and frequency of the radiation at the quark confinement can be measured here on Earth and yields the estimate, also noted in the section above, of nearly 10^{12} times hotter than the current -268°C temperature of space. Also, the corresponding radiant energy at the time of the Big Bang had a frequency ~10^{12} times greater than the radiation of today's observed CBR. The Universe was then about 900 thousand million (900,000, 000,000) times smaller and hotter than it is today. This means that the radiation from the moment of quark confinement has been stretched close to ~10^{12} times. The corresponding stretching of the light waves has slowed the frequency of the Cosmic Clock (i.e. expanded the perceived time between ticks of the clock) by a factor of 10^{12}.

On Earth we measure the age of the universe looking backwards in time with the Big Bang currently reckoned to have occurred approximately 13.9 billion (thousand million) years ago from our perspective. However, the Bible adopts this earthly perspective only from the time of Adam. God describes the history of the Universe differently because He was then the only observer. He is looking forward in time from the Creation in Cosmic Time which, as observed today, ticks approaching 10^{12} times more slowly than at the Big Bang, and this stretching of the radiation has caused our perception of time to change in proportion. The ~13.9 Billion years since the Big Bang are then equivalent in days as shown in Figure 8.4:

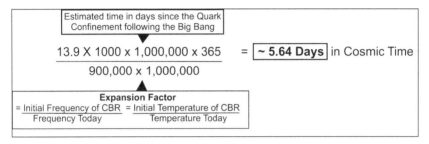

Figure 8.4: Calculating the equivalence of Cosmic and Earth Time.

Bearing in mind that the figures used here include approximate present-day estimates and that the expansion of the Universe is imperfectly understood, the close approximation of this figure to the 6 days recorded in Genesis Chapter One is impressive. It shows that the billions of years since the Big Bang as seen from our perspective when time is now ticking much more slowly, are equivalent to just a few days outside of our constraint. Schroeder (see web addresses below) has repeated this calculation in reverse assuming that Adam was created half way through Day 6 (instead of the last act of God's creation terminating this Day) to derive a close estimate of the Big Bang event of ~14 billion years. These calculations are constrained by the time of the Big Bang, the threshold temperature at which matter (comprising protons and neutrons) formed, the present background temperature of the Universe, and the number of days that the Earth takes to orbit the Sun. If any of these items had been substantially different, the number of days would be in conflict with the number of days given in Genesis - this is another example of fine tuning endorsing the Biblical record. The possible epochs embracing each of the Six Days will be evaluated in the next chapter.

8.9 The Biblical Timeframe of Humankind

8.9.1 The Birth and Ministry of the Lord Jesus Christ

BC/AD (Before Christ/anno Domini) is the universally-recognized pivotal point of historical time. Although always used to number years on the Julian and Gregorian calendars, this point was not fixed until A.D. 525. Whilst the Bible specifically tells us to commemorate the death and resurrection of the Lord Jesus Christ, we are never told the year in which He was born. The records of the Church Fathers are probably the most consistent extra-Biblical indication of the year of birth. Ireneus (~130-202 AD) who was trained by a student of the Apostle John, records it in the "41st year of Augustus' reign"; Augustus was adopted by Julius Caesar as his successor in 44 BC and began his reign in the Autumn of 43 BC, placing Jesus' birth in 2 BC. Tertullian (160-220 AD), a near-contemporary of Ireneaus, records that Augustus began his reign 41 years before the birth of Jesus and died 15 years after His birth, again placing this event in 2 BC (there was no year zero); he also notes that Jesus was born 28 years after the death of Cleopatra in 30 BC, further supporting the case for the birth in 2 BC. Eusebius (263-339 AD) records that Jesus was born during the 42nd year of the reign of Augustus and 28 years from the subjection of Egypt following the death of Anthony and Cleopatra in 30 BC; the 42nd year of Augustus' reign ran from the Autumn of 2 BC to the Autumn of 1 BC. The subjection of Egypt into the Roman Empire began in the Autumn of 30 BC.; this again places Jesus' birth in 2 BC.

The gospels make it clear that Jesus was born five months after John the Baptist whose conception and subsequent birth on, or about, the Festival of Passover can be dated from the position of his father Zacharias within the 24 courses of priests serving the Temple. When the Temple was destroyed by Titus in 70 AD, the first course of priests had just taken office. Since the course of Zacharias was the eighth course we can track backwards to determine that he would have ended his course on July 13th 3 BC; this dates his encounter with the Angel Gabriel. If the birth of John took place 280 days later, it would have been on April 19-20th, precisely at Passover to fulfill the prophecy of Elijah that his successor would appear on the Festival of Passover.

"Festival" in the Hebrew is literally *moedem* and correctly means "fixed appointment". The assignment of John's name ("God is gracious") ran against the family tradition and came with great promise as a herald of a Messianic age of deliverance (Luke 1:14-17).

Zacharias' wife Elisabeth had previously hid herself for five months when the Angel Gabriel announced to Mary both Elisabeth's condition, and that she would bear a son whose would be named "Jesus". Mary is recorded as going "with haste" to Elisabeth who was then in the first week of her sixth month (Luke 1:39), or the fourth week of December, 3 BC. If Jesus was born 280 days later this would place His birth on 28th of September of 2 BC which was also the beginning of the (7th) holiest month of *Tishrei*. The first two days of Tishrei are "Trumpets"; this is the fifth Appointed time (*Teshuvah*, "The Return", where five is the Biblical number of grace and redemption); the "Final Trump" is sounded on this day as one long blast on the horn, the *shofar*, following a month of daily soundings. A birth at the beginning of Tishrei would also imply His conception by the Holy Spirit in Mary nine months before on the 8th appointed time, the *"Festival of Lights"* (Hanukah) - eight being the number associated with Jesus' name and ministry (Chapter 2:3 and *2.3.1*), and Him being "the Light of the World" (John 8:12).

Tishrei is followed eight days later by the 6th Appointed time of the Day of Atonement, *Yom Kippur*. Since the eighth day after birth is the optimum time for circumcising a child, following Biblical tradition in would have been on this appointed day that Jesus was circumcised. Since the theme of this time is judgement and atoning for sin, it would signify Jesus alignment with humanity and the ultimate perfect atonement that His Crucifixion would achieve. The Gospel of John notes that He "tabernacled amongst us" (John 1:14). The *Festival of Tabernacles*, the *"Season of Our Joy"*, is the seventh and last of the seven Levitical festivals lasting for seven days and likely embracing days 15-21 of Jesus' life. It is immediately followed by the 22nd day, *"the Great Conclusion"* (*Hoshana rabbah*) defining the end of one religious year and the beginning of a new one.

Mary's purification would have been completed forty days after the birth according to Jewish custom and the family returned from Bethlehem to Nazareth (Luke 2:29). Only sometime later did the Magi from Persia arrive. They would have been familiar with the Messianic timeline from the prophecy of Daniel who in his time was one of their number, knowing that the birth had to be about 30 years before His ministry; they were also likely guided by the star sign prophecy given to a gentile prophet, Balak (Book of Numbers 24:17, Matthew 2:7). Immediately after this visitation the family left for Egypt following an angelic warning to Joseph (Matthew 2:13) before Herod began murdering the children of two years old and under. This timeline would probably link the death of Herod the Great to the eclipse recorded by the historian Josephus on January 9th in 1 BC, and not the more commonly quoted eclipse in 4 BC, with his painful death, also described by Josephus, as likely due to God's judgement for his slaughter of the innocents.*

The theme of the Great Conclusion is purification and the first miracle of Jesus' subsequent ministry is recorded near this day (John 2:6). Jesus began his ministry at the required Rabbinic age of "about 30" (Luke 3:23) in the 15th year of the Emperor Tiberius who commenced his reign in 14 AD. This would imply a ministry starting in the Autumn of AD 28 at the beginning of the new religious year. The timeline is consistent with the completion of His earthly ministry three and a half years later in the Spring appointed times of Passover to First Fruits (barley harvest), and then the fourth time of Pentecost (wheat harvest)

---

* *The information on the birth of Jesus documented here comes mainly from Koinonia House Ministries and is reported in some detail to clarify an issue about which there has been considerable confusion. The Roman General Pompey conquered Jerusalem in 63 BC and the historian Josephus records that Herod's reign began 27 years later in 36 BC. His reign is recorded as lasting for 34 years and although we do not know how long he lasted after completing this year, he died in his 70th year compatible with the lunar eclipse recorded by Josephus. The popular correlation with the eclipse in 4 BC is evidently untenable.*

in April of AD 32. This is the precise date implied by the 69 "weeks of years" prophecy given to Daniel in 536 BC (Johnson 2010). This prophetic timeline commenced with Nehemiah's rebuilding of the walls of Jerusalem and terminated with the ***"cutting off of Messiah but not for himself"*** (Daniel 9:25).

Every step in the unfolding of God's plan for humankind's redemption through the work of the Lord Jesus Christ has so far been precisely constrained to the timeline of the first four of the seven Levitical appointed times. The full unfolding of the implications of the last three Autumn (fruit gathering) times, *Trumpets*, *Atonement* and *Tabernacles; Hebrew names.... Rosh Hashanah, Yom Kippur and Succoth*) still awaits fulfilment. We anticipate that they will be the defining events of future history. They are usually attributed by Bible Scholars to the 70th Week of Years in Daniel's Prophecy (Daniel 9:24) ***"to finish the transgressions and make an end to sin"***, effectively seeing God winding up the present age. However, since the Jewish Lunar Calendar has been repeatedly adjusted to align it with the more common Solar Calendar, the actual times of the year when they will occur remain unknown.[*]

The 2 BC date for the birth of Jesus highlights a former insecurity in fixing the BC/AD boundary. The often-quoted calculation of the Biblical year of creation at 4004 BC also has an uncertainty of an unknown number of years. However, beginning with the creation of Adam in Genesis 1:27, there is no major dispute between Biblical scholars that a timeline of about 6000 years is present in the Old Testament generational record to bring us up to the present day. The

---

[*] *The 32 AD date for the death and resurrection of the Lord Jesus Christ used here is based on the calculations of Missler (1999) and Johnson (2010) from the initiation of the prophecy in Daniel 9. Some writings stagger the chronology by one year with a birth in 1 BC and the death by crucifixion in 33 AD. This may be due to adding a year for the year zero, although Phlegon of Trallesa, a Greek historian who wrote a 16 volume history called "Olympiads between 117-138 AD" records the dramatic events of the Crucifixion afternoon (Midday to 3pm) as follows:* **"In the fourth year of the 202nd Olympiad (33 AD), a failure of the Sun took place greater than any previously known, and night came on at the sixth hour of the day (noon), so that stars actually appeared in the sky; and a great earthquake took place in Bithynia and overthrew the greater part of Niceaea."**

Bible contains genealogies describing the descendants of Adam to the Jewish patriarchs through to the last kings of Israel and Judah, and then to events recorded in the histories of the Neo-Babylonian and Persian empires. Acknowledging that Adam was the first creation of God made in his three-fold likeness (Genesis 1:26-27) with body, soul *and spirit,* and therefore able to communicate with Him, is the Biblical basis for assigning Adam's creation to the origin of humanity.[*]

The first chapter of the Gospel of Matthew provides a chronology extending through the kings of ancient Israel and then Judah forwards in time from Abraham to Joseph the stepfather of the Lord Jesus Christ. This is a 14+14+13 person cycle with the implication being that the last and unstated 14th father would be God Himself. Matthew's gospel was written primarily for the Jewish people, noting the fulfillment of Old Testament prophecies and concerned with proving that Jesus is the legitimate Messiah of Israel. Matthew's genealogy is the Royal Line but could not be the true blood line because Jeconiah, the last king of Judah was the recipient of a curse that precluded this (Jeremiah 22:28–30); Joseph could therefore never be His natural father.

Luke was a physician of Greek-Syrian parentage and possibly entirely gentile. The third chapter of his gospel provides another genealogy, this time extending all the way back to Adam. Luke was concerned with Jesus' humanity to show that He was the perfect "Son of Man" and the only person qualified to correct the fall of Adam (Book of Romans 5:12) and become humankind's redeemer (Isaiah 53: 4-5). He avoids

---

[*] *The current Jewish calendar is ~240 years shorter than the popular Biblical calendar described here. When too many Jews were understanding that Daniel Chapter 9 accurately predicted the time of Messiah's death to be April 14th 32 AD, Second Century rabbis removed most of these years from their calendar in order to cause the 70 weeks prophecy of the book of Daniel Chapter 9 to line up with Rabbi Akiva's declaration that Bar Kokhba who revolted against Rome 132-135 AD, and not the Lord Jesus Christ, was the promised "star" out of Jacob. Rabbi Yosi changed the calendar to make Daniel's date embrace the interval from the destruction of the first to the destruction of the second Temple. He taught that the emperors Cyrus, Darius and Xerxes were titles of the same person to condense Persian rule from 210 years to only 24 years. As a consequence of these changes our year 2000 AD (~6004 on the Ussher-Lightfoot Calendar) was the Jewish calendar year 5760.*

the curse on Jeconiah by passing the line of succession through Nathan, the second surviving son of David and Bathsheba. This genealogy ends with Heli the father of Mary. It fulfils the prophecy given by God in Genesis 3:15 implying a virgin birth but including the contradictory statement "the seed of the woman". Since the seed is always in the man, only by Divine intervention could Mary conceive Jesus - the Virgin Birth is the most crucial truth central to Christian doctrine. Both Matthew and Luke would have obtained their genealogies from the Jewish familial records kept in the Temple in Jerusalem. After this was destroyed in 70 AD, no further records of this kind would have been possible.

The genealogies of Matthew and Luke both show that Jesus was descended from the line of Jacob's son Judah, the fourth son of Leah. She was the first wife of Jacob, and was at last able to stop grieving for her unloved condition and attribute "praise" for name of Judah (Genesis 29:35). On his deathbed Jacob prophesied over each of his 12 sons. He assigned the attributes of a lion to Judah and declared that his tribe would carry the sceptre of ruler ship over his people "until Shiloh shall come" (Genesis 49:10); the words "Shiloh shall come" have a gematria value of 358, exactly the same as "**Mashiach**" or Messiah. This was recognised as a Messianic prophecy by the priesthood. From the time of King David until the reign of the Herods a prince of Judah was always head over Israel (including Daniel in captivity). Even under foreign masters a measure of self-rule was retained until 7 AD; at this point, chaos resulting from the ineffectual rule of the sons of Herod the Great caused the Romans to take away the right to capital punishment. When this occurred the rabbis considered it to be a disaster of unfulfilled Scripture: the last vestige of the scepter had been removed from Judah and they had not yet seen the Messiah. Reportedly, the priesthood walked the streets of Jerusalem in sackcloth and ashes wailing "Woe unto us, for the scepter has been taken away from Judah, and Shiloh has not come." *(https://enduringword.com/bible-commentary/genesis-49/)*. They were not to know that the Messiah had already come and was now a youth dwelling up in the Galilee, although suffering condemnation for His supposed illegitimacy; this slur was vividly prophesied in Psalm 69 and repeated later during His ministry (John

8:33-39). The important implication of the removal of this last expression of self government was that the crucifixion of Jesus would now have to be the responsibility of both Jews and Gentiles (and ultimately of course, ourselves as fallen descendents of Adam). The condemnation of Jews as "Christ killers" by the Medieval Church would become a vile expression of anti-Semitism.

8.9.2 *Adam to the Present Day*

The best-known chronologies derived from the Old Testament record were made by John Lightfoot and James Ussher in the 17th century. The two assessments were close and yielded an adjusted age concluding that all creation took place in 4004 BC. Ussher first used the interval from the Creation of Adam to Noah (10 generations) and then from Noah's son Shem to Abram (also 10 generations) using the chronological data in Genesis 5 and 11. Abram was a unique man of faith and followed God's instruction to migrate from Ur of the Chaldees to the future Promised Land; here God expanded his name to "Abraham" by inserting the 5th letter of the Hebrew alphabet symbolic of grace. These two ten-fold generational cycles are separated by the Flood at ~2345 BC. The next step in the Ussher-Lightfoot chronology covers Abraham's migration to the Exodus including 30 years after he left Haran, and then 400 years up to the departure of the Hebrews from Egypt as recorded in the Book of Exodus. Thirdly, an interval of 480 years from the Exodus to the beginning of Solomon's temple in the fourth year of Solomon's reign is noted in 1 Kings 6. Collectively these 910 years span the interval from 1922 BC to 1012 BC. The fourth interval is the most difficult to calculate precisely due to difficulties in correlating the reigns of the kings of Judah and Israel, but Ussher was able to conclude this lineage using secular sources including the death of Nebuchadnezzar and the emperors of Persia. The Bible only records the age of each ruler in years. It does not include months and days so these estimates all have uncertainties of a few decades.

The Bible never recognizes grandfathers, only fathers, and it has sometimes been argued that generations are missed out from the Genesis account making the chronology derived from the listed ages of the patriarchs too short. The reader will find a number of internet sites investigating this possibility and the subject is analyzed in detail by Sexton (2018) who endorses the orthodox interpretation from Adam. In contrast, the Biblical scholar Victor Pearce (1993), who is also an anthropologist, has sought to place the creation of Adam as far back as ~10,000 BC in order to embrace the archaeological record from the first known farmers and town builders recorded in the Middle East. These could then all be regarded as descendents of Adam. However, this would require that there are major undocumented gaps in the genealogical record of Genesis and imply inaccuracy in the genealogy of the Gospel of Luke. There are a few places in Scripture where generations seem to have been deliberately excluded (Exodus 6:14-17, I Chronicles 26:24) and there are possible causes for disputes concerning the characters and their durations between Noah and Abraham. However the only case for significant changes of the order of multiple decades to the Ussher-Lightfoot chronology from Adam lies within the record of the Patriarchs predating Noah. Four arguments seem to argue against this possibility: (i) the New Testament apostle Jude, evidently with access to ancient documentation, tells us that Enoch was the seventh Patriarch from Adam, (ii) Enoch prophetically gave his son the name Methuselah meaning "When he dies it shall be sent" endorsing the ten generations including Noah, (iii) testaments of these Patriarchs are present in the records conserved by the Essenes in the Qumran archives and were likely preserved by Noah (Johnson 2017), and (iv) the ten father-son genealogies up to Noah in the Book of Genesis also hold a specific Divine message and a date for the Flood which can be substantiated by a range of independent evidence as described in Chapter *10.2.3*

Few scholars of the Biblical record would dispute the general scale of the Ussher-Lightfoot Calendar from the creation of Adam. The conflict arises by simply adding six days to derive the total interval of the Creation. However, such an immediate origin for mankind in the Garden of Eden poses an additional problem for Young Earth Creationism because Earth would have had to appear old when it is actually new - an apparent but nonexistent history (Whitcomb and Morris 1961). Plants and animals were already in a fully-grown state to serve as a food source; the plants would have to be created to appear fully germinated with the soil full of nutrients, a process that normally takes many years. The record of archaeology and anthropology is that multiple generations of humanoids, hunter-gatherers before becoming agrarians, preceded the time of Adam. Indeed, these would have overlapped with Neanderthals and Co-Magons, and the truth of the Biblical record must therefore hinge on the statement that Adam was a special creation (Genesis 1:27) with the whole of creation designed by God for him and his descendants. The narrative support for this claim has been made in the introduction to this chapter; the challenge for Biblical research is to show that the present families of mankind all have their origin with this special creation possibly about 4000 BC, but most specifically from ~2345 BC when the record tells us that just eight souls survived the Noachian Flood. The case for the latter event is examined in detail in Chapter 10.

There is a vast archaeological record of the pre-Noachian world embraced particularly by the civilizations of the Fertile Crescent of the near-East and including the Egyptian and Sumerian empires. In contrast, the Biblical record of pre-Noachian history from Adam is embraced by the lives of just the ten patriarchs in Genesis Chapters 4-6. These men have long recorded life spans and a genetic significance with implications leading up to the Flood described in more detail in Chapter 10. Schroeder (1990) has noted a rough check on this ancient Biblical chronology in the context of the known duration of the Bronze Age. The Bible first attributes the forging of metals (specifically "iron", *barzel,* in the Hebrew) to Tuval-Cain a descendent of Cain. The line of Cain was extinguished by the Flood and we can only estimate the duration of his life by reference to the surviving line of Seth through to Noah. Tuval-Cain was evidently a contemporary of Noah and likely to have been an active metal worker around 3000 BC. This is broadly compatible with the beginning of archaeological evidence for the start of the Bronze Age at ~3500 BC (*Wikipedia*). The Bible places the use of iron considerably before the traditional assignment of the Iron Age (Leviticus 26:19, Deuteronomy 3:11). Iron is not malleable and easily rusts away; although its use may have been a feature of a sophisticated pre-Flood civilization, the archaeological evidence attributes the craft of smelting to the Hittites in the post-Flood world (Pearce 1993 and see Chapter *10.2.2*).

There is a remarkable item of climatic evidence supporting the assignment of ~4000 BC to the creation of Adam. Although the global climatic cooling leading to the Pleistocene glaciations began millions of years back in Tertiary times, shorter term fluctuations in climate are caused by perturbations in the precession of the Earth and in fluctuations of eccentricity as it orbits the Sun; these are known as Milankovitch Cycles. When the Earth moves closer to the Sun, it warms and the greenhouse gas methane is released from environments such as permafrost and swamps; this is primarily a function of the ~22,000 year precession cycle. With a different cyclicity, this time depending on the eccentricity cycle, the key greenhouse gas carbon dioxide is released during warming cycles. Based primarily on evidence from Greenland ice cores, it has been discovered that both these cycles peaked about 11,000 years ago (Figure 8.4) leading to the warming conditions that ended the last Pleistocene glaciation. These cycles would normally continue smoothly taking the Earth into another glacial era at the present time. Instead, as William Ruddiman (2006) has found, the trends in carbon dioxide and methane production start to rise at ~6000 and ~3500 years ago respectively (Figure 8.5). The former is attributed to the rapid expansion of farming practices and the latter to the expansion of rice paddy agriculture. Although the influence of farming on global warming is detected somewhat before the Biblically-inferred creation of Adam, settlement and farming were already underway in the Middle East as documented by Pearce (1993).

However it was Adam and Eve that received God's instruction *"Be fruitful, and multiply"* (Genesis 1:22, 1:28). It was likely from this point that human populations rapidly expanded (Section 8.16) on a scale possibly to have a significant influence on climate to the point of preventing another glaciation (Figure 8.5). Human populations can only rapidly expand and flourish if they observe sanitary and dietary ordinances. These would likely have been taught to Adam by God and allowed his progeny to multiply; the instructions were later repeated to Moses in the Torah. Observance of sanitary rules, particularly the repeated washing of the hands, explains why Jewish populations tended to survive the plagues that have beset humankind much better than gentile populations. This often led to them being wrongly condemned for initiating the epidemics. It was only in the 1860's that medical practice introduced the washing of hands and sterilizing of equipment between operations in non-Jewish societies. The contrast between the paucity of the humanoid preservation before the approximate time of Adam and the extensive record of activities between the times of Adam and Noah (Chapter *10.2.2*) may provide a new Biblical perspective on the record of archaeology and anthropology.

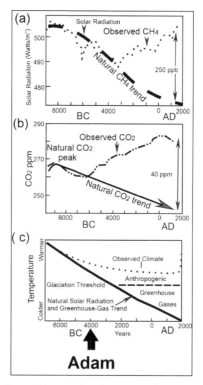

Figure 8.5: The likely effects of human (anthropogenic) activities on climate during the last ~10,000 years as shown by increases in (a) methane, CH4, (b) Carbon Dioxide, CO2, and (c) collective greenhouse gas increases. These have interrupted the natural cooling that occurred following previous inter-glacial periods, and may have prevented a further glaciation during recent times. Figure adapted from Ruddiman (2007). Note the correlation of trend-reversals with the conventional Biblical date for the beginning of the human family.

8.10 The Genetic Evidence for the Origin of Humankind

All primitive life in the Precambrian Earth comprised single celled organisms called "prokaryotes" and then "eukaryotes" (Chapter 9.4). Only with the explosion in the diversity of life forms during the Ediarcaran Era beginning ~630 Ma do we see definitive evidence for the appearance of multicellular organisms, although there is sporadic evidence that some may have appeared up to 300 million years earlier. Eukaryotes are a higher life form than the prokaryotes with a cellular nucleus embraced within a membrane that features subdivisions into 46 molecules. Each of these molecules has a specific function containing DNA molecules composed of two chains which coil around each other to form a double helix; these carry the genetic instructions (genetics being the study of DNA) required to drive development, bodily functions and reproduction. DNA continues to carry the instructions for life in all higher forms of animal and plant life up to humankind.

Chromosomes are the threadlike structures of nucleic acids and proteins in the nuclei of the molecules. During cell subdivision the chromosomes of each new cell line up as a set of "books" of information collectively comprising 3 billion "letters". These in turn divide into 46 molecules containing the genes defining the human genome. About 20,000 protein-coding genes comprise the human encyclopedia. A string of genes extending for a length of several feet is packed into a microscopic nucleus in every cell of the body. Mitochondrial DNA (mtDNA) is just a small part of the DNA located outside of the nucleus. It contains 37 genes and forms the "powerhouse" of the cell. It is made up of a loop 16,000 letters long comprising a few genes with the function of converting sugar from food into energy for the cells to use. The mtDNA is only inherited from the mother. It is when subdivision of the cells occurs that errors, or mutations, occur in the lining up of the letters.

8.11 The Two Models for the Growth of the Human Family

The Evolutionary Model for the origin of humankind has to explain the absence of genetic diversity in the human population. It addresses this by predicting a long Prehistory of human ancestors over the order of a

million years, traditionally regarded as sourced in Africa, and characterized by the continuing survival of only small populations endorsed by an
extreme paucity of skeletal remains. The human ancestors are then predicted to have suffered a crisis of population collapse leaving just a few
individuals (Figure 8.6). The lack of diversity in the human genome is
explained in terms of originating with a single mother, the "Mitochondrial
Eve" (Cann et al. 1987). The time of this crisis is usually dated by evolutionists at ~200,000 years ago followed by a rapid rise in numbers during
the last part of Pleistocene times (<2.6 million years ago). This time estimate makes critical, but highly questionable, assumptions. Specifically,
as discussed in section 8.14, it fails to accommodate the rapid accumulation of detrimental mutations.

The Creation Model begins with God's unique creation of Adam followed by His creation of woman from the rib of the man (Genesis 2:21-
22). This is a profound claim with genetic predictions: The name "Eve"
relates to the Hebrew name חַוָּה (Chawwah), derived from the Hebrew
word חָוָה (chawah) meaning "to breathe" or the related word חָיָה
(chayah) meaning "to live". Eve should be a clone of Adam including
copies of his blood cells and DNA. Just two portions of the 46 segments in the genome are unpaired and referred to as the X and Y chromosomes with males having the Y chromosome with a single X
chromosome and females having two X chromosomes - woman can
come from man but not man from woman; this accords with the
Genesis prediction. The Y chromosome is present in every one of the
millions of cells in the male and influences the genetic expression producing the male characteristics. It is the presence of the Y chromosome
in the male and the absence in the female that defines their genders. A
recent human origin in just two individuals limits genetic diversity and
explains why 85% of mtDNA is invariant with most variations confined
to just small people groups. This is the Biblical answer to the lack of
diversity in populations the world over, a lack of diversity which has
required the "population bottleneck" theory to accommodate the
Evolutionary Model (Figure 8.6).

The Biblical account of origins follows with a presumed rapid expansion in population accumulated over 10 lengthy generations of

patriarchs and then a catastrophic flood. According to the patriarch chronology given in Genesis, this would have occurred about 1600 years after the creation of Adam and it led to a collapse in numbers to just 8 people. In Genesis 9: 18-19 Shem, Ham and Japheth leave the Ark and breed to rebuild the human population. This is a second claim with profound genetic implications. A rapid rise in population over ~200 years to perhaps several hundreds of thousands of individuals was focused on the Plain of Shinar and the City of Babel (Babylon). It then experienced a confusion of languages and rapid dispersal by God. This forced the peoples to move away in tribal groups to inhabit the whole Earth and produce the rise in numbers to the global population that we see today. The tribes are summarized in Genesis Chapter Eleven where the time of "division" is linked to the patriarch Peleg.

It is the mtDNA and the Y chromosomes that collectively enable family trees to be reconstructed and show that all family lines on Earth go back to a single male and a single female. Noah would have given the same Y chromosome to all three of his sons; they were the source of all later populations and can explain why all males the world over have the same Y chromosome with just minor feature variations. An origin of the human family through 3 females, together with the possibility that Noah's wife had a daughter after the Flood predicts that there would be just three, possibly four, mtDNA lines in the world population. The number of X chromosomes depends more on random chance: Noah's wife could have passed on the same X chromosome to all of her sons but there is a possibility of up to 7 variants, or up to nine if Noah also had children after the Flood. Collectively these numbers yield the predictions that we should find a lot of diversity in the X chromosomes, only a little in the mtDNA, and none at all in the Y chromosome of humankind.

The last two of these predictions provide definitive tests distinguishing between the Biblical and Evolutionary models for the origin of humankind - they are demanded by the former but unlikely in the latter. Supporting the Biblical model, Y chromosomes are indeed found to be nearly identical in males the world over; in contrast the chimpanzee is only 70% comparable to the male, a difference comparable to the

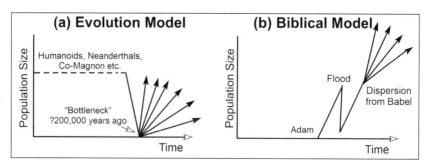

Figure 8.6: The Biblical and Evolutionary models for the growth
of the human population

contrast between a man and a chicken, with the latter not even a mammal. This conclusion is reinforced by the mtDNA evidence: only three main lineages assigned the letters M, N and R, are found the world over and they differ only in a few mutations. In Genesis 11:7-8 we are told that the renewed population, which had up to then remained focused and intermarrying on the Plain of Shinar for a time period of ~200 years, was confused in languages and scattered across the globe. Each population would have possessed a selection of the number of genes available in a population of perhaps tens of thousands, and this would predict that only limited diversity now exists between the racial groups on the Earth. The people groups across the world are indeed found to be ~99% identical to each other with the differences separating them due to mutations logically attributed to differences accrued within just a few thousand years.

One of the great achievements of modern Genetics is to show that we all share at least a third of the common gene pool. It is merely mutations within a tiny fraction of our genome that produce our outward features such as skin color. The physical contrasts between European, Ethiopian and Chinese Jews, all sharing the same genetic origin, is a classic illustration of how just ~2500 years of separation from the parent stock can change superficial appearances. Racial theories such those that dominated the thinking of Darwin, and the dangerous eugenic theories that it promoted in the latter part of the nineteenth century continuing through to the rise of Nazism, have been totally discredited. The Biblical implication of this is to show that we are all descendents of

Adam with a common issue of a fallen sinful nature: *" Wherefore, as by one man sin entered into the world, and death by sin; and so death passed upon all men, for that all have sinned"* (Romans 5:12). The heart of the Biblical message is God dealing with this issue.

8.12 The significance of Babel

In Chapter Ten verse 11 of Genesis we are given the descendents of the three sons of Noah and told that God divided the Earth into paternal divisions and therefore based on the Y chromosome. This statement makes two predictions: firstly, the Y chromosomes should show little diversity and be geographically specific. Secondly that the mtDNA inherited from the female with 7, or possibly 9, variants should show much more diversity and be randomly distributed across the world. The Y chromosomes indeed show very little variation, but the diversity that is found shows striking regional concentrations distinctive to Africa, Polynesia, Eastern Asia, northern Europe etc. In contrast the mtDNA through the female is globally dispersed and all 3 mtDNA lines are found scattered throughout all of the inhabited continents. The genetic evidence would therefore appear to have succeeded in rediscovering the Biblical account of the origins of humankind. However, this prompts a key question: "is this compatible with the Biblical timeline?"*.

The Biblical explanation for the genetic makeup of the modern world is related in Genesis Chapter Eleven to an event that occurred some 100-200 years after the Flood. Most of the descendents of Noah moved to the Plain of Shinar where, in the absence of stone, they built in brick (verse 3) and purposed to build a massive construction at the site of Babylon. In the Hebrew this is "Babel" meaning "confusion" but in the original Akkadian language is **bāb ilu** meaning "gate of the gods" suggesting some kind of occult portal. This concentration and purpose of the people defied God's instructions and what follows is recorded in the Tower of Babel incident in verse 6 to 9 of Chapter Eleven. It is described as a mirror-image chiasm reflecting the fact that God's

---

* *See work of Dr Robert Carter of Creation Ministries, references listed at the end of this chapter and YouTube presentations.*

judgment reversed the intentions of human rebellion (Fokkelman 1975). Words and phrases in the story have the consonant cluster **lbn** which refers to God's reaction to human rebellion. When God executes the judgment that reverses their plans He confuses **(nbl)** their language. This reversal of the consonants mirrors the reversal effected by divine judgment, an about-face also reflected in the chiastic structure of the record (Longman 2005):

A: All the people together with one language (Genesis 11:1)

  B: All people together with a unity of purpose (11:2)

    C: All able to communicate together (11:3a)

      D: Holding to common plans and inventions (11:3b)

        E: A unified intention to build a tower (11:4a)

          F: City and Tower building commenced (11.4b)

            Pivotal point: God's intervention (11:5a)

          F: God views humankind's rebellion (11:5b)

        E: The building and rebellion complete (11:5c)

      D: Now unrestrained counter-plans and inventions (11:6)

    C: God's patience exhausted, communication disrupted (11:7)

  B: God disperses the people over the Earth (11:8)

A: The common speech disrupted to give the many languages we have today (11:9)

The consequence of the Tower of Babel incident was that the population moved away in small people groups to occupy the rest of the world, a world that would formerly have been occupied by now-eliminated pre-Adamic peoples.

8.13 Mitochondrial DNA (mtDNA) and the age of "mtDNA Eve"

When a cell divides each chromosome will normally produce an identical chromosome and replicate its DNA; any mutations during replication will be passed on to subsequent generations of daughter cells so that the DNA accumulates more and more errors. Mutation rates of DNA are difficult to estimate with any degree of confidence. Mitochondrial DNA is the most reliable parameter for this purpose because it is only inherited via the mother: unlike nuclear DNA, mtDNA is not divided during cell division. It simply gets duplicated through a carbon copy-like duplication when cells divide, with the duplicate going to the daughter cell. During sexual reproduction, mtDNA passes down through the mother's lineage, so there is no complicating addition of paternal mtDNA.

Evolutionists have estimated mutation rates for human mtDNA by assuming that humans and chimpanzees had a common ancestor several millions of years ago. It was this approach that suggested one mutation every 6,000 to 12,000 years. Provided that the rate of mutation between the mtDNA of a mother and her offspring is constant, a direct link between ancestors can be estimated. When mtDNA sequencing discovered that all native Europeans shared unique markers, as did all native Asians, these markers were used to construct an evolutionary tree with African lineages suggesting that humans descended from an African woman 200,000 years ago (e.g. Gibons 1998, Zimmer 2001). There are serious problems with this age. Not only is the DNA of man and chimpanzee quite different, but it assumes that mutations in mtDNA are stable and exempt from natural selection, neither aiding nor hindering the organism. With these assumptions it was reasoned that one only had to count the number of mutants in the mtDNA between any taxonomic groups and decide approximately how long ago they diverged. However, evidence now shows that mtDNA is subject to natural selection. Furthermore, it is also found that mutations can accumulate very rapidly in small populations and instead of accumulating mutation-by-mutation over millions of years, mutations in mtDNA can become rapidly fixed in a population. This effectively destroys the assumption that mtDNA is very stable, and only changes slowly through the accumulation of neutral mutations over many millions of years. Major divergences in the mtDNA are now anticipated over thousands, instead of millions of years and more in line with the Biblical time frame.

Creationists have highlighted the flaws in the estimates of mtDNA mutation rates and note that current rates of mutation are much too high to explain an origin of modern humans hundreds of thousands of years ago (e.g. Jeanson 2015 and Carter 2018). Most people differ by an average of only 22 mutations; it is only when contrasted with small tribal populations that significantly larger differences are found. The male Y chromosome has a global uniformity explained by the men migrating for purposes of travel, conquest and colonization. In contrast the female mtDNA populations have regional characteristics reflecting their home-centered origins. A further argument includes the occurrence of heteroplasmy, a condition in which offspring inherit two different mtDNA sequences from the mother. Since heteroplasmy is the result of mtDNA mutation, the frequency of this condition in human populations gives insight into the rate at which mtDNA is mutating and can be used to calculate a much younger age for Mitochondrial Eve compatible with the Biblical figure of only a few thousand years.

8.14 The importance of Mutations: a Young but cursed Human Genome

Largely as a result of better diet, available medical treatment and less arduous life styles, humans have been typically living longer, healthier lives and growing to improved statures. In reality however, because of the effect of accumulated mutations, we are now less durable, and face a more restricted future, than our predecessors. A mutation is a random change to a highly-organized living organism and evolution has to assume that favorable mutations accumulate to transform living things into new organisms. In reality nearly all mutations have a detrimental effect and as they accumulate, and unless they remain "neutral" or are eliminated by natural selection, they ultimately lead to the extinction of the organism. The current reproduction rates of the human population are much too low to avoid our extinction (Lynch et al. 1995). Mutations are "spelling errors" in the genome; every time cells divide letter mistakes are made and each new child carries about 100 new mutations. They can occur as a result of the natural radiation emanating from the rocks and constructions around us; they are enhanced today by artificial radiation and numerous scientists have warned that the intense gigahertz radiation of 5G communications will have this consequence. However, up to the present time they have most commonly accumulated during chromosome copying: every time a cell divides mistakes are made in the 3 billion letters of the genome. Men pass on between a few tens to a few hundred mutations for each child that they father, and with ~100-300 new mutations occurring with the birth of each child, the present generational population of ~7 billion humans alone will have accumulated a minimum of 7×10^{12} mutations (Sanford 2005). Every possible genetic mutation now exists in the current human population. It negates the possibility that we have had a long-term evolutionary history and excludes the possibility of our long-term survival. Ironically the campaigns to reduce family size and promote abortion are only serving to rapidly accelerate this demise.

The rapid accumulation of defective genes in the human race is apparent in the Biblical record. Adam's descendents could marry their sisters, Abraham could marry his half-sister and even Isaac and Jacob could marry first cousins without genetic harm. However, by the time of the later Egyptian pharaohs the hazards of incest were becoming apparent and by Hapsburg times repeated close family unions were becoming lethal to the survival of the dynasty; it continues to be a health hazard in Islamic societies where marriage to close cousins is common. We share 50% of genes with our closest relatives and since these will include the same recessive alleles (pairs of genes on a chromosome that determine hereditary characteristics), the children are at a high risk of inheriting a recessive genetic disorder. More remote links do not seem to raise major health issues: until recent times the possibilities for travel were very limited and lower degrees of interbreeding were inevitable; thus it is reckoned that most naturally-born British people are unlikely to be removed by more than a fifth cousin relationship from each other. The cumulative effects of mutations require that the human population cannot be very ancient and thus refute the evolutionary model. They predict that the human race is unlikely to survive more than a few thousands of years. However, fallen humankind will have destroyed the atmosphere, land, and oceans long before then, and the Biblical books of Daniel and Revelation have a different record to tell us how God will actually wind up the history of the Earth and Universe at the end of His Arrow of Time.

Evolution has to assume that the negative mutations are concentrated in "junk DNA" but the overlapping codes present in the genome mean that this concept no longer has any validity. Since "deleterious mutations" always swamp any ability for natural selection to use the small number of positive mutations to correct the genome, our species cannot survive. As reproduction declines "mutational meltdown" will accelerate towards ultimate extinction. The lifespan of any organism, including humans, depends on the mutation rate. Carter and Sanford (2016) use an organism with a very high mutation rate, the H1N1 flu virus responsible for the 1918 epidemic, to illustrate this effect. Although this virus had a devastating effect, only those mutations which managed to pass the human immune system could survive. Natural selection has proved unable to reverse the rate at which mutations have accumulated in this version of the virus and it has subsequently become extinct. The effect is illustrated today as viruses build up resistance from the over-use of antibiotics. Initially few viruses have this resistance but this becomes critical once the battle with the antibiotics begins. The resistant progeny are those which are unable to transmit certain chemicals through their cell wall and are correspondingly resistant to antibiotics - these are the ones that survive to become more and more prominent in the overall population. The human immune systems require exposure to a pathogen to learn to recognize it and train our responder cells to rapidly counter an invasion. Vaccinations against measles and chicken pox for example, no longer allow our systems to build up a natural resistance to these diseases. We catch colds, and often influenza, each year because the viruses mutate much too fast for our immune systems to keep up with and vaccines based on the previous year are likely to prove ineffective. Although modern health care ensures that more of us can survive, as a species we are becoming inherently weaker and the mixing of people will make us more susceptible to dangerous pathogens, particularly as antibiotics become less effective.

The mutation rate of each species is implanted by the Creator of life. It is evidently very low for some organisms as applies to long-lived animals such as *Lingula* or *Nautilus*, but no population size, even large mega-populations, can escape ultimate mutational meltdown. This applies to all living creatures unless they are otherwise forced to extinction by natural catastrophes. It is a natural implication of the curse implicit in the Gap of Genesis 1:2 but it does not appear that this was God's original intention for his special creation of humankind. It is when Adam and Eve fell to the temptation of sin that we read: ***"In the sweat of your face you shall eat bread until you return unto the ground; for out of it you were taken: dust thou art, and unto dust you shall return"*** (Genesis 3:19); they were only then expelled from the perfect environment of the Garden of Eden and physical death would be the ultimate fate of them and their descendents. Unfortunately, Creationists have often sought to incorporate humanoids, Neanderthals, cave men etc. into the genetic history of Adam and his successors. This is unnecessary because these creatures inhabited Earth long before Adam. They emphasize the point made in the introductory paragraphs of this chapter: Adam was a special creation elevated above the animals.

8.15 The Animal Kingdom: The Ark and a parallel Young History to Humankind?

Stoeckle and Thaler (2018) have examined the variation in the mtDNA of animals representing 100,000 species to discover that the genetic diversity within most species is small, with only about 0.2% differences in the gene they examined. This was found to be true whether the species had a restricted geographical range or population size such as African elephants, or a large population and geographic range as has already been demonstrated for humankind. These authors concluded that this small portion of the mtDNA (inherited from the mothers) is a good practical marker for the species of many animals no matter what its current size or similarity to their fossils of any age. They concluded that the genetic diversity observed in mtDNA genomes of most species alive today can be attributed to the accumulation of mutations from an ancestral genome within the past 200,000 years: by tracing the mutations in one gene they tracked its origin back to the last common female ancestor of all living members. Working within an evolutionary mindset, the senior author records fighting against the significance of his own results which forced him to conclude "for the planet's 7.6 billion people, 500 million house sparrows, or 100,000 sandpipers, genetic diversity is about the same". The startling result of the study is that "nine out of 10 species on Earth today, including humans, came into being 100,000 to 200,000 years ago".

The evidence from the animal kingdom does not mean that all species started at the beginning of this proposed time, only that the genetic variation in the mtDNA has arisen within this timeframe. The cheetah species is an example of an animal with an ancient fossil record of Asian origin but young mtDNA. It evidently went through a population bottleneck experience and then moved to its present home in Africa - the mtDNA genetic "clock" was reset by the genetic bottleneck.

The time estimate of "100,000 to 200,000 years ago" is constrained by the same evolutionary assumptions noted for the human population above, and there are the same strong reservations concerning these assumptions. The academic discussion surrounding this discovery naturally eschews any thought of a Noah's Ark origin for common animal origins, but it is likely that the age could have been much younger and compatible with the Biblical timeline of this latter event. Much interest therefore attaches to the conclusion that the results only apply to "most" animal species because Genesis 7:2 records: ***Of every clean beast thou shalt take to thee by sevens, the male and his female: and of beasts that are not clean by two, the male and his female***. The animals following the "clean" definition stipulated in the Book of Leviticus would therefore have started with a much larger gene pool and not show the limited mtDNA signature exhibited by the majority of animals. The identification of the populations that fail to show the majority signature will prove to be a crucial test of the Ark proposition.

8.16 The Rapid Expansion of Human Populations

Several authors including Morris (1984), Grant Jeffrey (1996) and Batten (2001) have aimed to show that the size the present global human population can only be explained if it has very recent origins according with the Biblical model. Following the approach of Morris,

Grant performed calculations on a conservative basis assuming that mankind started at about the time of Noah's Flood in ~2345 BC with just one surviving couple producing only 2.5 children; he considered that an average 2.5 children per family would account for the natural depletion caused by war, disease and famine, and used an average generation of 43 years appropriate to an earlier age than our own. He found that the population would have grown to ~5 billion starting from the time of the Flood, a figure close to the global population in 1995. Morris (1984) came to a comparable conclusion.

This short term population growth was compared to a calculation using the same parameters but assuming that the human family began a million years ago. The 23,256 consecutive generations in Grant's calculation predicted an enormous present-day population of 10^{2019} people. This staggering figure, like that of Batten (2001), seems to provide strong support for the youth of the human population and is supported by the total absence of vast numbers of humanoid skeletons in the Pleistocene and Holocene (Recent) stratigraphic records. In contrast there are enormous numbers of *animal* bone beds preserved in this record (Chapter 10.3).

Yet more recent analyses by Carter and Hardy (2015) and Carter and Powell (2016) have endorsed the broad conclusions of Grant and Morris. A conservative model requiring a low 0.46% growth rate, or doubling every 156 years, involves just 150 breeding generations able to produce the present global population of 7 billion people in the ~4300 years since the Flood. The accounts of Genesis and Exodus describe 70 Hebrew family descendents of Jacob (Israel) travelling to Egypt and then leaving 430 years later as a population of at least 2.5 million including woman and children (Exodus 12:37). The 20th century alone saw the world population increase from 1.6 billion to 6.1 billion, equating to an average growth rate of 3.81% per year; this dramatic increase occurred in spite of the Spanish Flu epidemic of January 1918 to December 1920 which likely affected a third and killed between 3 and 6% of the world's population, genocides carried out by Communist, Nazi and Muslim regimes that have murdered more that 120 million people, and added to this, an average death rate up to the 1980's of a million people a year from starvation.

However, whilst the general implication of these calculations is apparent, it is important to stress that global populations are notoriously susceptible to natural events. Plagues can be particularly devastating. The Black Death for example, reached Europe in the late 1340s and killed an estimated 25 million people or between 30 and 60% of the total population. The Black Death lingered on for centuries, particularly in cities, and outbreaks included the Great Plague of London (1665-66) where one in five residents of the city died. The climatic consequences of the eruption of supervolcanoes can be particularly devastating. The eruption of the Toba volcano of Sumatra 75,000 years ago is probably the most explosive event witnessed by humanoids. It plunged the planet into a volcanic winter and is considered to have vastly depleted the early population, although the scale is disputed because a significant impact on African populations has not yet been recognised. The eruption of the Mount Tambora volcano, also in Indonesia, was perhaps the largest eruption seen in the last 10,000 years and caused 1816 to be "the year without a summer"; it was responsible for an estimated 80,000 deaths in the vicinity of the explosion and the agricultural impact caused widespread famine across the Northern Hemisphere. Provisionally however, it seems that no global event has impacted human populations since the time of the Noachian Flood to substantially affect the essential conclusion that the human population has grown very rapidly in recent times. Furthermore, the parameters used by Batten, Jeffery and Morris, as well as Carter and his co-authors, are actually very conservative and imply that the bulk of human populations in the past have been decimated by disease, warfare and natural disasters.

These conclusions are supported by investigations into the origins of language. No living primate apart from man is equipped to speak but Adam is recorded as naming the animals. Analysis of more than 6000 languages in use today shows that they actually have a range of common roots implying only 17 super-families all with apparent ages of no more than a few thousand years. Only the Asiatic family, which includes Hebrew, Arabic and Akkadian, seems to have an older pedigree (Ruhlen 1996). This would accord with a core origin in the area of Babel.

8.17 Summary

In this chapter we have summarised evidence defining the two time frames involved in the Biblical narrative. The first begins with the Big Bang initiation of creation and appears as billions of years from our Earth-bound perspective. God describes to Moses the six steps that He then took to transform chaos into order from His cosmic frame and outside of our restricted dimensional frame. The second is the historical record that follows from the creation of Adam; this is the normal timeline of history that he, and subsequently his descendents including ourselves, have experienced. Although both these time frames are subject to the Law of General Relativity, it is only in the former that this effect is significant. We show in the subsequent chapter how this effect can explain the history of the Earth and Universe in terms of God's description in Genesis Chapter One.

References:

Gibons, A., 1998. Calibrating the Mitochondrial Clock. Science, 279, 28-29.

Cann, R.L., Stoneking, M. and Wilson, A.C., 1987. Mitochondrial DNA and human evolution, Nature 325, 31-36

Carter. R.W., 2007. Mitochondrial diversity within modern human populations. Nucleic Acids Research 35(9):3039–3045.

Carter R.W. 2018. Effective population sizes and loss of diversity during the Flood bottleneck, Journal of Creation 32(2):124–127,)

Carter, R and Hardy, C., 2015. Modelling Biblical human population growth, Journal of Creation, 29, 72-79.

Carter, R. and Powell, M., 2016. The genetic effects of the Population Bottleneck associated with the Genesis Flood, Journal of Creation, 30, 102-111.

Fokkelman, J. P., 1975. Narrative Art in Genesis, Van Gorcum, Amsterdam.

Jeanson, N.T. 2015. "A Young-Earth Creation Human Mitochondrial DNA 'Clock': Whole Mitochondrial Genome Mutation Rate Confirms D-Loop Results." Answers Research Journal, 8: 375–378.

Johnson, Kenneth, 2010. *The Ancient Book of Daniel*, Charleston, South Carolina, 166pp., ISBN 1456306561.

Johnson, K., 2017. *Ancient Testaments of the Patriarchs: Autobiographies from the Dead Sea Scrolls, Bible Facts Ministries*, 167pp., ISBN 10:978-1975887742 and ISBN-13:1975887743.

Longman, T., 1987. *Literary Approaches to Biblical Interpretation (Foundations of Contemporary Interpretation, Vol. 3)*. Grand Rapids: Zondervan Publishing House.

Longman, T., 2005. *How to Read Genesis*, How to Read Series, Downers Grove: InterVarsity Press.

Lynch, M., Conery, J. and Burger, R., 1995. Mutation accumulation and the extinction of small populations. The American Naturalist, 140, 489-518.

Missler, Chuck, 1999. *Cosmic Codes: Hidden Messages from the Edge of Eternity*, Koinonia House Publications, Coeur d'Alene, Idaho, U.S.A., 535pp.

Pearce, E.K.V., 1993. *Evidence for Truth: Science*, Evidence Programs, Eastbourne, Sussex, 319pp.

Rokas, A., Ladoukakis, E., and Zouros, E., 2003. Animal Mitochondrial DNA Recombination Revisited. Trends in Ecology and Evolution. 18: 411-417.

Ruddiman, W. F., 2007. The early anthropogenic hypothesis: challenges and responses, Reviews of Geophysics, 45, 1-37, RG4001, doi:10.1029/2006RG000207.

Ruhlen, M., 1996. The Origin of Language: Tracing the evolution of the Mother Tongue, Wiley, 256pp.

Sanford, J. C., 2005. *Genetic Entropy and the Mystery of the Genome*, Elim Publishers, 214pp.

Sanford, J. and Carter, R., 2014. In light of genetics … Adam, Eve, and the creation/fall, Christian Apologetics Journal, 12:51–98.

Schroeder, Gerald, 1990. *Genesis and the Big Bang*, Bantam Books, 212pp.

Schroeder, Gerald, 1997. *The Science of God: the Convergence of Scientific and Biblical Wisdom*, Broadway Books, New York, 226 pp.

Sexton, J., 2018. Evangelicalism's search for chronological gaps in Genesis 5 and 11: a Historical, Hermeneutical and Linguistic critique, JETS 61.1, 5-25.

Shore, Haim, 2007. *Coincidences in the Bible and in Biblical Hebrew*, iUniverse Publishers, New York, 319pp.

Stoeckle, M.Y. and Thaler D.S., 2018. Why should mitochondria define species? Human Evolution, 33, 1-30.

Whitcomb, J.C., and Morris, H.M. 1961. *The Genesis Flood: The Biblical Record and its Scientific Implications*. P&R publishing.

Wikipedia. 2005. "Ussher-Lightfoot Calendar." http://en.wikipedia.org/wiki/Ussher-Lightfoot_Calendar.

Woodmorappe, J., 1998. Surprising New Evidence that Molecular Clocks Can Run Very Fast, /www.rae.org/essay-links/clocks/

Zimmer, C., 2001. *After You, Eve*. Natural History, 110, 32-35.

Chapter 9

The Six Days of Genesis Chapter One

9.1 Introduction

In the *first verse* of Genesis we have the primary verse defining God as the Creator:

> ***In the beginning God created the Heaven and the Earth***

In the Hebrew this verse has extraordinary properties alluded to in Chapters *2.6.1* and 3.4 which underscore a Divine origin. Accepting this statement as fact provides the core of belief. The believer will have no problem with the remainder of the Bible because God as supreme author of Creation, will both be responsible for the Laws of Nature and able to interrupt these laws with miracles as He desires to shape the destiny of humankind. Note that *this verse concerns the overall creation*; properly translated into English it is in the pluperfect tense: "God had created". It is the statement confirming God as Creator and has no relationship to the sequence of events described in the Six Days of verses 3 to 31. Earth is not mentioned again until Day 3; even the Sun is not mentioned until Day 4. The first chapter of Genesis uses the plural and generic name for God, ***Elohim***. This is the impersonal name defining Him as Creator of the material Universe and the source of life. In Chapter Two we find the personal and proper name of God, ***Yahweh***, introduced as He begins to interface with His ultimate creation, humankind. The first verse of Chapter One begins with the letter **Bēt, ב,** the second letter of the Hebrew alphabet. It is symbolic of a house and has a shape open on just one side (Hebrew reads from right to left); Rabbinic teaching has suggested this is because the verse encloses the known Creation and we are unable to understand what happened outside or before this. The emphatic claim of Genesis 1:1 is repeated in the New Testament in the Gospel of John (1:3).

Within microseconds ($<10^{-12}$) of the Big Bang the pure energy of the Creation was transformed into the matter which now makes up the more than 100 billion galaxies comprising the Universe (Chapter 8.5). There is one Hebrew word for creation from nothing. This is **bara** and it appears just three times in Genesis Chapter One referring successively to the creation of *matter*, *life* and *Adam* (Pearce 1993). The *act of creation of matter was essentially instantaneous* whereas the acts applied to this matter that followed during the Six Days of Genesis were *transformative* - they transformed chaos into order. This distinction is emphasised by the contrast between Genesis 1:1: "In the beginning God **_created_** the heaven and the earth" and Exodus 20:11: "For (in) six days God **_made_** heaven and earth".*

Until the creation of Adam only God was the observer. The events that followed embraced the formation and destruction of stars. This has been necessary to compress the primary hydrogen and helium into the higher elements such as carbon, with this latter element destined to become the building block of life. With each transformation the mass of each new atom would be slightly less than the mass of the combined individual atoms, and the excess mass would be converted into the nuclear energy of the star according to Einstein's equation. A multiplicity of explosions of supernovae would combine and recombine elements to produce the 92 elements that would ultimately be included in the makeup of planet Earth. During this long formative process each star and supernovae would possess a different gravity and speed. General Relativity tells us that a unique space-time reference frame would have applied, and continues to apply, to each one of the billions of stars. Quite simply, there was no common time frame.

---

* *Note that the word "in" does not appear in the original Hebrew of this latter verse. It was added by the KJV translators and is appropriately italicized.*

The *second verse* of Genesis 1 in expanded form reads:

> *But the Earth had become confused and an empty waste; and*
> *an unnatural darkness was over the abyss, the home of demons.*
> *And the Spirit of God brooded over the face of the waters.*

We have argued in Chapter 7 that this was an event of primary spiritual significance as God's perfect work of Creation was corrupted when the created angel Lucifer, the Light Bearer, fell as he declared that he would be like God (Isaiah 14:13-14); he became Satan and a third of the angels joined his rebellion. Again in English it is in the sense of "had existed". It is recorded as happening when Earth had been formed and has no direct relationship to the record of the Six Days.

Only when God both "made" and "created" Adam from the elements - *"the dust of the ground"* (Genesis 2:7) in Day 6, and breathed life into him could the reference time frame that we understand begin. From now on everything God describes is linked to humankind's Earth-bound timeframe - it becomes the timeline of history as we understand it. Day 6 is special because in the Hebrew it is the only day of creation with a definite article - *Yom Ha-Shishi* - THE sixth day. In the correspondence between Hebrew letters and numbers, six corresponds to the letter "vav" (Chapter 2). It is shaped like a hook and symbolically holds two things together so that normally *vav* is translated as "and". In the Hebrew this letter is referred to as the "vav of connection" implying that "the Sixth Day"—*Yom HaShishi (Yom Vav)*—connects the spiritual and physical with apparent implications to the creation of Adam with body, soul and spirit.

We have shown in the previous chapter how an estimate of the expansion factor of the Universe indicates that the ~13.9 billion years estimated to have elapsed since the Big Bang are closely equivalent to the Six Days in Genesis Chapter One when related to a cosmic timeframe. The ~900,000,000,000 times difference between our present perception of time and Genesis cosmic time is an average for the Six Days of Creation and uses the CBR to resolve this interval. Just after the Big Bang the Universe occupied a tiny volume, and the temperatures and frequencies of the radiation were intensely high. During the initial rapid expansion time would have moved very fast, but as the Universe expanded in size in all directions the temperature and frequency would have fallen away to become closer and closer to their present much lower values. This is a consequence of the accelerating expansion of the Universe. To assess how we view time as a consequence of this observation, Schroeder (1997) has assumed that each doubling in size of the Universe will slow down time by a half. The time required for the Universe to double in size then increases exponentially whilst the rate of change of the cosmic clock relative to Earth time decreases exponentially. The properties of the familiar expanding spiral described in Chapter 5.10 and shown in Figure 9.1 can then be used to determine the duration of each of the Genesis days as we perceive them in our present time frame.

To calculate the duration, D, of each cosmic day, t, in Earth days, Schroeder uses the equation 5.1 shown in polar form in Chapter 5. The equation becomes $D = (A_0/L)e^{(-Lt)}$, where $A_0 = 4 \times 10^{12}$ (the ratio of the frequencies of the cosmic microwave background at quark confinement compared to today) and $L = 0.693$, the natural logarithm of 2. Using these constraints (and qualifying the beginning and terminating dates of Creation according to Chapter 8), this equation yields time estimates for the durations of the Six Days as **Day One**: 13.75-7.75 Byr (Billion years), **Day Two**: 7.75-3.75 Byr, **Day Three**: 3.75-1.75 Byr, **Day Four**: 1.75-0.75 Byr, **Day Five**: 750-250 million years and **Day Six**: 250 million years to 6000 years. The Cosmic Spiral is sketched in visual form in Figure 9.1. The beginning of the first day is placed at the Big Bang event and the end of the last day is placed at the time of the creation of Adam as determined from the Biblical record of the Ussher-Lightfoot chronology discussed in Chapter *8.9.2*. The latter date represents the pinnacle of God's creative work defining the end of this Day Six. These values imply that cosmic day One lasted for roughly 8 billion Earth years, Day Two for 4 billion years, Day Three for 2 billion years, Day Four for 1 billion years, Day Five for 500 million years and Day Six for 250 million years.

Each time the universe doubles in size, the perception of time halves: as we project back towards the time of the Big Bang, the fractional rate of change - the rate of doubling - would have been very rapid in the early history of the Universe. Although the actual expansion rate is assumed to be constant, the fractional rate of change decreases with time. This is because it takes longer and longer for the overall size to double as the universe gets larger and larger. For this reason, the length of time occupied by each Day rapidly decreases - the first day is immensely long whereas the last day is relatively short in the context of Geological Time.

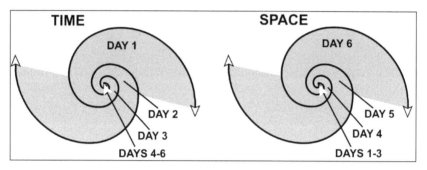

Figure 9.1: The logarithmic Spiral of Space-Time: as space expands exponentially, time contracts. The logarithmic spiral was called the "Spiral mirabilis" by Jacob Bernoulli or "the marvelous spiral" because of its unique property: with each successive curve the size of the spiral increases but its shape is remains unaltered.

Critiques of Schroeder's analysis come from two sources. Young Earth Creationists (*https://answersingenesis.org/creationism/old-earth/gerald-schroeders-new-variation-on-the-day-age-theory-1/*) are evidently disappointed that the Six Days of Genesis can now explain the long time periods that science has resolved for Earth and Cosmic histories - the conflict between science and the Bible sustained for decades appears to be without foundation. However, they present no counter arguments to suggest a flawed scientific analysis. Authoritative comments critical of the physics used by Schroeder (e.g. *http://www.talkreason.org/articles/schroeder.cfm*) relate primarily to the assumptions he has used to evaluate time dilation. Unfortunately the criticisms of the secularist scientists have an agenda - to them Evolution is sacrosanct whilst the Bible is simply a collection of myths and no scientific authority can be assigned to it. Accordingly, the details of the Hebrew text are ignored and much emphasis is placed on the pre-Adamic archaeological evidence which is not relevant to the case if, as we

(Chapter 8.1) and Schroeder have argued, Adam was a special creation made in the image of God, and therefore the first living creature to relate to Him personally. The most serious scientific reservation concerns thermodynamic issues. Clearly Schroeder is simplifying a complex and poorly-understood phenomenon that applies only to the Universe that we can see: the expansion of space into a pure vacuum would not by itself cause the temperature drop used to define the expansion factor. Instead a high proportion of the thermal energy of the primordial explosion resulting from the Big Bang would have been converted into other forms of energy, including the energy converted into the masses of stars, galaxies and cosmic dust according to Einstein's equation. Also we do not know how much Universe (if any) exists beyond our ability to detect.

Nevertheless, the key foundations of Schroeder's analysis remain: Einstein's Law of General Relativity has been confirmed by multiple experiments, the accelerating expansion of the Universe is confirmed by observation, we know that we are living in four dimensions including time, and time dilation depends on the reference frames. The largest uncertainty in the parameters used to determine the durations of the Six Days concerns the expansion factor. The calculation noted in the previous chapter yielding an overall age for the Universe approaching the number of six days in cosmic time suggests that this is unlikely to be very wide off the mark. Accordingly, we devote the remainder of this chapter to comparing the inferred durations of the Six Days according to the doubling-halving model of Schroeder (1997) with the Geological and Cosmological record. We qualify this analysis by acknowledging the physical limitations of the model and uncertainties in defining the boundaries between some of the days and the ages assigned to them. Revisions will clearly be required as we learn more about Hubble expansion and the ways that the Universe has changed.

Genesis Chapter 1 only tells us what happened within each day, not at what point things happened. The sequence however, correctly accords with the geological and cosmological record: **1. Light (v. 4), 2. Firmament and waters (v. 6-8), 3. Plants (v. 11-13), 4. Animals (v. 20-23)** and **5. Man (v. 31).** The number of permutations (possible order) of these five observations is given by the factorial of five: *there are 119 ways of getting this order wrong, just one possibility of getting it right.*

9.1 Day One: ~13.9 - 7.75 Billion Years - Creation of the material comprising the Universe and the first stars and galaxies.

The first of the Six days is described in verses 3-5 of Genesis 1:

> *And God said, Let there be light: and there was light. And God saw the light, that it was good: and God divided the light from the darkness. And God called the light Day, and the darkness he called Night. And the evening and the morning were the first day.*

The Hebrew for "first day" here is better translated "Day One", *Yom Echad* (Schroeder 1990) in contrast to the succeeding days where "second", "third", etc. are appropriate. Two creative acts of God, matter and Adam, begin and end the Six Days. As the photons broke free from matter only ~380,000 years after the Big Bang we have the division implied in this verse: radiation was now decoupled from matter. As the temperature fell below about 3000°C atoms could form without being torn apart and matter could be created from the primeval plasma: this would go on to be moulded into the stars and galaxies. The text implies that the Universe now became transparent to light although the "light" referred to here would actually have mostly been ambient radiation at much higher frequencies than the visible spectrum that our eyes are sensitive to. The verses describing Day 1 can logically be taken to record cosmological history from this creation of matter but before the making of the "firmament" on Day 2 in verse 6 onwards. From our current perspective of ages, it likely embraces the time interval between the point when time and space were created ~13.9 billion years ago, and the earliest star and galaxy formation. The time of this latter event is disputed but is likely to have occurred more than 7.75 Byr ago. The earliest part of the cosmological record associated with this Day is also the part with most uncertainties. Thus Cosmologists tend to regard the acceleration of the Universe as beginning only about 5 Byr ago. Before that expansion may have been due to the attractive influence of matter. The density of dark matter in an expanding universe is reckoned to halve as the volume of the universe doubles. It decreases more quickly than dark energy and eventually the dark energy dominates as matter converts to energy.

9.3 Day Two: ~7.75 - 3.75 Billion Years - Expansion of the Universe, Formation of the Solar System and separation of the waters

The Second day is given in verses 6-8 of Genesis 1:

And God said, Let there be a firmament in the midst of the waters, and let it divide the waters from the waters. And God made the firmament, and divided the waters which were under the firmament from the waters which were above the firmament: and it was so. And God called the firmament Heaven. And the evening and the morning were the second day.

This is the first day in which the words "heaven" and "firmament" are introduced. There is no singular equivalent for the plural word for **heaven**, *samayim*, in the Hebrew. It is used some 522 times in the Old Testament and the significance has to be interpreted in context; translators of the KJV used the singular 414 times and the plural 108 times. The word **Firmament** is frequently translated as "expanse" and used just 17 times in the Old Testament; the Hebrew *raqia* comes from the root *raqa*, meaning "to hammer" or "pound out", "to expand". Hence these verses appear to refer to the spreading out of the heavens comprising the stars and galaxies, and implied by the verses in the Book of Isaiah as described in Chapter 8.5. This time interval embraces the formation of the Solar System with formation of Earth following within only about 100 Ma (Wood 2011). Age determinations on meteorites and the rocks of the Earth indicate an age of formation of 4.54 Billion years with an uncertainty currently reckoned to be ± 50 million years.

Whilst there are rare indications that continental rocks were forming on the Earth as early as ~4.0 Byr, no crust could survive the intense impacting by meteorites before the ending of the Late Heavy Bombardment phase at ~3.8 Byr. All water would have been in a gaseous atmosphere until the Earth had cooled sufficiently for water to condense and form the oceans at ~3.8 Byr near to the inferred boundary between Days 2 and 3. This is also the age of an oldest substantial record of continental crust and by ~3.0 Byr some 20% of this crust had formed. It had aggregated into a supercontinent known as 'Protopangea' by ~2.9 Byr and with peripheral modifications, it survived as a quasi-integral crust ('Palaeopangaea') until the beginning of Day 5 (Piper 2018). Whilst this implies a separation of continents and oceans, it is a factor altogether smaller in scale than the firmament and waters implied by verses 6-8 and more likely refers to the first verse of Day 3 described below.

Whilst the levels of water referred to in verses 6 and 7 are not clearly interpretable, the interval embraces separation of water from the Universe, from the Solar System and from within the Earth. Since hydrogen is the most common molecule in the Universe, it is unsurprising to find that waters are pervasive in space. The "ice giant" planets Uranus and Neptune are also thought to have supercritical oceans of water beneath their gaseous surfaces. Disks of volatiles blown out from distant exoplanets also contain water. Whilst the inner planets Mercury and Venus appear to be dry, Mars has icecaps and possible subsurface water reservoirs, and water has even been discovered on our own Moon. Jupiter's moon Europa has a thick surface layer of ice with the possibility that tidal forces warm this to liquid water at depth; the companion moon Ganymede may have a similar structure, whilst there are signs that Saturn's moons Titan and Enceladus also have water. The comets are balls of ice and dust left over from the formation of the Solar System (Chapter *6.12.2*) and the heavy bombardment of Earth by meteorites at ~3.8 Byr, as evidence by the crater history of the Moon, suggests that great volumes of water were delivered to the Earth by comet impacting. This event near the proposed end of Day 2 was likely responsible for the water now comprising our oceans and atmosphere.

9.4 Day Three: ~3.75 - 1.75 Billion Years - Formation of oceans, emerging continents and creation of single celled life.

Verses 9-16 of Genesis 1 read:

> *And God said, Let the waters under the heaven be gathered together unto one place, and let the dry land appear: and it was so. And God called the dry land Earth; and the gathering together of the waters the Seas: and God saw that it was good. And God said, Let the earth bring forth (grass), the herb yielding seed, and the fruit tree yielding fruit after his kind, whose seed is in itself, upon the earth: and it was so. And the earth brought forth grass, and herb yielding seed after his kind, and the tree yielding fruit, whose seed was in itself, after his kind: and God saw that it was good. And the evening and the morning were the third day.*

The descriptive focus is now narrowed down to the Earth. The boundary between Day 2 and Day 3 alluded to in the first two verses embraces the formation of the oceans and substantial continental crust by ~3.8 Byr as noted above. From high ratios of oxygen isotopes $O^{18}:O^{16}$ it has been inferred that clay minerals, and by extension soils, were not forming prior to ~3.2 Byr - the continental crust was still then submerged. As implied by verse 9, only during this Day did the continental crust begin to emerge. This is also the first Day where living things are introduced. The earliest positive evidence for bacterial life on Earth comes from ~3.7 Byr sedimentary rocks in Greenland deposited contemporaneously with, or soon after, the preservation of the first oceans. Subsequently bacteria may have begun to live on land after ~3.2 Byr. Temperatures prior to ~3.8 Byr were likely too high, and meteorite impacting too strong, for permit water, and by extension life, to survive for long.

The problem issue with interpretation of the Day 3 verses in Genesis arises because the life forms that appeared during the interval assigned to this day were primitive single celled organisms - algae and bacteria - much less complex than the grass, herbs and fruit trees referred to. The only plant life on Earth remained this way for the next two billion years. The Hebrew word *deshe* noted in parenthesis above however, is incorrectly translated as "grass". In fact, it refers to something green and is relevant to the blue-green algae which appeared at this time. Schroeder amplifies this issue by noting that these algae actually have as much as a hundred times the amount of genetic information in their DNA per cell compared with mammals. Thus, we find the more complex organisms appearing first in the geological record because plants need to have the ability to create chlorophyll to receive and convert the Sun's rays into energy; animals do not require this complex sun-converting process. The early plant forms could therefore have contained the genetic information that would also be present in all the plants that subsequently appeared, including the land plants at ~400 Myr in Devonian times (inferred Day 5) and the flowering plants that appeared in Cretaceous times ~130 Myr ago (early in Day 6). The chronology of plant life that appeared in Day 3 and in subsequent Genesis days is all condensed into this Biblical record of just two verses. Plant life serves as a food and for other material uses for the animal kingdom, and it is with this animal kingdom that the subsequent text is primarily concerned.

The earliest life forms were prokaryotes, bacteria adapted to living with an early atmosphere that was likely a thick mist of water vapor, nitrogen, methane and carbon dioxide. They were anaerobic, meaning they could not have survived in an oxygen atmosphere and were shielded from the ultraviolet radiation by living in water. Prokaryotes do not have a nucleus and replicate by cell division. They were likely programmed by RNA (Ribonucleic acid with a single helix). This era thus records the first extraordinary creation of life: without protracted time available for any kind of chance mechanism to bring it about. Molecules with long, ordered and complex chains within cells, which are programmed to organise the extraction of chemical energy from ingested foods, had appeared. These produce 20 different types of amino acids to generate a multitude of proteins and then use them for the maintenance, growth and reproduction of the cell.

The primitive prokaryotes could only survive if *their life form had already been created* because they obtain the energy for life by fermentation which requires no oxygen. The larger molecule simply divides by the cutting of the chemical bonds; this generates energy which is split into energy used by the primary cell, and potential energy left in the fragments of the discarded parts of the original cell. In fermentation chemical changes are brought about by the action of enzymes able to extract energy from carbohydrates in the absence of oxygen. Enzymes are proteins only produced by living cells - *life is required to produce life* - their activity consumes carbon dioxide but does not produce oxygen in the simple prokaryotes. The presence of both bacteria and enzymes thus requires that a diverse range of organic systems had already been created by the time of the formation of the first oceans. This conversion process is a microscopic example of order moving towards disorder to create and distribute energy.

The key feature required for the transition from Day 3 to Day 4 was the conversion of the primitive atmosphere from a reduced (anoxic) condition to one which is oxygen-rich enabling higher forms of life to survive. Bacteria were key to this process. The atmosphere had by now become sufficiently translucent for some prokaryotes, the blue-green cyanobacteria, to capture the Sun's energy and release oxygen by photosynthesis as a waste product. This would have been immediately dissolved into the surrounding water. There was much soluble ferrous iron dissolved in the primitive oceans able to combine with the oxygen and precipitate as insoluble ferric iron in rocks known as "banded iron formations". These first appeared at ~3.7 Byr, a time correlating with the earliest evidence for oceans and bacteria. However, they were deposited on an enormous scale between ~2.2 and 1.8 Byr to produce the vast deposits that now provide some 60% of global iron ore resources. The cyanobacteria continue to thrive today and produce much of the global oxygen.

The appearance of the much more complex eukaryotes is a milestone correlating with the boundary between Day 3 and Day 4. These are organisms with the cell now comprising a nucleus containing DNA - molecules with a double helix, and they can reproduce sexually. There is sporadic evidence for them from around 2.2-2.1 Byr, although positive identification has only been achieved in rocks from ~1.5 Byr. Eukaryotic bacteria are about ten times the size of the prokaryotes and obtain their energy for life by a two-stage process. The first step is the simple partition seen in the prokaryotes, but light-harvesting pigments absorb water and carbon dioxide from the environment and convert it into chemical energy; this produces oxygen by photosynthesis. The energy produced is stored as carbohydrates and released for growth and reproduction of the bacteria.

The oxygen-producing process is much more energy-efficient than the simple cell division and fermentation in the prokaryotes and would have been highly effective in rapidly reducing the carbon dioxide levels in Earth's early atmosphere. Since oxygen is a reactive element and easily combines with other elements, it is readily extracted from the atmosphere. Continuous production of oxygen is required to sustain the oxygen levels later required for advanced life forms; at the same time this must be balanced by the oxygen-consuming processes so that it does not become elevated to a level at which it becomes poisonous (Chapter 4.5). Eukaryotic bacteria have been found to be remarkably versatile with a species now discovered that garners energy from methane (CH_4) to both produce and consume its own oxygen; these would have been effective at removing toxic methane from the atmosphere at the same time as restraining the oxygen production. The eukaryotic bacteria have no obvious pre-genitors and are seemingly another example of God's specific work.

9.5 Day Four: ~1750 - 750 Million Years - Transformation of the atmosphere followed by the "Boring Billion"

Verses 16-19 of Genesis 1 read:

And God said, Let there be lights in the firmament of the heaven to divide the day from the night; and let them be for signs, and for seasons, and for days, and years: And let them be for lights in the firmament of the heaven to give light upon the Earth: and it was so. And God made two great lights; the greater light to rule the day, and the lesser light to rule the night: he made the stars also. And God set them in the firmament of the heaven to give light upon the Earth, and to rule over the day and over the night, and to divide the light from the darkness: and God saw that it was good. And the evening and the morning were the fourth day.

Unlike the previous and succeeding days, the verses for Day 4 make no reference to life. They refer to a purely physical transformation and correspond to the major physical transition which initiated this Day. Schroeder's date of ~1.75 Byr provisionally assigned to the beginning of this day is somewhat later than the geological evidence. This comprised the Great Oxygenation Event ~2.2-2.0 billion years ago, when the atmosphere changed from reducing to oxidising. The atmospheric concentration of photosynthetically-produced oxygen rapidly rose and would ultimately prepare conditions for diverse multicellular life to appear on Day 5. The increase in oxygen was mimicked by the largest carbon isotope ($\delta^{13}C$) signature in the geological record (the "Lomagundi-Jatulian" event), a pulse event dated ~2.2-2.05 Byr. Organisms preferentially take up the lighter carbon isotope ^{12}C and a large increase in the ambient heavier $\delta^{13}C$ isotope is the signature of a dramatic increase in the abundance of life forms at this time. The oxygenated atmosphere now permitted much more vigorous organic activity but it remained simple and mostly single celled (unicellular). The signatures of the Great Oxygenation and Lomagundi-Jatulian events is sudden rather than gradual in geological terms and points to a motivating catastrophe. There are two probable candidates. The first is the possible appearance of the efficient oxygen-producing eukaryotes at this time; the second it an overturn of the Earth's mantle dated at 2.2-2.0 Byr when the primeval continental crust was translated through ~90° from the pole to the equator and likely released nutrients and gases stimulating this explosion of oxygen-producing activity (Piper 2013).

With the Day interval now reduced to a thousand million years, as if to affirm Schroeder's analysis, we reach a time interval actually referred to as the "boring billion" by geoscientists mystified by the absence of Evolution (*https://en.wikipedia.org/wiki/Boring_Billion*). Characterized by little change, the oxygen in the atmosphere was stuck at a lower, although variable, level than the present, whilst much of the global ocean was entirely devoid of oxygen leading to inhospitable seas rich in iron and toxic hydrogen sulphide.

Before this time the atmosphere would likely have been similar to Venus or the gaseous outer planets. A thick veil of vapors including water, nitrogen, methane and carbon dioxide was firstly left over from the primeval meteorite bombardment, and then from the massive Achaean and early Proterozoic volcanic activity which is recorded by the "greenstone belts" (~3.8-2.2 Byr). This atmosphere would mostly reflect the radiant energy from the Sun but would progressively have become more translucent. The transmission of radiation to provide the energy driving the bacterial activity converted the atmosphere into a composition which would ultimately become favorable to higher forms of life.

The greater (Sun) and lesser (Moon) lights of verse 18 are not specifically named, probably because pagan societies in Moses' time were worshipping them as gods. The Hebrew description of Day 4 implies that the Sun, Moon and Stars had already been created, but they would now be visible on the Earth as the atmosphere transitioned from opaque to transparent. They appear to us as exactly the same size and periodically able to create perfect eclipses although this has only applied during the brief period of humankind's presence on Earth (Chapter *6.12.3*) and seems to be another example of God's design. From the beginning of Day 4 onwards day and night would be clearly evident with the Genesis text implying that the seasons would also now become apparent. A hydrological cycle incorporating rainfall (Genesis 2:5) could now begin as the atmosphere transformed away from the thick mist of earlier times.

9.6 Day Five: ~750 - 250 Million Years - Creation of multi-cellular life and the modern animal phyla

Verses 20-23 of Genesis 1 read:

> *And God said, "Let the waters bring forth abundantly the moving creature that hath life, and fowl that may fly above the earth in the open firmament of heaven". And God created great (whales), and every living creature that moveth, which the waters brought forth abundantly, after their kind, and every (winged fowl) after his kind: and God saw that it was good. And God blessed them, saying, Be fruitful, and multiply, and fill the waters in the seas, and let fowl multiply in the Earth. And the evening and the morning were the fifth day.*

For more than two billion years life forms had been mostly just unicellular with simple morphologies. Multicellular organisms comprising blue-green algae may have appeared as early as ~2.0 Byr, but their morphology was restricted to simple mat-like forms, notably static mound-like features flourishing in intertidal waters called "stromatolites". Defining the beginning of Day 5, Earth was to experience two extraordinary creative events that introduced the metazoans, animals that originate as a single cell but then develop into multiple cells with different purposes organized into a range of different organs such as nerves and muscles. The first event is assigned to the Ediacaran Period (635-541 Myr) and comprised a range of more than 100 genera of soft-bodied organisms. Due to the absence of hard body parts they are preserved as impressions in fine grained and slowly-deposited clay and silt-rich sediments with worm-like, leaf-like, disc and immobile bag-like impressions (Figure 9.2). They seem to have no direct links to succeeding faunas and appear to be unique to this ~100 Myr time period. The beginning of the Ediacaran is defined by the end of the previous interval of episodic frigid climates (the Cryogenian) and not by the first appearance of the Ediacaran fauna. It is therefore likely that the appearance of this fauna occurred earlier, although suitable rocks to confirm this are unfortunately rare.

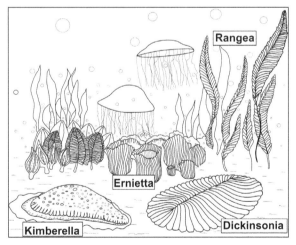

Figure 9.2: Examples of the multicellular life forms that appeared in the Ediacaran Seas about 635 Ma ago. These are preserved as impressions in fine-grained rocks and were soon (in geological terms) to disappear and be replaced by the modern phyla of fauna and flora in the "Cambrian Explosion" at ~541 Ma.

The second creative event, the "Cambrian Explosion", began at 541 Myr and within an interval constrained to little more than 20 Myr all the present animal phyla seem to have appeared. The phyla of the animal kingdom are progressively subdivided into classes, orders, families, genera and finally species. These subdivisions comprise animals that were subsequently to change, appear, adapt and disappear throughout the succeeding stratigraphic rock successions, but the basic body parts defining the number of phyla appear to have remained the same.[*]

The significance of the Hebrew in the text of Day 5 is "Let the waters swarm with swarms of living creatures." The word for swarm is repeated to add extra emphasis and in English this could be interpreted as "swarms and swarms and swarms" giving the impression of enormous numbers of a wide variety of creatures. The fourth Century teacher Basil interpreted the verse as: "Let the waters bring forth abundantly the moving creature that hath life." These creatures are described as living creatures or in Hebrew *nephesh chayyāh* and include creatures with life defined by blood דם - *dahm,* a word with a gematria of 44, just one short of Adam's number 45 (Chapter 8.1). The word *nephesh* (נפש) refers to life where Leviticus 17:11 notes that *"the life of the flesh is in the blood"*. Day 5 emphasizes the great difference between animal life and plant life of Day 3. Plants are food machines that can self-replicate, whereas it is the animals that use this plant material in a hierarchy through plant-consuming to meat-consuming. Hebrews 9:22 declares *"without shedding of blood there is no remission for sins"*. This is why the blood of certain animals could be offered as a covering for sin as a type of the future Messianic sacrifice, whereas plants could not: God could accept Abel's offering but not Cain's (Genesis 4:4-5).

The first insects appeared in Early Ordovician times simultaneously with the plants required for their food and life cycle. The translation

---

[*] *Of the 36 recognized animal phyla, not all can be positively traced to the base of the Cambrian; the present record of the Rotifera (microscopic organisms with ring-shaped heads) for example, only goes back to the Eocene.*

Figure 9.3: Impression of the "swarms and swarms and swarms" of animals that appeared with the Cambrian "Explosion" and all including phyla that are still present with us today. Even if Evolution were true it could never have produced such an amazing diversity of life forms within such a brief time span.

'winged fowl' noted in parentheses above is correctly derived from the Hebrew as 'flying creatures', not birds, and would appropriately refer to winged insects which first appear in Devonian times at ~405 Ma. Pollen-bearing plants (angiosperms) essential for the life style of these insects again appear simultaneously in geological terms during a great diversification of plant life found at this level in the Geological Column. Since insects and angiosperms are essential to the life cycle of each other, they had to appear at the same time. A further issue in the KJV translation is the use of the world 'whale' also noted in parentheses above. The whale is a marine mammal. It did not appear until Day 6 at ~32 Ma together with many other large mammals defying attempts to link it to a land-living predecessor. The Hebrew *tannim* actually refers to 'great sea monsters' and can embrace the amphibians and the early marine reptiles such as the ichthyosaurs and plesiosaurs which appear in the geological record from Permian times towards the end of Day 5.

9.7 Day Six: ~250 Million Years - 6000 years ago: Preparing the modern environment, creation of mammals and ultimately Humankind

Verses 24-31 of Genesis 1 read:

> *And God said, "Let the Earth bring forth the living creature after his kind, cattle, and creeping thing, and beast of the Earth after his kind: and it was so. And God made the beast of the Earth after his kind, and cattle after their kind, and everything that creepeth upon the Earth after his kind: and God saw that it was good. And God said, Let us make man in our image, after our likeness: and let them have dominion over the fish of the sea, and over the fowl of the air, and over the cattle, and over all the Earth, and over every creeping thing that creepeth upon the Earth". So, God created man in his own image, in the image of God created he him; male and female created he them. And God blessed them, and God said unto them, "Be fruitful, and multiply, and replenish the Earth, and subdue it: and have dominion over the fish of the sea, and over the fowl of the air, and over every living thing that moves upon the Earth". And God said, "Behold, I have given you every herb bearing seed, which is upon the face of all the Earth, and every tree, in which is the fruit of a tree yielding seed; to you it shall be for meat. And to every beast of the Earth, and to every fowl of the air, and to everything that creepeth upon the Earth, wherein there is life, I have given every green herb for meat": and it was so. And God saw everything that he had made, and, behold, it was very good. The evening and the morning were the sixth day.*

This is the longest description of a day and is first to mention a mammal, in this case a domesticated animal (cattle). However, the primarily concern of the text is the creation of man. The date assigned to the beginning of Day 6 coincides with the catastrophic mass extinction event at the end of the Permian Period, around 252 million years ago. It defines the boundary between the Palaeozoic Era where large mobile life forms were dominated by invertebrates, and the

Mesozoic Era dominated by reptiles. The leading cause was likely the eruption of the Siberian basalt traps spanning around 2 Myr at ~251 Ma. This event produced an immense volcanic province with associated gas emissions that devastated the climate. Contributory causes may have included one or more large asteroid impacts, and climate changes brought about by large releases of underwater methane or methane-producing microbes. The extinction affected up to 96% of all marine species and 70% of all terrestrial vertebrate species; as a result ~57% of all biological families and ~83% of all genera became extinct. The consequent loss in biodiversity and collapse in the food chains devastated the environment for land-dwelling organisms. The ecosystems took 10-30 million years to stabilize - significantly longer than after any other extinction event.

Of most importance to the Biblical perspective is the preparation of Earth for the Class Mammalia - the mammals. This class would be distinguished by the presence of mammary glands, which in females produce milk for feeding, nursing and caring for the young. Other distinguishing features are a covering of fur or hair, a neocortex (a region of the brain) and three middle ear bones. The earliest known examples of the mammals appeared within a hundred million years of the inferred start of this day at ~160 Myr in Jurassic times and were small rodent-like animals. Genesis 1:29-30 concludes by stating that plant and animal life were created for humankind with the plant life also given for the cattle to bring forth meat (also noted in Psalm 104:14).

Following a dearth of impacting for a billion years, asteroid activity increased by about two and a half times close to the start of this Day at ~290 Ma. This level of bombardment persists today, and has been attributed to an ancient collision of objects in the asteroid belt between Mars and Jupiter which caused a large asteroid to break up into smaller pieces. The climatic consequences of asteroid impacts can be a primary cause of extinction events and six such event are recognized between 252 and 66 Ma. However, it would take the largest of these impacts defining the Cretaceous–Tertiary (K–T) boundary at 66 Ma to destroy the dominant reptilian fauna including the dinosaurs, and prepare Earth for the dominance of mammals and ultimately humankind. The cause of this second mass extinction is now confidently attributed to a massive comet or asteroid 10 to 15 km in size. The impact is linked to the 180 km Chicxulub crater on the Yucatán Peninsula in the Gulf of Mexico. Possible contributory causes include the near-simultaneous eruption of great volumes of lava comprising the Deccan Traps in India and climate change resulting from a rapid drop in sea levels. The impact debris and gaseous aerosol reduced solar transmission by 50-80%, closing down photosynthesis in plants and plankton for months and reducing surface temperatures for years. These effects combined with acid rain, and a disrupted ocean stratification and circulation, devastated the global environment mainly through a lingering winter (Pope et al. 1998). A large part of all animal life was forced into extinction: in addition to the dinosaurs, this included numerous terrestrial organisms including certain mammals, pterosaurs, birds, lizards, insects, and plants. In the oceans it extinguished the plesiosaurs and giant marine lizards at the same time as devastating fish, sharks, and mollusk populations (notably the ammonites, which became extinct) as well as many species of plankton. Overall at least 75% of all species on Earth vanished.

The last Tertiary Period of Geological Time encompasses the dominant age of the mammals. The latter part witnessed global cooling leading ultimately to the Pleistocene ice ages during which the hominids with a likeness to created Adam appeared. According to the conventional Ussher-Lightfoot chronology this Day would have ended about 6000 years ago with the creation of Adam being God's last transformative act (Chapter *8.9.2*). In the last verse (31) of Genesis One God reflects on His work of converting chaos into order with the statement: *"God saw everything that He had made, and, behold, it was very good"*. The latter part of this verse was alternatively translated by Onkelos (~35-110 AD) the distinguished Roman convert to Judaism, as *"it was a unified order"*, or in Young's literal translation: *"God blesseth the seventh day, and sanctifieth it, for in it He hath ceased from all His work which God had prepared for making"*. This becomes the first mention of the Sabbath Rest of God, instituted by Moses in the Torah and subsequently kept by the Jewish people (and most of the rest of humankind) ever since. Unlike the descriptions of the preceding Six Days, Genesis has no statement telling us that Day 7 had ended. The Book of Hebrews (4:3-4) tells us that this Sabbath rest is continuing - we are apparently still in Day 7 as order progressively runs down to disorder and ultimately chaos.

It is the essence of any hypothesis that it should be subject to testing leading to its rejection or continuing acceptance in the way that the Young Earth proposition is evaluated in Chapter 6. A preliminary test of the analysis we have presented above can be made with Schroeder's (1997) proposition that each doubling of space will lead to a contraction of time by half. This is tested in Figure 9.4 by comparing the days according to this doubling-halving model with the most important transitions in cosmological and geological history. If we were selecting these times on the basis of our present scientific understanding of the ages assigned to the key major events defining the limits of the Six Days, the likely candidates would be (in reverse order) (i) the creation of Adam ~6000 years ago, (ii) the Palaeozoic to Mesozoic boundary at 252 Ma preparing the world for the rise of the mammals, (iii) the explosion of complex metazoan life during the Ediacaran Period (635 Ma), although with an original date not yet well defined, (iv) the purely physical event of Day 4 defining the change of the atmospheric composition from reducing to oxidizing, an event with a central timing of ~2.1 Byr, (v) the appearance of the first life when the first oceans were formed at ~3.8 Byr, (vi) the formation of the Earth and Solar System estimated to be ~4.5 Byr and (vii) the event immediately after the Big Bang when heat and light were converted into matter from which the Universe would subsequently be built.

The significant differences are seen to be the ages assigned to the boundaries between Days 2 and 3 associated with the formation of the Solar System, and the boundaries between Days 4 and 5 linked to the transformation of the atmosphere from toxic to oxygenating. The latter age is rather broadly constrained by the geological evidence and the difference is not large enough to warrant doubt about the interpretation of Day 4. In contrast, and as described in Chapter 6, we can only currently infer that age of the Solar System, likely defining the beginning

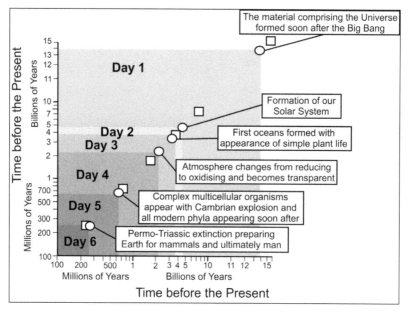

*Figure 9.4: The logarithmic expansion of space and contraction of time shown on a log-log graph where the **squares** are the ages deduced from the Doubling-Halving model of Schroeder (1997) and the **circles** are the current ages assigned to the events likely to the define boundaries of the Six Days of Genesis Chapter 1 from present understanding of the Geological and Cosmological evidence.*

of Day 2, as older than 4,500 Ma but less than 10,000 Ma. This remains the biggest uncertainty in constraining the intervals occupied by the Six Days and, as noted above (9.1), there is much uncertainty surrounding cosmological history during this earlier phase of Universe evolution. Nevertheless modern science teaches us that the history of the Earth and Universe has been punctuated by seven pivotal events (Figure 9.4) with the last being the Creation of Humankind. This is just what the Bible tells us as it frames them within the six transformative days of Genesis Chapter One. We are told that each of these days ended; we are not told that Day 7 has ended - this is still with us today.

References:

Pearce, E.K.V., 1993. *Evidence for Truth, Volume 1, Science*, Evidence Programs, Eastbourne, Sussex, 319pp.

Piper, J.D.A., 2013. A planetary perspective on Earth evolution: Lid Tectonics before Plate Tectonics, Tectonophysics, 589, 44-56.

Piper, J.D.A., 2018. Dominant Lid Tectonics behavior of continental lithosphere in Precambrian times: Palaeomagnetism confirms prolonged quasi-integrity and absence of supercontinent cycles, Geoscience Frontiers, 9, 61-89.

Pope, K.O., Baines, K.H., Ocampo, A.C. and Ivanov, B.A., 1998. Volatile production and climatic effects of the Chicxulub Cretaceous/Tertiary Impact, Journal of Geophysical Research, 102, 21645-21664.

Schroeder, Gerald, 1990. *Genesis and the Big Bang*, Bantam Books, 212pp.

Schroeder, Gerald, 1997. *The Science of God: the Convergence of Scientific and Biblical Wisdom*, Broadway Books, New York, 226 pp.

Wood, D., 2011. The Formation and Differentiation of Earth, Physics Today, 40-45.

Chapter 10

The Real Flood of Noah

10.1 Introduction

This chapter seeks to establish the case for a recent and devastating, but extremely brief, event in Humankind's early written history. The Flood of Noah has been widely derided by secularists, parodied by Hollywood and falsely used by YECs to explain the geological record. Nevertheless, although the direct record left by the Flood is sparse, evidence coming forward over just the past few decades shows that it may be explained by a geophysical event occurring precisely on the date the Bible predicts. This event proves to be endorsed by the contemporaneous archaeological record. In addition, and independent of this evidence, the Biblical record of the Flood contains a remarkable signature of the redemption of humankind of such breadth that it is difficult to escape the conclusion that it has a Divine origin. It now appears as a pivotal moment in our history, only to be surpassed ~2300 years later by the death and resurrection of the Lord Jesus Christ.

10.2 The Case for the Flood Event

10.2.1 Mankind has recent genetic origins

We have explored in Chapter 8 the evidence that humankind has a recent origin with genetic evidence defying Evolution and requiring that the generations were reset in relatively recent times, likely as recently as the Biblically-recorded time of the Flood. Genesis Chapter Six tells us that the Flood was necessitated by a near-total corruption of humankind by sin, which in turn resulted from some kind of cross breeding (Genesis 6:4). Biblical scholars have produced two contrasting explanations for this corruption.

The first proposal is that it was brought about by the separate inter-breeding between contrasting families, namely an ungodly line of Cain and a "godly" line of Seth with the latter ultimately preserved during the Flood through the family of Noah. There are two difficulties with this explanation. It requires that all the progeny of a supposedly-righteous line of Seth, with the exception of Noah, were judged by the Flood as well as Cain's evil line. Also it provides no explanation for Genesis Chapter Six with the introduction of the "mighty men of renown" bringing in "giants", and also the introduction of an extra-ordinary knowledge to the world predating the Flood.

The second explanation is that the human genome was being progres-sively corrupted by a source with angelic origins. The Bible testimony has no accommodation for aliens; instead it attributes this corruption to fallen angels (literally translated from the Greek angels are "messen-gers") from another dimension invading humankind prior to the Flood. These "Sons of God" - a term more correctly translated "associates of god" - are commonly referred to as the "Nephelim" or "fallen ones". This word appears in the Septuagint Old Testament as the word "gigantes" and leads to their association with impressive stature and mythological traditions of the Middle East. In the Masoretic text the word again appears in the post-Flood world (Numbers 13:33) suggesting that some aspect of their genetic makeup survived the Flood, a point expanded on below. The angelic beings of the Scriptures come from a dimension outside of the created world of Genesis Chapter One, which has a time-frame subject to decay as order moves to chaos. Angels are created but eternal and Jesus emphasizes that they do not breed (Matthew 22:30). The Book of Jude, the penultimate book of the Bible, and written in a time which still had access to many ancient writings since lost, refers to this in verse 6 as *"angels which kept not their first estate, but left their own habitation"*. To be able to breed they would need to have sacri-ficed a property which may be implied by the Greek word *"oiketerion"* ("dwelling") to occupy a human body; a contrast is seen where this same word occurs in the hope of the redeemed person in 2 Corinthians 5:2: *"for in this we groan earnestly desiring to be clothed upon with our heavenly body which is from heaven"*.

The impact of the Nephelim on humanity before the Flood is described in the apocryphal books of Enoch and Jasher. These books are not included in the canon of Scripture because they are not regarded as Divinely-inspired in their entirety, and at least the former has clearly been corrupted (Johnson 2012), although they are referred to in the Bible as sources of additional history. The Dead Sea scrolls preserved by the Essenes include a "Book of Giants". It is also likely that the great wealth of ancient knowledge held in the Great Royal Library of Alexandria would have been able to shed more light on this era. Sadly in 640 AD when the Arab legions swept across North Africa during the Islamic invasion the warlord Amr ibn Al-Aas asked Mecca what to do with the scrolls; he was told that if it was not in the Quran it was not worth keeping and the entire contents were used to fuel the water for Alexandria's 4000 public baths over several months. Nevertheless we have the historian Josephus who equates the Nephelim with the Titans of Greek mythology, a mythology that went on to pervade Middle Eastern and circum-Mediterranean societies including Rome. The apocryphal sources imply that the watchers indulged in genetic manipulation so that their offspring would no longer have the breath, the *neshama,* of God, as hinted at in Genesis 6:3. The effect of this invasion was to cause *"all flesh to be corrupted"* (Genesis 6:12).*

According to this explanation Noah and his family are considered to be the only line left that remained genetically pure; the long period of 500 years that he alone of the pre-Flood patriarchs had to wait before he could find an untainted wife, and then have his children seems to be an indication of this. The books of the Old Testament up to the time of

---

* *Jewish tradition holds that the Book of the Patriarch Enoch was carried by Noah in the Ark and passed on to Shem. Today we have three versions of the Book of Enoch. Enoch 1 was recovered from an Ethiopian source by James Bruce in 1773, stored in the British Museum, and translated from the Coptic by R.H. Charles in 1893; it contains the item quoted by Jude. Enoch 2 written in Aramaic is known as the "Slavonic Enoch" whilst Enoch 3 is known as the Hebrew Book of Enoch from evidence that it may originally have been written in Hebrew. The Books of Enoch contain much prophetic material, some already fulfilled, much awaiting fulfillment, which accords with the Biblical record, although items which are clearly unbiblical appear to have been inserted later by Gnostics (Johnson 2012, and see also "Who were the Watchers?" by Dr A. Nyland, Ancient Mysteries Publishing Company).*

King David and even later to the Prophet Ezra continue to record the "gigantes" in the inhabitants of Canaan. Canaan is the only grandson of Noah mentioned in Genesis 9:18. Noah cursed him but not his own son Ham, (Genesis 9:25) suggesting that it was Ham's wife and Canaan's mother who was not genetically pure. Possibly for this reason a corrupted gene crept through into the post-Flood generation to explain references to genetic hybrids. The Bible records their sinful character and why God required the destruction of descendents of Canaan; their habitation in the land of Canaan extended to the "cities of the Plain" including Sodom and Gomorrah. However the curse evidently did not apply to the other children of Ham (Cush, Mizraim and Put) who are recorded as moving off to inhabit Africa and Arabia; any racist slur that their races were inferior has no Biblical foundation.

10.2.2 *The evidence for a vanished civilization of superior technological achievement*

There is widespread archaeological evidence that a civilization with extraordinary technological abilities was wiped out by the flood. In spite of the explosion of knowledge in our own day we still have no idea of, for example, how the geoglyphs or the walls of Cuzco in Peru were precision cut and set, how the 2.5 million finely shaped blocks weighing between 2 and 70 tons of the Great Pyramid of Giza was both engineered and placed with extraordinary astronomic properties, how the huge serpent mounds stretching from Ohio down to the Gulf of Mexico were precisely engineered, and how the great pillars and blocks of Baalbek in Lebanon (some of the latter as heavy as a frigate-sized ship) were cut and smoothed. Ancient Egypt alone, records an outstanding number of artifacts perfectly shaped and smoothed, many transported hundreds of miles from the Aswan granite quarries; these were cut from granite and quartzite of such exceptional hardness that they could never have been cut and shaped with copper and bronze tools, and smoothed with sand, according to the conventional skills traditionally assigned to the Bronze Age. The Smithsonian Institution archives document extensive evidence for burials of giant figures in the latter part of the 1800's. This evidence has been subject to obfuscation in more recent times, perhaps because it does not accord with the evolutionary view of humankind from hunter-gatherers and cavemen. However, these pre-Flood civilizations achieved technological feats some of which we are still unable to replicate today; this knowledge disappeared with the Flood. Chapter Four of Genesis briefly alludes to the technological and artistic achievements of Cain's generation, and even Noah would likely have required superior metal tools to construct something as large and complex as the Ark. Although beyond the scope of our analysis here, the record of these vanished pre-Flood peoples and the impact of the Nephelim is the subject of much ongoing scholarly research by Christian investigators, notably Derek Gilbert, Tom Horn, L.A. Mazulli and Steven Quayle. The reader can follow up this research in an expanding body of their books and websites. The surface preservation of this extraordinary pre-Flood record clearly precludes any implication that the Flood was responsible for the Geological Column (see Chapter 6).

10.2.3 The record of the Ten Patriarchs

There are 10 patriarchs recorded in Genesis from Adam to Noah where 10 is the Biblical number of Divine Order, Law and Testimony. Their names record God's post-Flood plan for humankind's redemption. The patriarchs were each assigned names with specific Hebrew meaning leading up to the Flood Event. In order these are:

1. **Adam (אָדָם)** = "Man"
2. **Seth (שֵׁת)** = "Appointed"
3. **Enosh (שׁוֹנָאֱ)** = "Mortal man"
4. **Canaan (כנע)** = "sorrow; low; humble; depressed"
5. **Mahalaleel (מהללאל)** = "praise of God; God is splendour"
6. **Jared (יִדְרָ, יֶדְרָ)** = "descent; shall come down as a theophany" (a theophany refers to an appearance of God to man)
7. **Enoch (חנוך)** = "Wise teacher; dedicated; disciplined; profound"
8. **Methusaleh (מְתוּשֶׁלַח)** = "His death shall bring judgement; scourging; smitten"
9. **Lamech (לְמֶךְ)** = "To lament; despairing"
10. **Noah (נֹחַ)** = "Comfort; rest"

Taken in sequence these names record God's intention to send the Messiah to deliver mankind by His own sacrifice in the post-Flood world:

"Man[1] is appointed[2] mortal[3] sorrow[4] but the Splendid God[5] shall come down to man[6] wisely teaching[7] that His death shall bring smiting and scourging[8] and to the despairing[9] comfort (rest) [10]"

Methusaleh, whose name implies judgement, lived longer than all the other patriarchs; his longevity is likely a measure of God's grace and patience. Consistent with the name assigned by Enoch, Methusaleh is recorded as dying just before the flood began.

10.2.4 *The Divine properties of the Biblical Text*

The Biblical text reporting the event has remarkable geometrical properties each pointing to the theme of Redemption:

- ➤ The length of the Ark was **300** Cubits. **300** is the 24th (**8 + 8 + 8**) Triangle number.
- ➤ Furthermore **300** is the sum of the first **24** numbers (= 1+ 2 + 3 + 4 + 5 +…+ 24) where **24** was the Biblical number of the courses of priesthood in the ancient Jewish First and Second temples and becomes symbolic of the priesthood of believers, the people that are redeemed in the Book of Revelation Chapter 4.
- ➤ The Height to Width to Depth of the Ark was **300** to **50** to **30.** *In proportion, these are the typical dimensions of a man.* They are a signature of the deliverance of the 8 people carried safely by God through the Flood: Only with the extensive building of steamships in the 19th Century was it found that these are also the optimum dimensions for a seaworthy craft.
- ➤ The **Volume of the Ark** = **300** x **50** x **30** = **45** x **10,000** cubic cubits. This number is the gematria of Adam (man) multiplied by the number of ordinal testimony multiplied (Chapter 5). The end of the ark, 50 by 30 cubits, is in the ratio of 5 to 3, or 1.666, the golden ratio.
- ➤ The Gematria of "Noah" (נח) is **58** where: **58** = **3** (Trinity) + **10** (the Patriarch Cycle) + **45** (Adam, man)
- ➤ The whole Flood episode saves the faithful few from judgment and prefigures the redemption of humankind by the Lord Jesus Christ:

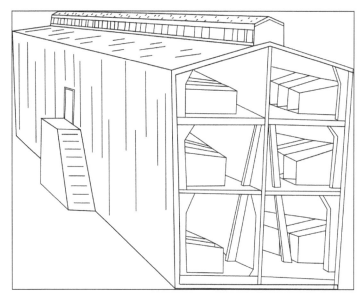

Figure 10.1: A sectioned sketch of the likely form of the Ark. Images and reconstructions of the Ark usually show it incorrectly with rounded prows. In reality it was designed to float and not to move through the water.

(a) Since the length of the Ark (**300** cubits) is the 24th triangle number and **24 = 8 + 8 + 8**, it is also a reflection of **8,** the Biblical number of resurrection and new beginnings. The Ark saved 8 souls and the Greek Gematria of Jesus is **888**

(b) The Ark was constructed of wood; the cross was made of wood.

(c) The volume of the Ark equaled Adam's number. Jesus was the second Adam come to redeem Adam's failure where Paul declares: ***"For as in Adam all die, even so in Christ shall all be made alive"*** (1 Corinthians 15:22).

(d) There is symbolism to the single door in the side of the Ark: Jesus declared ***"I am the door...the way the truth and the life"*** (John 14:6). On the cross His body was unbroken but He was given a single wound in the side shedding His atoning blood. We are told that it was God that shut the door of the Ark (Genesis 7:16).

(e) The Ark delivered humankind through judgment to a new life, Jesus would later come to redeem humankind for eternity

(f)   The Biblical record is a chiasm (Wenham 1978, 1987) - a cyclic 7-fold repetition of theme comprising a prophetic revelation of God's judgment followed by the redemption of humanity:

1. Noah and his sons Shem, Ham and Japheth (Genesis 6:9-10)
   2. Promise of the Flood and establishment of a Covenant (6:12-18)
      3. Preservation of life and food for sustenance (6:19-22)
         4. Command to enter the Ark (7:1-3)
            5. Waiting for the land to flood (7:4-10)
               6. Waters increase on the land and the Ark rises 7:11-17)
                  7. The waters cover the land for 150 days (7:18-24)

God remembers Noah (8:1)

                  7. Waters cover the land for 150 days (8:2-4)
               6. Waters drain away and Ark comes to rest (8:5-6)
            5. Three periods of 7 days waiting for the Land to dry (8:7-14)
         4. The command to leave the Ark (8:15-22)
      3. Multiplication of life and food for sustenance (9:1-17)
   2. Promise by God to remember the covenant and never again to bring judgment by flooding (9:8-17)
1. Noah and His Sons Shem, Ham, and Japheth (9:18-19)

This highly symmetric seven-fold structure characterizes the reporting of many themes in the Scriptures. Here it is a literary framework for a cataclysmic historical event. *Seven* is the biblical number of perfection and completion, *forty* is the number of trial and testing, *150 = 3 x 50*, or the *Trinity Number* times the *number of Jubilee, deliverance and restoration,* and there are *seven* pairs of each clean animal. Every one of these numbers carries a divine signature.

10.2.5   *The significance of the wood and the pitch*

The symbolic issue of redemption continues with the wood and the pitch used for the Ark. Lignins are a complex group of organic compounds found in the cell walls of plants that give structural rigidity to their growth and form - they make hardwood trees hard. The sulphur-bearing lignins form the structural basis of all hardwood trees and this botanical fact amplifies the significance of Genesis 6:14. The Ark allowed Noah and his family to survive the impending global Flood and repopulate the Earth. He is specifically commanded, "Make yourself an ark of gopher wood." The meaning of the Hebrew word **גֹּפֶר**, or gôpher, is unknown; this is the only place in the Bible where it is used and the KJV leaves it unspecified although other versions speculate different kinds of wood such as cypress.* "Gôpher" is a root of the word *gophrîth*, **גָּפְרִית** translated seven times in the Old Testament as "brimstone" in the context of fiery judgment on human wickedness including Genesis 19:24 in the context of Sodom and Gomorrah. The New Testament Greek equivalent of gophrîth is θεῖον, or *theion*, and is again used seven times in the context of Divine judgment of wickedness. The number seven also has a reference to God's displeasure of humankind's sin as stated in Proverbs 6:16: ***"These six things the Lord hates, yes, seven are an abomination to Him."*** By using the Greek word *theion* for brimstone, used interchangeably with the word for sulphur, θείο, or *theío*, God is telling Noah to use a form of plant material with sulphur-bearing lignin. The word for "wood" is plural in the Hebrew since wooden ships are typically built of several types of hardwood. Some woods work well for the hull, whilst other kinds of wood are used for support structures and decking but all would be sulphurbearing trees.

Noah is told in Genesis 6:14 to cover the Ark inside and outside with pitch. The word "cover" is the Hebrew word **כָּפַר**, or *kâphar*, which literally means "to cover" or "to insulate" or "to atone for". It is applied in the Mosaic Law to describe the priestly atonement for the sins of the people as on Yôm Kippûr (the "Day of Atonement"). A similar word used for pitch, **כֹּפֶר**, or *kôpher*, describes the "covering" payment of a ransom for a person's life. The Ark is therefore not only a symbol of protection

---

* *The antiquity of the Flood account is suggested by several other words with usages that had evidently lapsed by the time of Moses. They include "ark" which is a different word from "Ark" of the Covenant and "Tosher" (Genesis 6:16) which might have meant "window" or "ventilator" (see Pearce 1993).*

from the judgment of the floodwaters, but the materials used in the construction are, at a deeper level, a covering protection from a sulphurous fiery judgment. The Bible foretells only one judgment by flooding (Genesis 8:21) but predicts a second one by fire (2 Peter 3:6-7) so that Noah and the Ark become a foreshadowing of the ultimate atonement achieved by the Lord Jesus Christ *(https://www.icr.org/article/11276/)*.

10.2.6 *The world-wide record of Flood Traditions*

Over 270 ancient traditions record a great Flood from every one of the six inhabited continents. The diverse records of a flood event can be explored on websites such as *www.talkorigins.org/faqs/flood-myths.html*. The best-known flood story is the Babylonian Epic of Gilgamesh, recorded within a segment from a poem on 12-tablet IX dating from ~1200 BC; some tablets hinting at the event may be as old as 1800 BC, although well after the time of Abraham. Gilgamesh was an historical king of Uruk who reigned in the Early Dynastic I period and the first tablet records him rebuilding the city walls destroyed by the Flood; he is therefore likely to date from a generation soon after the Flood occurred. The Gilgamesh boat is a most unseaworthy cube-shaped and only seven days were given for the building, gathering all the animals and for rainfall to cover the Earth. In a myth from Hawaii a man named Nu-u made a great canoe with a house on it and filled it with animals. In this story, the waters came up over all the Earth and killed all the people; only Nu-u and his family were saved. One of the Chinese legends explains that the flood was caused by an argument between a crab and a bird. Fuhi, his wife, three sons, and three daughters escaped a great flood and were the only people alive on Earth. After the great flood, they repopulated the world. In a Greek myth the first race of people was completely destroyed because they were exceedingly wicked. Deucalion is told to build a chest to survive a flood; the fountains of the deep opened, the rain fell in torrents, and the rivers and seas rose to cover the Earth killing everyone except him and his family. They survived due to his prudence and piety to form the link between 'the first and second race of men'. He loaded his wives and children on to a great ark with the animals. The animals came to him, and by God's help, remained friendly for the duration of the flood. The flood waters escaped down a chasm opened in Hierapolis.

The global sample of so many flood stories appears to record memories of a real cataclysmic event carried down orally by ancient traditions that lacked a written language. To the skeptic Noah's Flood would be just one of many myths and may even have been derived from an older tradition. However, the oldest recorded example seems to go back to only 400-500 years after Noah's epic adventure, whilst Noah's Flood has a Biblical record with the extraordinary Divine signature that defies human invention. Although these stories from around the world differ, particularly in ways that they embellish the characters, they date from an era after God had confused the languages (Genesis 11:7) and are likely to have been modified with each oral transmission; unsurprisingly, they often do not want to acknowledge that the Flood was an act of judgment.

10.2.7 The record of Jesus

The most compelling reason for us to believe that the Flood was a real event is that the Lord Jesus Christ Himself confirmed it. This occurs in the Gospel records of Matthew and Luke and describes the Flood as an act of Divine judgment. The historian Luke records:

"They did eat, they drank, they married wives, they were given in marriage, until the day that Noah entered into the ark, and the flood came, and destroyed them all". (Luke 17:27).

With the reality of the Flood repeated by the Apostles:

"By faith Noah, being warned of God of things not seen as yet, moved with fear, prepared an ark to the saving of his house; by which he condemned the world, and became heir of the righteousness which is by faith". (Hebrews 11:7).

"Which sometime were disobedient, when once the longsuffering of God waited in the days of Noah, while the ark was a preparing, wherein few, that is, eight souls were saved by water". (1 Peter 3:20)

"And spared not the old world, but saved Noah the eighth person, a preacher of righteousness, bringing in the flood upon the world of the ungodly". (2 Peter 2:5)

10.2.8 The purpose of the Flood

The Hebrew word **Mabbul** occurs thirteen times in the Old Testament in the exclusive context of Noah's Flood; this distinguishes it from **nachal,** the word used to describe the typical flood experience of humankind. Amplifying on section (*2.1*), we note that the implications of these verses is that God tolerated a corrupt civilization until he was forced to act in judgment, with the exceptional longevity of Methusaleh's life reflecting His patience and compassion. Many Biblical scholars consider this corruption to have been of a genetic nature and concerned the "Nephelim". By the time God acted in judgement only Noah's line remained genetically pure - the New Testament records Noah as a "preacher of righteousness" (2 Peter 2:5), but due to the reprobate nature of his world he only succeeded in saving seven people. Jesus warned that the time of His Second Coming would be like the days of Noah (Luke 17:26-30). The expanded implication of His statement is that society would then become totally self-absorbed with no thought for its eternal destiny; in the context of the nephelim, an additional implication may be that it indulges in genetic manipulation.

There is an indication of this in the gematria of the four named people saved by the Flood. **Noah (נח = 58), Shem (שֵׁם = 340), Ham (חם = 48) and Japeth (יפה = 490).** The sum of these numbers is **936** which is a multiple of **13**, Satan's number (see Table in Chapter 5). However, when Ham's number is subtracted we have **888**, the number of Jesus and resurrection. Ham was the progenitor of the Canaanites, and the Israelites of the Exodus found "Anakim" and "Rephaim" apparently descended from them when they made their reconnaissance of the Promised Land (Book of Numbers 13:28-29). The Anakim are traditionally linked with the Nephilim, the "giants" of Genesis 6:4). Particularly problematic was their adoption by their descendents of the worship of the deity Molech who required child sacrifice, a practise later recorded in civilisations such as Carthage. It would even taint ancient Israel and Judah, and would go on to become a key reason for their judgements (Chapter *1.2.1*). It would have been for this reason, and not for any vindictive trait, that God required the destruction of the descendents of Canaan.

10.2.9 *The timing of the End of the Flood*

Moses records in Genesis 8:4 that the Ark came to rest on the Earth on the *17th* day of the First Month of the year. As Moses led the Israelites out of Egypt it was on this *17th* day of the same month that they emerged from crossing the Red Sea and the Egyptian Army was destroyed. The manna which had fed the nation of Israel for 40 years in the wilderness stopped on the 16th of Nisan and from the 17th onwards Israel feasted on the new grain of the promised land (Joshua 5:10-12) - another picture of new life that came on the 17th day of the month. A thousand years after Moses, the Jews of the Persian Empire were delivered on this **17th** date of the same month from the genocide plotted by Haman who was condemned to death instead (Book of Esther 3:13, 4:11, 5:1). These were all to be examples of the greatest event of deliverance that would occur on this day: on the **17th** of this Jewish month (Nisan, the Appointed time of First Fruits - the Barley Harvest) 32 AD Jesus rose from the dead following three days in the tomb. Each of these events is viewed as an example of God moving to thwart Satanic aims to frustrate His ultimate redemption of humankind. Seventeen is the seventh prime number and the Biblical number of eternal security (see Table 5.1 in Chapter 5).

10.3 The Physical Record of the Flood

There are so many Divine signatures to the Biblical record of Noah's Flood that it seems inconceivable that they could have been brought together by chance human design. Nothing comparable has been demonstrated from all the other ancient records of a cataclysmic flood event. If we adhere to the Genesis record of the generations from Noah through to Abraham, and then through the Israelite people up to the record of historical times from secular sources, the Flood proves to be a surprisingly recent event occurring at ~2,345 BC according to the Ussher-Lightfoot chronology (Chapter *8.9.2*). Adam's son, Tubal Cain of the pre-flood generation is recorded in the Hebrew as a "hammer, a copper worker in copper and iron" (Genesis 4:22). The Copper Age is regarded as the period between the Neolithic and Bronze ages and is traditionally assigned to the ~1000-year period between ~4500 and 3500 BC, broadly consistent with the Biblical record. Either because it was so tough to beat out or because of the Flood, iron seems to have fallen into disuse until the Hittites discovered the art of smelting in ~1500 BC. It is always possible to speculate, as many have done, that generations are missing from the Bible account and that events occurred considerably earlier (Chapter *8.9.2*). However this would seem to conflict with the Divine message within the overlapping genealogies noted in (*2.3*) above and it seems to be unnecessary in the context of the geophysical and archaeological evidence described below,.

We consider the case for the physical record of Noah's Flood under four headings:

10.4 The Ark and the extent of the Flood

Whilst the evidence for pre-Flood civilizations is extensive, evidence for the Ark itself is not compelling. Repeated attempts to locate the Ark of Noah on the volcano Mount Ararat on the Turkey-Armenian border can be explored on various web resources but remain unconvincing. This is probably because the explorers are looking in the wrong place. The assignment of the name "Ararat" to this location appears to date only from medieval times. The Bible records that the Ark landed on the *Mountains* of Ararat (Genesis 8:4) and that the survivors moved _westwards_ to the Plain of Shinar in the Tigris-Euphrates valley (Genesis 11:2). The actual landing place of the Ark would therefore seem to have been in Iran much further to the east of the location which has been the focus of so much, apparently fruitless, investigation. However, continuing pursuit of remains of the Ark is not without merit because Noah was instructed to coat the gopher wood with pitch both on the inside and outside (Genesis 6:14) and the potential for preservation should be good. The centre of bitumen production in Noah's time was likely the region of Hit ~130 km west of Baghdad; it is still found here in pools along a line of hot springs connected by a fault to a hydrocarbon reservoir at depth.

Whether or not the Flood covered the whole Earth (and therefore at what altitude to look for the Ark) has long been debated by Biblical scholars without a clear answer. The Hebrew records *kol eretz* where *kol* means "all" but *eretz* can mean "earth", "land", "country" or "ground". The most common usage is "land" and may signify that the Flood did not cover the whole global land surface, although Genesis 7:19 uses the expression "under all the heavens" and implies a global impact. A wide-ranging discussion of the location, depth and extent of the Flood can be found at the website *godandscience.org* where unfortunately, no unified model emerges that could aid in the search for archaeological evidence. The Hebrew word for "mountain" ר ה can also refer to "hills" as in Deuteronomy 11:11 and the KJV translates Genesis 7:19 as "all the high hills". If God had wished to make it clear that the entire planet was covered with flood waters, the Hebrew word for the whole earth—tebel ('world')—would likely have been sufficient. In the New Testament the Apostle Peter refers to the fact that "the world of that time *was deluged and destroyed" (II Peter 3:6)*. The Greek phrase used here—tote kosmos—indicates that it refers to the world known to Noah when the Flood occurred. Whilst it might then be argued that God could just have told Noah to move to higher ground, this would seemingly have destroyed the redemptive message behind the Flood narrative: to tell Noah to hike up to where he would be safe from God's judgment is to teach that man can save himself by his own two legs.

10.5 The Record of Geomorphology

Since the Flood was such a short event with a total duration of no more than 150 days, it is unsurprising that little obvious geomorphic evidence remains after more than 4000 years of topographic degradation. Any sediments deposited during such a brief flood would have been washed away by now - such sediments would otherwise have required thousands of years in a stable and subaqueous environment for them to be lithified into hard rock and identified today. Nevertheless, there are possible geomorphic signatures. Most river systems are 'misfits' meaning that their present volumes and meandering geometries are much smaller in scale than the geometries of the embanking topography. This is attributed to much larger volumes of water draining through them and cutting broad drainage channels that bear little relationship to the rivers that they now host. In addition, porous terrains composed of rocks such as limestone and chalk have entire topographies cut by valleys which are now dry.

These geomorphic signatures are usually attributed to flood waters during the melting of the Pleistocene ice sheets between ~15,000 and 9,000 years ago and during subsequent post-glacial pluvial (wet) periods; it would therefore be difficult to isolate any effects of landscape molding during the draining of the short Noachian Flood.

The issue thus becomes one of distinguishing the effects of draining flood waters due to a very brief event ~4350 years ago from the deposits of other much more protracted, post-glacial melting and pluvial events. An interval of wet climatic conditions before the time of Noah's Flood in North America for example, is known as the "Neopluvial Period" and was characterized by wet intervals between ~6000 and 3000 BC; a succeeding wet period in Europe known as the "Piroa Oscillation" occurred between 3200 and 2900 BC. These pluvial events were controlled by the global climatic zones and were not global in their impact. However, together with the vast volumes of water produced by the protracted melting of the Pleistocene ice sheets after 11,000-10,000 years ago in the northern hemisphere, they lasted long enough to cut massive valleys and gorges, and deposit sediments of a clearly multiple-episodic nature spanning long intervals of time. It would be difficult to isolate the impact of these melt waters from a single brief flooding event occurring only a few thousands of years later.

10.6 The Geophysical Causes

The Noachian Flood would have been a miraculous event not subject to rational explanation but the cause and the source of the water are legitimate sources for enquiry. One possibility is that the water came from the Earth's interior. The surface plates of the Earth (Chapter 6.12) are rigid but move over a Transition Zone between 410 to 660 kilometers deep where the Mantle approaches closest to its melting point and exhibits long-term plastic behavior as it moves the plates above. It is when rock melts from here that magma is produced to rise to the surface and produce volcanic activity that adds to the crust at the mid-ocean ridges (see note on *constructive plate margins* in Chapter 6.12). Minerals formed by the high pressures at this depth in the Earth squeeze the olivine, a 'dry' mineral and the characteristic content of the Mantle above, into a new crystal configuration called "wadsleyite". Wadsleyite together with the succeeding mineral stable in the pressures at greater depth called "ringwoodite", are hydrous ('wet') and can hold up to 3 percent of their weight in water. Diamonds recovered from the Transition Zone are found to contain water in a high-pressure form known as ice-VII. The estimated viscosity of the transition zone matches the predictions of a rock containing these minerals and saturated with water. Since this zone is a 250-kilometer-thick shell accounting for about 7 percent of Earth's mass, it is estimated that it contains several times the volume of the water in the surface oceans. It could be the source of the water related to the verse in Genesis Chapter 7 stating:

"...in the second month, the seventeenth day of the month, the same day were all the fountains of the great deep broken up, and the windows of heaven were opened". (Genesis 7:11)

However, from evidence compiled a hundred or more years ago but only now becoming widely known, there appears to be a more plausible cause of the Flood which both correlates with the Biblical date, and may not necessarily involve the need for the water from the Earth's interior. Pearce (1993) originally proposed that an abrupt shift in the axis of rotation of the Earth could have been responsible for the Flood because this would lead to a dramatic redistribution of the seas and drown large areas of land surface in a mega-tsunami-like event, even potentially briefly covering high mountains. Whilst there is no evidence for a recent movement of the magnetic poles that he proposed, there is evidence for a short-term shift in Earth's rotation identified from changes in the obliquity of the ecliptic. The ecliptic is the angle of tilt of the Earth's axis as it moves around the Sun. The Obliquity of the ecliptic is the inclination of Earth's equator with respect to the plane of rotation of the Earth around the Sun. It is currently approximately 23.4° and is responsible for the seasons as well as necessary for the annual renewal of organic activity (Chapter *4.3.8*). It is currently decreasing by about 0.013 degrees per hundred years due to planetary perturbations. These slow secular changes in the obliquity are described by an internationally-accepted formula derived by the Canadian-American astronomer Simon Newcomb (1835-1909). His formula incorporates all the forces known to govern the regular slow movement of the Earth's axis

The obliquity of the ecliptic is resolved by comparing the length of Sun's noonday shadow on the longest and shortest days of the year. Painstaking compilations of these observations in the ancient literature by the South Australian Government astronomer, George Dodwell (1879-1963) found that the obliquity of the ecliptic had deviated in a large but systematic way from the values predicted from Newcomb's formula. Dodwells' data are sparse before 1000 BC (Figure 10.2) but appear to yield an exponential curve of recovery of the Earth's axis from a sudden movement to an ecliptic angle of at least 26.5° back to the present 23.4° value. By fitting a Sine curve to his data Dodwell determined that this sudden shift occurred in about the year 2345 BC which, within an uncertainty of a few years, coincides precisely with the Biblical date of the Flood (Chapter 8.9.2 and Figure 10.2). Dodwell recognized that this curve expresses a behavior like the response of a spinning top when it is recovering after being struck by an outside force (Dodwell 2010). Evidently following a sudden and dramatic change in tilt, the Earth began to wobble and has gradually recovered only recently (~1850) to reach back to the value predicted by the Newcomb Formula.

Whilst it has been speculated that the Earth's axis was suddenly displaced by a major astronomic impact at the instant of the Flood, no atmospheric impact (see Chapter 9.6) due to such a cause is recognized at this time, and since no other extra-Biblical cause has yet been identified, it may rank as a Divine intervention. It does appear to be alluded to by the Biblical reference in Isaiah 13:13 linking a movement of the Earth to a Divine judgment: *"Therefore I will shake the heavens, and the Earth shall remove out of her place, in the wrath of the LORD of hosts, and in the day of his fierce anger".*

No attempt seems to have yet been made to model the effect of a sudden change in the angle of tilt of the Earth. The minimum shift was ~3° but it is clear from Dodwell's data (Figure 10.2) that it could have been considerably larger. As regions formerly near the poles speeded up and equatorial regions slowed down a redistribution of water would follow; an obvious consequence would have been a tsunami accompanied by the flooding of large areas of land and a shifting of the climatic belts. Whether this event alone, without any ancillary cause, could have produced a tsunami of sufficient amplitude to sweep over higher ground and eliminate all ancient settlements to complete God's judgment is unclear. Genesis Chapter Seven implies that the Flood came up from the deep, mentioning but not emphasizing, the contribution of the rain; this is alluded to in Psalm 104:6-9 and in the ancient Book of Job (38:8-14) noted below. The Babylonian and Sumerian tablets also say that the 'Flood came up' from the oceans. The implication of these texts is that the Flood was initiated by a tsunami and that the waters lingered; the rain, which lasted for only 40 days, was a relatively minor factor and may have been initiated by the accompanying shift of the climatic belts.

The scale of the Flood would have depended on the suddenness of the event, whilst the duration would have been a function of rate of decline of the obliquity (Figure 10.2) and the latitude of the location. The Bible

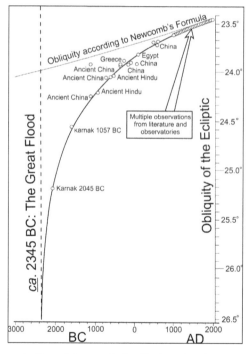

Figure 10.2: A reproduction of George Dodwell's data showing the variation in the obliquity of the Earth's Ecliptic during historic times. The sine curve fitted to his results predicts a large and sudden shift in the ecliptic near the conventional Biblical timeline of Noah's Flood

provides two records. Noah's log summarizes the impact of the entire episode in the Middle East (Pearce 1993): the rains first fell for 40 days (Genesis 7:12) and the waters continued to rise for another 110 days (Genesis 7:24). A further 74 days were occupied by the "going and decreasing" after which Noah waited 40 days before sending out a raven to test for the presence of dry land. Over three successive periods of 7 days he sent a dove to test for land and only after the third time did the dove fail to return. After another 29 days the waters had "dried from the Earth" (Genesis 8:13) implying that the entire episode lasted for ~314 days.

God's description of the event to the Patriarch Job (38:8-13) is more poetic but less factual as he questions Job's knowledge: *"Who shut up the sea with doors, when it broke forth, as if it had issued out of the womb? When I made the cloud the garment thereof, and thick darkness a swaddlingband for it, and broke up my decreed place for it, and set bars and doors, and said, "hitherto thou shalt come, no further and here shall thy proud waves be stayed?"* (The oceans are constrained, released, but then ordered to return to their former place). *Hast thou commanded the morning since thy days; and caused the dayspring to know his place* (the position of the Sunrise is altered due to the changed position of the Earth's axis) *that it might take hold of the ends of the earth and the wicked might be shaken out of it?* (Judgment).

Psalm 104 of unknown authorship, also refers to the Flood (verses 6-9) and acknowledges a Divine control: *"Thou covered with the deep as with a garment: the waters stood above the mountains. At thy rebuke they fled and at the voice of thy thunder they hastened away. They go up by the mountains; they go down by the valleys unto the place which thou hast founded for them. Thou hast set a bound that they may not pass over that they turn not again to cover the Earth".*

There are aspects of this episode about which the Bible has nothing to tell us. We are not told how eight people coped with looking after the animals. We are only told that God was "with Noah". It would have required His guidance to bring the animal "kinds" (not species), to the Ark. Possibly they were induced into hibernation or their bodily functions were paused whilst they were on the boat - these would have been lesser miracles than the Flood itself.

A further possible consequence of the shift in the pole of rotation is the change in the duration of the Earth's rotation around the Sun. Noah's calendar in Genesis Chapter 7 comprised 360 days with the 12 months each comprising 30 days. It is possibly because the Earth circled the Sun in 360 days that the Ancient Sumerians divided the circle into 360 degrees, and further to give us our hour and minute divisions of 60. Evidently because the cycles of the Moon are readily monitored, the tradition died hard and 360-day years also appear in the ancient Hindu, Maya and Chinese calendars, with the latter one adding a separate period of five and a quarter days to match the present length of the Solar year. The change in the length of the year cannot positively be linked to the time of the Flood because the 360-day years persisted in post-Flood Jewish, Persian and Egyptian calendars as well with appropriate adjustments at intervals to accommodate our present Solar cycle. The ancient 360 day year also continues in the Biblical prophetic discourses (see Table 5.1, Chapter 5) and with the institution of the seven Levitical Appointed Times. These would be postponed for a whole month if the barley harvest was not ready for the Feast of First Fruits and would serve to bring the Lunar and Solar calendars into alignment at intervals.

10.7 Holocene Times and the Archaeological Record of the Flood

The Holocene is the current geological epoch and embraces the last ~11,000 years since the end of the last Ice Age. It embraces the time interval over which humanity has practiced agriculture and laid down organized settlements. It has been a time of turbulent natural events which incorporated the extinction of many large mammals, including ~80% of a mega-fauna including the mastodons and mammoths. Extensive animal bone beds are found all over the world but the challenge is to recognize those resulting from the Flood from earlier cataclysms (Montgomery 2013). Much interest has been attached to the sudden catastrophe that froze the mammoths of Siberia. However, these mammoth graveyards are dated 43,000-28,000 and 12,000-9,000 years old, much too early to be a consequence of the Flood. An event with dramatic environmental implications at ~11,000 BC appears to have been caused by the impact of asteroid debris with an impact site identified in NE Greenland. This event is speculated to have brought an end to a period defined as the Younger Dryas (~12,800-11,600 BC) which brought about a rapid collapse of the last ice sheets and had commenced at ~15,500 BC. The earliest signs of settled civilizations such as Gobekli Tepe in Turkey are identified soon after the end of Younger Dryas where the archaeological evidence shows that the pre-Adamic hominids were accomplished masons and copper workers.

Biblical authors, notably Pearce (1993) and Langford (2011), have proposed that aspects of the early Holocene record, including widespread extinctions and the cutting of deep gorges and canyons like those in the western United States, correlate with Noah's Flood. Unfortunately, theirs, and many other attempts, to constrain the location and extent of the Flood (documented for example, at *godandscience.org*) have confused it with the extensive evidence for the melting of the Pleistocene ice sheets and associated rise in sea level. Not only did these events have durations much longer than the Flood, but according to the Biblical chronology they would actually have occurred several thousand years earlier. The extensive bone beds which include the extinction of the large megafauna, are normally attributed to dramatic, and sometimes sudden, climate changes during the end of the Pleistocene and beginning of Holocene times. Pearce (1993) quotes multiple examples from Europe and the Americas of dramatic faunal changes in post-Dryas times with extinctions followed by barren intervals of several thousands of years. These include the disappearance of mammoths, horses, lions, tigers and camels from the Americas and the scattering of whale bones over the surface as far north as Alabama. However, these bone beds are all now dated with multiple ages in the range of up to ~10,000 years before the present; they can only be linked to Noah's Flood if Dodwell's evidence is dismissed and generations are missing from the Genesis account. Pearce (1993) attributes the Flood to the time following the Copper Stone, or 'Chalcolithic' Period (~5000-4100 BC), which saw the spread of agriculture from Western Asia comprising earlier phases of the Ubaidian

Culture, which then spread throughout Southern and Central Europe. Evidence for the Early Bronze Age where the smelting of bronze is accompanied by urban settlement and proto-writing began about 3300 BC. The cultural gap between the two periods was an obvious candidate for the impact of Noah's Flood. Unfortunately, although the impact of this period (variously known as the 'sterile epoch' or 'yawning millennium') may well be attributable in part to flooding, this would relate to the last stages of sea level rise following the decay of the Pleistocene ice sheets and occurred more than 2000 years before the Flood of Noah. It marked the Atlantic Phase when the British Isles separated from the continent to produce the marine sediments separating the Neolithic and Bronze periods. An overtopping of the current sea level is seen in the drowned forests found around many of our shorelines. At about the same time cataclysmic flooding of the Black Sea occurred as waters poured thorough the Bosporus from the Mediterranean at ~5,600 BC (Ryan and Pitman 1998) during an earlier event lasting much longer than Noah's Flood.

More promising, although undated, evidence for Noah's Flood comprises the widespread occurrence all over Western Europe and Russia of fissures containing jumbled bone beds with diverse animal types and sometimes human relics. Clefts in the limestone terrains of the Mediterranean coast of France are crammed with bones of animals from diverse environments including wolves, bears, oxen, cave lions, rhinos, horses etc. likely to have been brought together by a cataclysm. Similar fissure deposits are found in Wales and South West England, whilst fissures within the Rock of Gibraltar are also filled with remarkably fresh bones, apparently not gnawed but nevertheless all splintered and broken. Examples from Malta have numerous sea birds crammed in with a diverse range of other animals; since these could otherwise have flown on to nearby land, the bones seem to be the signature of a sudden catastrophe.

In North America comparable fissure and cave deposits are found in localities as widely dispersed as Lincoln County in Wyoming, Organ Mountains in New Mexico, Cumberland Cave in Maryland, the Red Deer River in Canada and the San Pedro Valley of California. Some of these examples include human relics whilst the latter location has a varied marine fauna all mixed up with land mammals and birds. Each one of these examples gives the impression of diverse animals being driven together by a common danger and then perishing in a single catastrophe. Since Pleistocene ice sheets were absent from Australia, comparative examples from that continent at Wellington Valley and elsewhere indicate a cause other than the end of global glaciation; confused mixtures of multiple animal types have evidently been thrown together into crevices by a sudden event (Gray 2008).

With more precise temporal confidence, archaeological evidence for the destruction of earlier civilizations by the ~2345 BC Flood and the resetting of human habitation is now extensively documented in the journal *Chronology and Catastrophism Review,* in the proceedings of the 1997 Society for Interdisciplinary Studies (SIS) conference in Cambridge, and also at various websites such as *www.freerepublic.com/focus/fr/ and www.catastrophism.com/intro/search.* The devastating climate signature recognised by Michael Baillie in the dendrochronological (tree ring) record at 2345 BC was the key independent evidence supporting Dodwell's conclusion. A highly unusual growth defect was also discovered in trees which grew in the fenlands just south of Lough Neagh in Northern Ireland; these showed a change in character of growth from normal ring porous to diffuse porous over a decade-long period consistent with prolonged inundation. The chronology derived from volcanic tephra deposited from outpourings of the Hekla volcano in Iceland have also defined a catastrophic event dated 2310 +/- 20 BC.

This time is seen as defining the end of Early Bronze Age and appears to correlate with the disappearance of the lush lake and river systems that formerly occupied the present-day Sahara Desert; the Legend of Atlantis is also attributed in some literature to an "Atlantic Tsunami". Contemporary changes in the climate of Africa and the Near East resulted in the cessation of a Neolithic Wet Phase about 2350 BC. In Ancient Egypt it correlates with the end of the Old Kingdom whilst in Mesopotamia it defines the end of the Akaddian Empire where the record of this civilization is succeeded by the products of erosion that show no trace of human activity. The Third Dynasty of Ur as well as civilizations on Crete and mainland Greece, and the great city states of

Mohenjo-daro and Harappa in the Indus Valley are all recorded as collapsing close to the date of the Flood. In northern Syria there is very specific evidence for the Flood in a chaotic deposit dated ~2350 BC including items of mud-brick construction that were thrown together as if " by an air blast". The global impact of the Flood is best summarized by a statement of Dr B. J. Peiser from the SIS Conference: *"...Most sites in Greece, Anatolia, the Levant, Mesopotamia, the Indian subcontinent, China, Persia/Afghanistan, Iberia which collapsed at around 2200 ± 200 BC, exhibit unambiguous signs of natural calamities and/or rapid abandonment. The proxy data detected in the marine, terrestrial, biological and archaeological records point to sudden ecological, climatic and social upheavals which appear to coincide with simultaneous sea- and lake-level changes, increased levels of seismic activity and widespread flood/tsunami disasters"*.

Sediment deposition during the later stages of the Flood would have been susceptible to erosion in later times and can rarely be identified with confidence. The excavations of Sir Leonard Woolley in the Euphrates Valley during the earlier part of the last century seemed to provide a possible record of this. Rapid recent sedimentation around the City of Ur has buried a thick but uniform record of Early Dynastic Period III Sumerian settlement; this lies above a ~3 meter layer of pure clay apparently of marine origin, and beneath this clay there is a record of earlier settlement characterized by extensive hand-made pottery dated ~2750 BC from an Early Dynastic Period I. A similar clay occurs well above the flood plain and was subsequently identified, although in more attenuated form, up to 250 km inland from the Persian Gulf; it was not found at much higher elevations (Keller 1956). However, subsequent excavations have found that the Persian Gulf was subject to several flooding events during these times and probably only the youngest might be attributable to the Flood. Similar reservations apply to the clay layers excavated below the ancient city of Nineveh. An intriguing possible signature of waning stages of the Flood was discovered when Abjullah Al Mamun, son of the Caliph of Bagdad, broke into the Great Pyramid of Giza in 820 AD. He found that the walls and floors inside were encrusted with salt as much as an inch thick. The casing stones around the outsides of the pyramid (unfortunately mostly since removed for the rebuilding of Cairo) showed watermarks reaching more than halfway up the sides of the 147-meter-tall structure. (https://sacredsites.com/africa/egypt/the_ great_ pyramid_of_giza.html, also see Prophecy in the News, February 2002).

The aftermath of the Flood is recorded by a prolonged period of drought (see *https://en.wikipedia.org/wiki/4.2_kiloyear_event*) possibly lasting for the entire century 2200-2100 BC. It is recognized in settlements across North Africa, the Middle East, the Red Sea and Arabian Peninsula, the Indian subcontinent, and in midcontinental North America, whilst glacier advances over a much wider area yield indications of a global impact. It has been used to define the last "Meghalayan" division of time starting around 2200 BC.

There are several possible implications to the analysis presented in this chapter. Firstly, the global climatic disturbance may be a signature of the disturbance of the ecliptic; secondly the disparate scattered settlements imply substantial dispersal of some Flood survivors; thirdly the concentration of the majority surviving population in the Flood plain of the Tigris and Euphrates was likely necessitated by the widespread impact of the drought. The Babylonians told Alexander the Great that Babylon began when their astronomical records commenced in 2234 B.C. Nebuchadnezzar had also in-scripted on a plaque that this first king ruled 42 generations before ~500 B.C. and implied that the establishment of Babel (Babylon) by the infamous priest-king of Uruk, Nimrod, occurred about 2200 BC (Chapter 8.12). The literary history of Gilgamesh which includes the celebrated, albeit corrupted, version of the Flood begins with Sumerian poems about Bilgamesh ("Gilgamesh") the king of Uruk from the Third Dynasty of Ur dated ~2100 BC. According to the historian Eusebius of Caesarea, Egialeus, the first king in Greece, began his reign in 2089 B.C. One of the legendary Xia Dynasty heroes of China named Yu the Great (Da Yu) lived around 2200 – 2100 BC, and engineered a massive land reclamation project suggesting that residues of the deluge may have left trapped water that needed to be drained. Up to the time of the Flood the evidence for major urban development is all concentrated in the Middle

East. After the Flood rapid population growth in China began to over-
take developments in the west, so that by ~1600 BC Yinxu in China
became the largest city in the world. Extra-Biblical evidence for the
divergence and dispersal of the descendents of Noah's sons Shem, Ham
and Japheth can be found at the website *https://ancientpatriarchs.
wordpress.com/*. The author of this site also speculates on how the religious foundations instituted by God and given to Noah were progressively corrupted into the pagan religions of the Mediterranean and
Middle East, and led to the classical mythologies. It seems likely that
all the earliest civilizations were monotheistic and only later lapsed into
polytheism (Pearce 1993).

Further Reading:

Dodwell, G.F., 2010. The Obliquity of the Ecliptic: Ancient, mediaeval,
and modern observations of the obliquity of the Ecliptic, measuring the
inclination of the earth's axis, in ancient times and up to the present,
http://www.setterfield.org/Dodwell/ Dodwell_Manuscript_1.html#note

Gray, J., 2008. Surprise Witness: Global events during the Flood, Teach
Services Inc., 234 pp., ISBN-13 978-1-57258-554-6.

Harrison, James, 1995. The Pattern and the Prophecy, Isaiah
Publications, Peterborough, Ontario, Canada, 399pp.

Jeffery, Grant R., 1999. *The Handwriting of God; Sacred Mysteries of
the Bible*, Frontier Research Publications, Toronto, Canada, 280pp.

Johnson, K., 2012. *The Ancient Book of Enoch*, Charleston, South
Carolina, ISBN 1480102768.

Keller, W., 1956. *The Bible as History*, Hodder and Stoughton, 429pp.

Langford, J.W., 2011. *The GAP is not a theory*, Xlibris Publications,
252pp.

Montgomery, David R., 2013. *The Rocks Don't Lie: A Geologist
Investigates Noah's Flood*, W.W. Norton and Co. 320 pp., ISBN
978-0-393-34624-4.

Pearce, E.K.V., 1993. *Evidence for Truth: Science*, Evidence Programs, Eastbourne, Sussex, 319pp.

Ryan, W. and Pitman, W., 1998. *Noah's Flood: The New Scientific Discoveries about the Event That Changed History*. New York: Simon & Schuster.

Wenham, G. J., 1978. *The Coherence of the Flood Narrative*. Vetus Testamentum XXVIII, Facsimile 3: 336-348.

Wenham, G.J., 1987. *Word Biblical Commentary, Vol. 1: Genesis 1-15*. Nashville: Thomas Nelson.

Summary and Conclusions

This book emerged from a conviction that a very diverse range of evidence can show that the Bible is the inerrant Word of God in its entirety. For the secular reader approaching this subject for the first time there are probably two extraordinary claims to emerge from the analysis. The first is that humankind was a special creation of God, beginning with Adam, and representing the first and only life form able to relate and converse with Him. The second is that the natural propensity towards sin in the mind of humankind has its roots in a Satanic Realm, and has required a unique intervention by God to provide a Redeemer. To support these claims we have documented in Chapters 1 and 2 the origins of the Biblical record and the unique properties to endorse a Divine authorship. This has involved selecting material from years of investigation by dedicated Bible researchers. It has aimed to show that the Bible has been most carefully recorded and preserved, and has Divinely-inspired properties beginning with the first verse of Genesis and only ending with the last verse of the Book of Revelation. We believe the existence of a benevolent God with concern for His Creation, and most specifically for His special creation of humankind, will have created the Earth in a way that is uniquely suited to life. We consider that this is why all aspects of Creation are so finely tuned as summarized by the evidence in Chapter 4. Chapter 5 continues with this theme by describing the perfection of design in Creation.

The information compiled in this book presents two major challenges. The first is to show that the conflicts between the findings of modern science and the Bible, so avidly promoted by the media and most of academia, are illusory - this has to follow if God created science as well as everything else. The second challenge is the testament of the Bible to our modern society - if the Bible is indeed true and Divinely-inspired then instead of being marginalized, or even eliminated, it should be at the heart of our world today.

Considering the first challenge: from childhood we have each grown up grown up within an ethos where the Theory of Evolution was an unquestioned article of faith. Our school history books often showed the "tree of life" with side branches moving off into progressively higher animal forms, and then showing man standing triumphantly at the top. To question whether this was really true was to invite astonishment or even ridicule. Indeed, in our academic circles it was the required foundation of our thinking on the origin of life, and refusal to accept it could threaten marginalization - it proved best just to keep alternative views to oneself. We nevertheless had to privately question how brilliant academic minds could view the origin of life as originating from pure chance, a chance which even their own probability calculations showed them was so near-infinitely remote that they had to force it out into space into another time and another world. To accept that the perfection of the cell and the amazing ordering of DNA can be accommodated by a chance process has become an issue of faith, an alternative religion - one which does not need to acknowledge a Creator, sin or eternity, and favors self-preoccupation but offers only a pointless future and a depressing outlook on the world.

Of course, as we were trained from childhood to accept Evolution as fact, we likely still confessed ourselves to be Christians and would probably reconcile the contrasting perspectives of Creation and Evolution by accepting that God used Evolution to create the diversity of life. Adam and the Garden of Eden would either be accepted as a mythological story or viewed as the pinnacle of Evolution. However, decades of intensive research have on the one hand failed to produce the required stratigraphic evidence from the geological record, and on the other hand have recovered remarkable evidence from DNA and the extraordinary complexity of living things, that together totally fail to support a chance process. There is a dichotomy here between a modern scientific understanding which is forcing an increasing number of scientists to privately or publically question Evolution, and the Mainstream Media which continues to promote it as an established fact. Sadly, it is the latter that primarily influences the present generation of politicians and decision makers, and even the populace at large.

Now that we understand the deeper significance of the Hebrew of the first verse of Genesis and the ensuing text, we recognize that God is specific in declaring that He Created - He did not evolve. This is the motivation of Chapter 3 compiling a range of evidence supporting Creation and disproving Evolution. To this point we agree with a wide range of evangelists and creation ministries that have extensively highlighted the flaws in the supposed "Theory" of Evolution. They have done much to challenge secularists, and to reinforce the belief of Christians that they are indeed a special creation with a destiny provided by the messages of both Old and New testaments of the Bible.

Unfortunately, most of these same ministries have raised an artificial barrier between Science and the Bible by promoting a very young Earth with a history spanning just 6000 years which either denies or falsifies so much established science. In large measure this has negated their powerful arguments against Evolution - if science confounds Evolution, why should it not also demonstrate a Young Earth? The YEC position continues to be the most common view of the relationship between Science and Scripture held by much of the evangelical community and, unfortunately but understandably, it is the view of science that most non-Christians associate with Christianity. For scientifically literate non-Christians, it presents an obstacle to Christian faith, and for new Christians who have been raised to equate YEC with the teaching of Scripture, it can destroy their faith altogether when its falsity is discovered. This crisis has become acute in recent decades as an informed populace views the evidence for Intelligent Design and seriously questions the origin of Life by a purely chance process, but at the same time realizes that the evidence for an Old Earth and Universe is now beyond question. If God is indeed the Creator He must also be responsible for every aspect of the physical creation as well as the Laws of Nature. We believe it is simply unacceptable to use the large canon of scientific evidence to refute Evolution whilst at the same time rejecting the vast amount of evidence refuting a Young Earth. Addressing this conflict has been the motivation for Chapter 6.

It also seems paradoxical that the Young Earth Creationists should have focused their attention on a brief 150-day flood event (which evidently occurred after Day 6 of Genesis Chapter One) instead of aiming to explain the successive events of the Six Days of Genesis 1. As we have shown in Chapter 9, even without accepting the timeline described by Dr Schroeder and ourselves, the events defining the Six Days can be shown to correlate well with successive major events of cosmic and geological history. In contrast, the correlations attempted with Noah's Flood are untenable and simply open to ridicule.

There are a few residual issues promoted by Young Earth Creationism that merit discussion. The most important is the issue of sin and its link to the creation of Adam. Genesis Chapter 3 does not imply that the Curse introduced the death of all creatures. The potential for corruption extended way back prior to Day 3 with the fall of Satan and a third of the angels in the GAP. This is alluded to in Genesis 1:2 and elsewhere in the Scriptures such as the books of Isaiah Chapter 14, Luke Chapter 10, Revelation 9, and as also discussed in Chapter 7 of this book explaining the significance of the GAP. All life apart from humankind has no conscience - actions are motivated by the will to survive; death for them is no penalty for sin and the sacrifice of a Redeemer has no relevance. It might be significant that most excavated settlements prior to the probable time of the creation of Adam were actually unwalled and there seems to have been no strong motivation for open warfare (Pearce 1993). In contrast God had to provide His special creation of Adam with free will. Otherwise we would simply be automatons and unable to properly relate to Him and love Him by choice. However, with free will comes the potential for deception and the knowledge of good and evil (Genesis 3:22). Orthodox Biblical interpretation is that it was the propensity of Adam and Eve to sin that led to ruler ship of Earth falling into the power of Satan. The primary purpose of the Biblical narrative from Genesis Chapter 3 onwards is God's unfolding purposes for redeeming fallen humankind with the future restoration of the Earth and God's authority over it, being the primary subject of the Book of Revelation from Chapter 4 onwards. Paul confirmed this in the Book of Romans: ***"by one man sin entered into the world, and death by sin; and so death passed upon all men, for they all have sinned. For until the law sin was in the world but sin is only imputed when there is no law."*** (Romans 5:12-13). Here Paul is specific that death from sin applies only to humankind - he does not consider the death by sin applying to pre-Adamic life.

Similarly, there is nothing in the text to confine us to the interpretation that the ground was only cursed from the time of Adam's fall (and c.f. Genesis 8:21) or that thorns and thistles were not around before then: the implication of Genesis 3:15-19 is that because of their sin, life would now become hard graft for Adam and Eve and their offspring - something that has generally persisted to our time. Rain is mentioned in Chapter 2 of Genesis where God is reflecting from Day 7 on the description of the days already given in Chapter 1. Rainfall impressions are present in sediments deposited on land way back in the geological record although Genesis 2:5-6 implies that there was no rainfall before plant life; this is readily explained by the preceding "mist rising from the Earth" alluding to the transition defining the beginning of Day 4 as proposed in Chapter 9. The rainbow of Genesis 9:13 is a signature of God's blessing in providing the water from rainfall essential for life - there is no need for rainbows to have been absent before humankind was created. The remaining issue that continues to be contended by YECs is the preservation of DNA and soft tissue material in ancient fossils. Although present scientific evidence may explain this, the research is at an early stage. Nevertheless, the multifaceted and over-whelming evidence for vast cosmic and planetary ages as documented in Chapter 6, and the long history of the Earth as described in Chapters 8 and 9 give confidence that a full secured explanation will be forth-coming in the future.

The Introduction noted an ancient prophecy given to the Prophet Daniel implying that the Bible was a sealed book, but that knowledge would increase rapidly at the end of the present Age with the "to and fro" implying the explosion in travel that we are seeing in our day. To previous generations lacking the scientific knowledge the Biblical message was open to straightforward acceptance - as noted in the Book of Romans Chapter 1, the observed diversity and perfection of the world around would have been enough to convince the observer of the existence of a Creator. With the environment of enquiry that accompanied the Age of Enlightenment we find the Bible competing with an ever-expanding canon of scientific knowledge. It has been a contention of the present text that, if the Bible is Divinely-inspired, it must conform to this knowledge and the analysis has aimed to seek this conformity. At the same time we observe that revelation of accord between the Bible and Science unfolds gradually as implied by Daniel's prophecy. In part this is to be expected because scientific knowledge is ever-changing as hypotheses are proposed, and then often abandoned as evidence accumulates. In contrast, the Biblical text is unchangeable.

Eastern religions and philosophies regard history as cyclical and subject to endless repetition. The Bible however, describes a beginning and an end to history. Only within the last hundred years have we discovered that this latter view is the correct one: Science has told us that the Universe had a beginning and is moving towards an end of infinite entropy. Even more recently we did not understand DNA or the details of the perfect order in living matter. The corresponding perfection of order in the inorganic world of crystal structures had only been known a few decades earlier, mainly since the achievements of Lawrence Bragg in the field of X-ray crystallography first published in 1913. The extraordinary depths of the Biblical text too, have been revealed to the non-Jewish world only since the beginning of the 20th century, and initiated by the research of Ivan Panin. Wider dissemination of a correct understanding of Equidistant Letter Spacing (ELS) has had to wait just until the last three decades; at present this is due mostly to the dedicated research of Yacov Ramsel and Grant Jeffrey, but now that computer programs for the analysis are available, new examples are emerging all the time, especially from Jewish sources. The genetic evidence for humankind's unique origin and short lifespan has similarly only been unraveled over a recent time span.

Since revelation is ongoing and science is always evolving, no analysis like the one presented in this book can ever hope to be complete. From the era of Noah onwards we can have confidence in the Biblical timeframe within an uncertainty of just a few decades. We are now able to highlight Dodwell's research, remarking on its tight correlation with the time of Noah's Flood according to conventional Biblical chronology, and expand on the extraordinary Divine signature behind this event. We believe that this, together with the large body of geological and cosmic knowledge that we have given, should however end the false correlation of the Flood with the Geologic Column promoted by Young Earth Creationism.

Nevertheless, whilst we have been able to demonstrate a conformity between recorded geological and cosmic time and the Six Days of Genesis Chapter 1, an understanding of the expansion of space and contraction of time is an enormous subject still very imperfectly understood by minds vastly superior to this author. It is acknowledged that the analysis presented in Chapters 8 and 9 will no doubt merit refinement in the future. However, the text compiling the extraordinary range of evidence for the fine tuning and age of the Earth and Universe, the perfection of God's design and the confounding of Evolution, show that the apparent conflict between Science and the Bible, so avidly promoted by Academia and the Media, is without foundation. To the enquiring mind open to understanding the most important book in the history of humankind, a whole new understanding of the world and our place in it becomes possible.

Finally, to the second challenge: Just within a single generation we have lived through an extraordinary transformation as the society we were privileged to be born into, and much of it achieved by the sacrifices of the so-called "greatest generation", has moved at a frenetic pace to dismantle its Christian heritage. Even prestigious universities like Harvard, Yale, Oxford, and Cambridge founded on Christian principles where a comprehensive Biblical knowledge was once required for acceptance, have been going to great lengths to minimize, or even deny, that Christianity had anything to do with their esta-blishment. Despite the modern tendency to dismiss the influence of Christianity by pretending it merely existed prior to the modern world, the truth is the opposite: the entire modern secular scientific world relies on the foundations and formulas developed or improved upon by Christians. James Clerk Maxwell had the words of Psalm 111:2 placed above the entrance to the Chadwick Laboratory in Cambridge (in Latin): *"The works of the LORD are great, sought out by all them that have pleasure therein".* The Marxist-secularist influence on education over the past century has caused us to forget that the privileges of our civilization are new and undeniably superior to the alternatives in human history. Whenever other great civilizations like the Chinese, Indian, Japanese or Korean encountered Christian missionaries, they revamped their cultures to align themselves with Christian principles, because the benefits that Christianity brought were so blatantly superior to the average person, as well as to the state. They abandoned slavery and polygamy, set up charities, hospitals and universities, implemented scientific instruction and widespread education of the masses to make literacy universal, reduce or eliminate the absolute power of the monarch, and established rules detailing the inherent rights of their citizens – even if they rejected the Christian doctrines directly responsible for these benefits in the West. In earlier centuries formerly-violent peoples like the Celts, Saxons and Vikings had been similarly convinced. An exhaustive study by the Oxford anthropologist J.D. Unwin (1895-1936) of 6 major civilizations and 80 societies covering 5000 years found that only civilizations which practiced traditional Judeo-Christian values of monogamy, gender equality and family integrity were able to flourish; whenever they lapsed into polygamy and sexual deviancy they inevitably declined. To his evident disappointment, he was forced to refute the teaching of Freud that these values are restrictive and repressive *(https://archive.org/details/ b20442580)*.

Christianity is why we have laws that are universal among all civilized nations. Without it, there would be no freedom of speech, freedom of, and from, religion, freedom of travel, freedom of assembly and property rights. The world did not get them from Islam, Hinduism, Buddhism, Sikhism, Shintoism, Taoism, or the Baha'i — they came from Christianity and from those whose moral compass was guided by it. This is why people are able to leave, and even ridicule, the dominant religion without fear in the west, but will suffer serious consequences and even death if attempting to do so elsewhere. The Christian milieu in Europe and North America over the past 500 years has given the world the notions of human rights. It has forced the abolition of human sacrifice, slavery, infanticide, and cannibalism wherever its influence has prevailed and has driven the criminalization of pedophilia, rape, and torture. It is responsible for developing universities, hospitals, universal literacy, education degrees, academic accreditation, property rights, intellectual property rights, separation of church and state, freedom of speech, and many more benefits that we take for granted including most inventions that we enjoy today. In the absence of Christianity modern science and technology could never have been founded. It was only Christianity's theology and cultural practices that allowed their establishment and spread throughout the world.

The brilliant scientific minds of the likes of Newton, Euler, Gauss, Leibniz, Kepler, Pasteur, Faraday, James Clerk Maxwell, Marie Curie, Fleming, Einstein, Bohr, Teller, Heisenberg, Schrödinger, Dirac, Planck, Hubble, Crick and many others, although not all Christians, were able to flourish in a rational Western Christian environment giving them liberty to do their research and encourage free inquiry. It gave them recognition, honor and financial reward for their advances to knowledge. It enabled them to obtain an education within institutions created by Christians, and provided them with the means to formulate and refine their ideas, which could then be circulated around the world. There were no Moslem, Hindu, or Buddhist figures outside the Christian West that have impacted the whole world in ways comparable to these figures. Whilst men like physicist Sir C.V. Raman, the wide-ranging scholar J.C. Bose and the astrophysicist S. Chandrasekhar have made immense contributions to science and literature, their achievements were made within Western societies established by Christianity. Similarly the unsurpassed abilities of the Jewish people (just ~0.2% of the world's population gaining more than 20% (206) of the Nobel Prizes) did not flourish in Greek, Roman or Ottoman empires; they flourished in societies transformed by the example and sacrifice of the greatest Jew of all, Jesus Christ.

To visualize the impact that Christianity has had on society we need only to view what the world was like before the Apostolic Age, and then before the great revivals which ultimately came out of the Reformation that recovered Biblical truth. Without Christianity the world would have been an uglier and much more dystopian place; half of our children would die before their fifth birthday, our average life expectancy would be below 40, and one out of every four of us would die violent deaths. Most of us would likely be peasant farmers ruled by superstition, and only a minority would ever know how to read. In the light of the evidence from history it is surely foolish to pursue the present rapid secularization of society and abandonment of our Christian heritage – as noted in the Introduction, the fruits of this process are already becoming apparent in moral decay, dissatisfaction and mental depression. The accelerating degradation of the environment and the increasing concentration of the worlds' wealth within a narrowing number of people (only about 60 billionaires now possess more wealth than half the world's population) reflects the fallen nature of humankind. In contrast the Bible encourages care for the Creation and concern for our fellow beings. During good years of harvest enough food has been produced to feed 10 billion people and the frenetic efforts to curb human populations cannot be justified, either on moral or numeric grounds. The Christian message has had the greatest positive impact on the world and everyone, regardless of country, race, religion, or culture, has directly benefitted from its influence. If, as this book has aimed to show, the Biblical narrative is indubitably truth of Divine origin, it is surely foolish to marginalize it.

Milton Keynes UK
Ingram Content Group UK Ltd.
UKHW020254111023
430276UK00011BA/117